Rural Sociology

Rural Sociology

S.L. Doshi
P.C. Jain

RAWAT PUBLICATIONS
Jaipur • New Delhi • Bangalore • Guwahati • Kolkata

ISBN 978-81-7033-522-1 (HB)
ISBN 978-81-7033-523-8 (PB)

Reprinted, 2023

Published by
Prem Rawat for **Rawat Publications**
Satyam Apts., Sector 3, Jawahar Nagar, Jaipur - 302 004 (India)
Phones: 0141 265 1748 / 265 7006
E-mail : info@rawatbooks.com
Website: rawatbooks.com

New Delhi Office
4858/24, Ansari Road, Daryaganj, New Delhi 110 002
Phone: 011-23263290

Also at *Bangalore, Guwahati* and *Kolkata*

Typeset by Rawat Computers, Jaipur
Printed at Nice Printing Press, New Delhi

Contents

Preface 9

1 **What is Rural Sociology ?** 11
- Newly Acquired Significance of Rural Sociology
- Sociology, Social Anthropology and Rural Sociology

2 **Nature, Subject Matter and Methods of Rural Sociology** 37
- Nature of Rural Sociology
- Subject Matter of Rural Sociology
- Methods and Tools of Rural Sociology
- Tools of Data Generation

3 **Studies in Rural Sociology** 51
- Decade of the Flood of Village Studies

4 **Some Key Concepts of Rural Sociology** 70
- Changing Language of Rural Sociology
- Emergence of New Methodology
- Dominant Caste
- Village Unity
- Sanskritisation
- Westernisation
- Little and Great Traditions
- Parochialisation and Universalisation

5 **Sociology of Rural Life** 98
- What is Rural?
- Rural People
- Determinants of Rural Social Formations

6 **Agrarian Social Structure** 114
- Study of Agrarian Structure
- What is Agrarian Social Structure?

- History of the Study of Agrarian Structure
- Gandhi's Approach to Land Problem

7 **Land Tenure System and Land Reforms** 125
- Areas under Agrarian System
- Land Tenure System
- Land Reforms

8 **Rural Social Stratification: Caste and Class** 150
- Social Stratification
- Forms of Social Stratification
- Rural Social Stratification
- Theoretical Approach to the Study of Rural Stratification
- Changing Rural Caste Stratification
- Scheduled Castes, Scheduled Tribes and Other Backward Classes in the Changing Rural Caste Stratification
- Rural Class System: The Changing Patterns
- Caste-Class Nexus

9 **Rural Social Institutions: Family, Kinship, Marriage and Religion** 179
- Social Framework of Village Community
- Rural Institutions and Their Types

10 **Rural Aesthetics** 213
- What Does Aesthetics Mean?
- Art Forms
- Status of Art in Rural Society

11 **Agrarian Unrest** 223
- Importance of Peasantry in India
- Some Basic Statistics about Indian Villages
- Some Erroneous Assumptions about Peasantry
- Who is a Peasant?
- Peasant Movements in Pre-Independent India
- Santhal Insurrection (1855-56)
- Peasant Revolt in Punjab (1930)
- Champaran (Bihar) Movement (1917-18)
- Kheda Peasant Struggle (1918)
- Bardoli Satyagraha (1928)
- Moplah Rebellion in Malabar (1921)
- Peasant Movements at the Eve of Independence and Afterwards

- Naxalbari Peasant Struggle
- Some Other Contemporary Peasant Struggles

12 **Rural Development** 265
- Rural Development Before Independence
- Rural Development After Independence
- Impact of Development Programmes

13 **Village Cooperatives** 293
- Meaning of Cooperation and Cooperative Societies
- Basic Characteristics of Cooperatives
- Types of Cooperative Societies
- History of Cooperative Movement in India
- Some Important Kinds of Societies
- Politics in Cooperative Societies
- Sugar Cooperatives in Maharashtra
- Milk Cooperatives in Gujarat
- Status of Cooperatives in India

14 **Village Environmental Crisis: Forest, Landuse, Water and Fuel** 314
- Environment, Ecology and Development
- The Policy Framework
- Extent of Environmental Degradation
- Causes of Environmental Degradation
- People's Movement for the Protection of Environment
- The Government Initiative

15 **Panchayati Raj: An Era of Empowerment** 329
- Why Study Panchayati Raj?
- Historical Backdrop
- Functions of Panchayati Raj
- Empowerment of Women
- Empowerment of Weaker Sections
- A Critique of 73rd Constitution Amendment Act

16 **Changing Rural Society** 345
- Subsistence to Market Economy
- Rural Society and Technology
- Abolition of Intermediaries
- Emergence of Various Associations and Institutions
- Contemporary Rural Cultural Changes

Index 357

Preface

The Indian society has a euphoria for village life. The village society is considered to be an old society which has a rich culture. Village people are said to be honest and hard working. Their robust commonsense is very rich. This society is in the process of new social formations. There came a watershed when the country decided to launch with development programmes to lead the villagers to the road of progress. Millions of money has been spent on the development of villages. What we want to do with the villages is that we want to make them self-sufficient and also link them with the wider society at regional and national levels.

The Constitution of India gives certain provisions to the villagers in the form of special development programmes. The village poverty has to be eradicated. There needs to be an end of the exploitation of villagers. Our national leaders throughout the struggle of independence reiterated that in independent India, first priority would be given to the village development. By village development we understand development of agriculture, irrigation, health, education, cooperatives and panchayat system. What is required is to empower the people so that they can make their own decisions. In real sense, the development is that, which the villagers term development. Despite the diversification of village economy from subsistence level to market, the villagers continue to practise agriculture as their main source of livelihood. The age-old agriculture has now become capitalistic and the village capitalism has multiplying effect. The land tenure system, land control, and above all land relations occupy an important place in rural society. Not only the village economy has witnessed tremendous transformation, there has also been vital cultural transformation.

Thousands of social workers, change agents, government agencies and NGOs, are working in our more than five lakh villages. The villages are at crossroads. On the one hand they want to maintain their identity and on the other hand they want to establish link or nexus with the urban society. It should be mentioned that both rural and urban communities, though distinct, are parts of a wider Indian civilisation.

In our enthusiasm for leading the villages towards development, we should be intelligent enough to understand thoroughly, the rural society. Sociologists have spent thousands of days in the study of rural society. Surely, there is no well-tested all-embracing theory for rural development but with so much of accumulated rural empirical data, sociologists and for that matter rural sociologists have made certain empirical generalisations. These generalisations are found in concepts like sanskritisation, westernisation and dominant caste. Those working in the rural society must benefit from such conceptual constructions. The sociologists have also analysed the social formations which have taken place in the rural society followed by development programmes.

We admit that those who work in the field or want to familiarise themselves with the village situations should not be guided by the rule of thumb. Conjectures and wild guesses hardly help us to get favourable response from the villages. Our emphasis is that before launching a village development programme we should have an appropriate understanding of the rural society. The present work is a sincere effort to look at the village life from the objective point of view. We present some of the important findings in the form of conceptual framework and analysis which can be useful for students of rural society. The book as we have prepared is thus a guide to those who are concerned with the development of our villages.

S.L. Doshi
P.C. Jain

1 What is Rural Sociology ?

India has a nostalgia for rural life. The literature available in Hindi and regional languages, very adequately provides profile for the rich and simple life. The fictions created by Prem Chand on village life are said to be the bestial of humanity in the phase of industrialisation and consequent social erosion and at times, the scenes reveal exploitation and resultant dehumanisation. His perception of village life and the prescriptions given by him, are so impressive that one of the critics observed that without spending any huge sums on village development, it was sufficient to distribute, free of cost, Prem Chand's literature on village life. His Hori, Surdas and innumerable characters provide adequate material for developing comprehension about village people.

Maithilisharan Gupt, our national poet, has portrayed the humane and simple face of village life. So has been done by Pannalal Joshi in Gujarati and Rabindra Nath Tagore in Bengali. Tagore was so much in love with the village community that he established Shanti Niketan far away from the crowded city of Calcutta. Gandhiji, too, had an extravagant love for village life. He founded Sabarmati Ashram, a little away from Ahmedabad city. There is also enough literature on the exploitation of peasantry and the village masses. In fact, Indians have enough good to say for the village life. It was Gandhiji who pleaded the case of village development. It is reported in the press and the debates in Constituent Assembly that when the first draft of India's Constitution was referred to Gandhiji, he immediately tore it of commenting that there was nothing substantial for the betterment of village people. It was at the instance of Gandhiji that the Constitution provided Panchayati Raj in the Directive Principles of State Policy. Any agenda for village development—may it be five year plans or village industries---is not an obligation to the village people. All our efforts for improving the standard of life of the village masses is but a constitutional obligation.

India means rural India. It was at the census of 1901 that about 89.2 per cent of Indians live in villages. Historically, therefore, India has been overwhelmingly an agricultural country. However, the shift in the population from rural to urban community has been conspicuous since 1901. In the first census of 1951, after independence, the rural population had a sharp shift towards urban life reducing the percentage of rural people to 82.7. According to 1991 census three-fourth of India's population (74.3%) lives in villages. The process of urbanisation has, thus, been accelerating.

Newly Acquired Significance of Rural Sociology

One of the common observations of the masses of people in our country is that the village people are excessively immobile. They die on the same soil where they are born. The village society is characterised as highly static society. But, this kind of common understanding is believed in the context of large scale five year plans and liberalisation and the revolution in mass media. The earlier village life which did not have any political and economic power, has now acquired adult franchise, democracy and accelerating transformation. During the last five decades rural people have witnessed massive changes. It is in this context that we shall have to assess and evaluate the significance of rural sociology. Study of rural life, now, no more continues to be a romantic narration—full of natural life, hills and forests, streams and rivers, and folklore and folk-tales. The village life has today reached a stage where the glamour of urban life has made its inroads inside the village life.

It is argued by David Pocock and Louis Dumont that there is nothing special about Indian rural life. Both rural and urban communities are a part of the larger civilisation of the subcontinent. They argue that the urban community is nothing but an extension of rural community. Basically, rural and urban communities are the two sides of the same coin. Whether it is Rampura or Kanpur, the Hindu marriage is basically a Hindu marriage. It does not change with the change of community. Similarly, there is nothing like rural family or urban family. Family is a basic Indian institution and in the paraphrase of I.P. Desai, family in India means joint family.

The observations made by foreign anthropologists in the *Contributions to Indian Sociology* appear to be oversimplified. The facilities, comforts and the sources of income found available in urban community are in a degree wanting in rural community. It is this disparity which makes rural communities different from urban communities. Admittedly, in the domain of religion and culture, the difference in the two communities might not appear conspicuous, but there are several differences in the basic life pattern of the people.

1. *Class Formation and Power Transformation*

The relevance and the significance, which rural sociology assumes in contemporary India, is due largely to political transformation and the resultant class formation. The implementation of five year plans and the emergence of green revolution in 1960s and 1970s have given rise to new class formation. The agricultural bourgeoise which came into prominence during this time, eventually, claimed due share of political power.

Agricultural development has been accompanied by the growth of an increasingly assertive class of rich capitalist farmers, comprising newly rising rich *kulak* peasants and the middle class peasants who have expressed their interest through political power. Actually, the class formation and class differentiation in rural India has not been even. This uneven development of agriculture has resulted in conflict and contradiction at the village level. This has also given rise to communalism and brought in power the political parties that are non-secular.

2. *Panchayati Raj and Its Impact*

Yet another reason for the significance of rural sociology is that of the new power given to the Panchayati Raj. The prominence accorded through the policy of reservation to the scheduled castes, scheduled tribes and women has strengthened the newly emerging social formation in village life. The proverbial village unity has been thrown to winds. The structure and functioning of Panchayati Raj and the inbuilt contradictions between the progressive castes and the *dalits* have also affected the rural structure. It warrants the application of scientific approach to the comprehension of village community.

3. *Poverty Removal Programmes*

The slogan for the removal of poverty has taken a variety of forms.

The peasantry is up in arms against the big or *kulak* farmers. The peasant movements are an indication to this new struggle. There are problems of struggle over wage-land to the tillers, distribution of wasteland, agrarian relations in the context of commercial crops and above all class discrimination.

A variety of poverty removal programmes, both at the central and state levels, require an indepth understanding of the village community. The schemes of Integrated Rural Development Programme (IRDP), Spatial Livestock Production Programme (SLPP), Drought Prone Areas Programme (DPAP), National Rural Employment Programme (NREP), Training of Rural Youth for Self Employment (TRYSEM) and a number of other such schemes have provided opportunities for generation of new income. These programmes need a new perspective of rural sociology for churning out successful stories of development. Perhaps, in all programmes of poverty removal, the significance of rural sociology has assumed new dimensions.

4. *Changing Ecosystem and Environmental Dilemma*

The forest and forest land are passing through an environmental erosion. Deforestation has been more than enough. Most of the forests are at the verge of ruin. The forest land has been encroached upon by unscientific and unsystematic mining. Not only the urban sector but perhaps much more the rural sector is facing devastation of eco-system. The debate on development and sustainable environment has assumed new significance in the country. It is argued that plans of development should not be made at the cost of environmental degradation and disequilibrium in eco-system. If big dams provide ample opportunities for irrigation, they also ruin the forest, mineral wealth and turn thousands of farmers as oustees. The problem of rehabilitation of oustees becomes an agricultural disaster. On the other hand, the developmentalists and, particularly the state and the central governments, put forward a counter-argument that these human resource 'losses' are at the cost of development. There is a consensus in the country that development in all conditions should be eco-friendly. The significance of rural sociology assumes importance in the present situation of vast development and environmental decay in rural life. It must be said that the plans of rural development can hardly be implemented by the sheer rule of thumb understanding. Rural sociology, as a scientific social science, has a kit of concepts along with theoretical formats which can be of substantial importance for the development of village life.

5. *Constitutional Constraints*

As observed earlier, the development of rural communities is not a happy-go-lucky desire of state or the central government. It is an obligation on the part of these governments which has to be implemented as desired by the Constitution. The Constitution of India lays down certain Directive Principles of State Policy which, though not justiciable, are "fundamental in governance of the country". And it is "the duty of the state to apply these principles in making laws". In constitutional paraphrase the state is required to build a social order in which justice-social, economic and political-prevails in all the institutions of the national life. "The state shall direct its policy in such a manner as to secure the right of all men and women to an adequate means of livelihood.... " Some of the other important directives relate to the provision of opportunities for "the organisation of village panchayats" and improvement in the standard of living. There are various objectives of five year plans and the development policies but the basic focus is on the improvement of the living standard of the millions of villages. In this context it is obligatory to foster development in the rural segment of society. And, if development is the idiom of our planning, the perspectives of rural sociology need to be applied thoroughly. If, in the context of post-modernity in Europe, experts have power, the rural sociologists and for that matter being experts, assume the status of power. There is no alternative to rural sociology. If the life in villages has to be improved, the poverty has to be removed as our goal of development.

6. *Accelerating Proletarianisation of the Village People*

It was during the British Raj that the land was made a personal property. One could own his personal land and dispose it off at his will. The concept of land as a property was unhistorical for the country. By the process of succession going through one generation to the other in a period of decades, land today has become a scarce commodity. It has resulted into depeasantisation. The higher agriculture technology, which is beneficial for big peasants, hardly suits to the small owners.

This has compelled the poor peasantry to take to agriculture labour, wage earning and frequently migration. If three-fourth of India's population is rural, a large number of them survive below poverty line. Actually, the common man in the village is a proletarian. The slogan---land to the tiller---is a simple extension of proletarianisation of the marginal and small farmers. The plight of the rural proletariats requires to be studied with the help of sociological perspective so that the schemes which are meant for them are utilised by them only. To ensure such a condition of development, rural sociology needs to be applied. For all purposes it should be clear to the government and the advocates of development that rural sociology is not a fiction. Nor is it a pedagogy only. It is worth its application.

7. *Multi-Ethnicities*

India has multi-ethnicities: it is a land of diversities. Such a multi-ethnic situation makes it obligatory to understand the village life thoroughly. We do not have India's villages like the homogeneous villages of Japan. It would not be an exaggeration to say that in terms of ethnicity, dialect, fairs and festivals, and if not each village, surely a cluster of villages is different from other villages. In the north-eastern villages, namely, Bodos and Nagas, sometimes, a single village has its own dialect, own autonomy and above all own ethnicity. It clearly brings out the fact that we should have thorough knowledge of rural anthropology and rural sociology. And it is here that these two branches of sociology assume crucial importance.

8. *Role of Non-Governmental Organisations (NGOs)*

An authentic decentralisation of power means that the non-governmental organisations should occupy a pivotal status in the implementation of development plans. One plus point with the NGOs is that they are closer to earth and the people. They have better understanding of the village life. We have some substantial data to indicate that in comparison to government agencies, the NGOs have better record of success stories for the awakening among the village people. The NGOs though not professionally holders of the knowledge of rural sociology but definitely they apply the perspective of rural sociology for a deep comprehension of village life.

9. *Gandhian Scheme of Rural Development*

Any critique of Gandhian philosophy would accept that Gandhiji was clear about the plight of the village people. Definitely, he had his personal experiences about the village community, but he was closer to the rural people. He is credited to have developed the concept of *Gram Swaraj*, i.e., village autonomy. He pleaded for the self-reliance of the village people. Gandhiji's village autonomy was not segmentary. It was, for all purposes, an organic autonomy where an isolated village was a part of the organic whole, i.e., the wider community. *Gramdan* and *Bhoodan* villages, created by Vinoba Bhave, are the models of village development imagined by Gandhiji. Rural sociology carries within its belly a large number of such experiences pertaining to village development. These must be put into practice.

10. *Widening Horizons of Rural Sociology*

Some five decades back, rural sociology consisted only of the study of rural life, its simple composition and ordinary way of life caused with absence of transport and communication. It was a place of romance and merry-making. Gone are all these features of village life. Its horizons have extended. In its new incarnation, it includes agrarian relations, land reforms, agricultural labourers, wage reforms, stratification, rural leadership, environment and above all peasant movements and struggles. There are problems of rural people pertaining to exploitation and antagonism between lower peasantry and upper peasantry. The peasant struggles are formulated into Marxist framework, namely, conflict and contradictions.

Rural sociologists have recently shifted their emphasis from caste, ritual and village solidarity to agrarian relations and peasant movements. Such a widening zone of rural sociology provides attractive feedback to an appropriate rural development.

11. *Social Science Research as a Major Growth Industry towards Village Economy*

It would not be wrong to say that beginning from 1950s, sociologists and social anthropologists conducted extensive studies in the field of rural sociology. The research trend in rural studies continued till the early 1960s. The dominant concern of these studies was the examination of the interrelationships between different dimensions of rural organisation. M.N. Srinivas (1960), McKim Marriott (1955), S.C. Dube (1955) and D.N. Majumdar (1955) among others contributed substantially to the field of rural sociology. Some of the earlier writings of this genre appeared in the *Economic Weekly* between October 1951 and May 1954. These studies have employed both sociological and social anthropological perspectives.

The researches conducted in the field of rural sociology by sociologists and social anthropologists have focussed on green revolution, problems of cooperative system, land tenure, caste system, panchayat system and voting behaviour. Even now rural sociology continues to be the field of enquiry for sociologists and social anthropologists, though, there has been a shift in these enquiries. This shift is observable in the unit of investigation, change in the theoretical analysis and interdisciplinary thrust concept building. Recently, Myron Weiner has done a holistic analysis of social science research and public policy in India. He observes that studies in rural sociology are sponsored by central and state governments, UGC, ICSSR, ICHR and a number of other non-governmental agencies. The Anthropological Survey of India and Registrar General of India also make intensive studies in the field of rural life.

We have now reached at a stage where some serious exercise is required. Whatever rich data that we have in the domain of rural sociology, should be put to theoretical construction. Though, we have certain hypothetical formulations regarding rural life such as caste mobility, dominant caste, parochialisation—universalisation, effort should be made to bring these findings closer to the students and social workers. This makes the study of rural sociology all the more significant for developing certain hypotheses and laws for improving the standard of life of the masses of rural people. It is in this context that Weiner considers social science research as a major growth industry in India.

12. *Growing Urbanisation, Industrialisation and Migration*

The popularity of rural studies which reached its peak in the middle of 1950s to the end of 1960s now has assumed fresh relevance. With the passage of time industrialisation has increased in rural India. Consequently, as the census of 1981 shows, the process of urbanisation has also accelerated. In the census of 1981, it is reported that 23.43 per cent of population resides in urban areas. The speedy industrialisation and urbanisation have pushed the rural people to urban market. The burden on land and the unemployment at the rural level has compelled the rural proletariats to migrate to city. What is important in this respect is that the importance of rural sociology has assumed greater significance in the sense that how do we meet the challenge of unemployment and burden on land which the rural people face.

To conclude, in the present context of liberalisation and the role of market, we only wish to stress that in the web of political and economic transformation, village studies, i.e., rural sociology should acquire a priority status among the social sciences. The experts, whether engineers, technocrats, bureaucrats or nutritionists, are now required to develop their skills and knowledge in the domain of rural sociology.

Sociology, Social Anthropology and Rural Sociology

At a broader plane rural sociology is a branch or sub-discipline of sociology and social anthropology.

If we evaluate the researches conducted in the field of rural sociology, it would be easily found that social anthropology has contributed substantially to the field of rural sociology. Village studies of the kind of *Indian Village, India's Villages, Village India* have all been written by social anthropologists. Viewed from this perspective, if rural sociology is a branch or sub-discipline of sociology, then it is also a sub-discipline of social anthropology. Therefore, rural sociology is basically two-dimensional—sociological and anthropological.

Sociology

On a general plane, it is said that when sociological perspectives are applied to the analysis of rural society, it is the sub-discipline of rural sociology. Such a definition of rural sociology is only simplistic. First, we should delineate what do we mean by sociological perspectives. In other words, one should be clear about the meaning of sociology. If the correct and precise meaning of sociology is made out, we would be certain about its perspective.

There are several definitions of sociology. When this discipline emerged it was defined as the science of society. Auguste Comte (1789-1857), who is said to be the Father of Sociology, defined it as a composition of two words---the Greek 'logos' meaning word, speech, reasoning or calculation, and the Latin 'socius' meaning companion. The Greek word 'logos' means a scientific study. Thus, in Augustine paraphrase, sociology is the study or theory of companions, concerned with what goes on when people get together in groups and interact with one another.

Perhaps, the master ideas concerning the definition of sociology have been given by the founding-fathers of sociology. Emile Durkheim did not accept sociology as a study of society. Such a definition was vague. He, therefore, provided a focus to the definition and said that sociology is the study of social facts which are exterior to one's mind and have a constrain on him. Durkheim defined sociology precisely and narrowed down the area of study limited only to social facts.

Max Weber, however, defined sociology in an interdisciplinary usage. For him, sociology is both subjective, i.e., psychological and sociological. He said that it is social science which analyses social action. Social action is typified as goal-oriented, traditional, formal and charismatic.

Karl Marx did not define sociology in specific terms but whatever he has argued in his works, is that sociology tries to analyse the class formulations resulting from the behaviour of the actor. For him sociology or in wider terms all social sciences must be emancipatory. Man is the ultimate reality of society.

In a single sentence, reviewing the definitions of sociology given by all these master thinkers, one could safely say that sociology studies man as a member of society or a group, may it be caste or clan. All the three agree that sociology is not an arm-chair exercise. It is for the emancipation of the mankind. Sociology has its uses. If it is devoid of any use for the society in the Durkheiminian paraphrase, it has no right to survive for a moment in the society. It all means that sociology is about interaction—human behaviour which takes place among individuals. Secondly, its prime objective is to improve the status of individual or society in wider context.

During the last four or five decades a few other master sociologists have emerged. These include Talcott Parsons, Robert K. Merton, Kingsley Davis and a few others. These new sociologists are better known as functionlists. They define sociology with the perspective of system. Each system has its actors and the activities of these actors either maintain the system or create dysfunctions for its devastation. For these sociologists, in a broader sense, sociology is the study of social functions and social systems. Such a sociology is characterised by the perspective of consensus of the society. They go with the assumption that the society is cohesive, it is autonomous, it is integrative and above all one.

During the last half a decade a new crop of French and German sociologists-anthropologists has emerged. Among them may be included Jurgen Habermas, Michael Foucault, Jacques Deridda and Pierre Bourdieu. These sociologists are also social anthropologists and philosophers. They are also advocates of post-modern sociological theory. Though, they disagree among themselves, they share the view that sociology has certain concepts, methods and verifications which put it to the status of scientific discipline. Bourdieu, for instance, argues that though sociology is a divided discipline, it is interested to find out the 'hidden' aspects of human actions. It is concerned to find out the vital interests of social groups. In his words: Sociology uncovers the hidden foundations of human domination or strives to publicise its findings.

Bourdieu, quite like his European counterparts, has elaborately taken up the exercise of defining sociology as a science and its uses for the surrounding society. We shall discuss him in a little detail.

Bourdieu is a contemporary philosopher-turned sociologist-social anthropologist from Paris, France. He conducted his fieldwork among the tribals of Algeria. It is out of his fieldwork and other experiences that he has developed certain theoretical concepts, discourses as he calls from these experiences. Basically, he was a farmer, close to nature and land. This developed in him an authentic sociologist. He is currently much talked about and referred in Europe and USA. His interpretation of the meaning and content of sociology is both current and contemporary.

He argues that sociology is the only science which puts at stack the interests, sometimes the vital interests, of social theory. This concern for social group makes sociology very difficult both to produce sociological discourse and to transmit it. What is important for a sociologist is to find out the hidden foundations of human life and strive to publicise the findings. The sociologist can expect little help in his effort to make known what he has learned, from those whose job it is, day by day and week by week, to produce---on all the required subjects of our time, 'violence', 'youth', 'drugs', 'the revival of religion', and so on---the not even-untrue discourses which become ritual essay subjects for high school peoples. Bourdieu argues that sociology:

> ...has a great need of being helped in this task. For truth has no intrinsic capacity to prevail, and scientific discourse is itself caught up in the power relations that it uncovers. The transmission of that discourse is subject to the very laws of cultural diffusion that it sets out. Those who possess the cultural competence needed to appropriate that discourse and not those who would have most interest in doing so.

Bourdieu could further be elaborated but what he emphasises strongly is that sociology is a social science which uncovers the hidden truth of society. The society owes its continuance to its cultural capital and, therefore, Sociology falls in the domain of cultural analysis. For Bourdieu access to culture or what Bourdieu calls cultural practices, are manifold. Normally, there are cultural practices followed by the general people. But, there is also a counter-culture, perhaps, the culture of the proletariat. Generally, the proletariat counter-culture is defined negatively by the un authentic sociologists. The objective of sociology is, therefore, to unveil the hidden culture of the society. It is the prime concern of sociology, as Bourdieu observes:

> In that sense my book is both a cultural and a counter-cultural book. More generally, I think a genuine counter-culture ought to supply weapons for use against the soft forms of domination, the advanced forms of mobilisation, the gentle violence of the new professional ideologists, who often rely on a kind of quasi-scientific rationalisation of the dominant ideology, against the political uses of science, the authority of science---physical science or economic science, not to mention the biology or sociology of the advanced forms of racism.

Bourdeau is really a post-modernist in his access to the definition of sociology. When he talks about counter-culture, he emphasises that the culture of the proletariat should be studied in depth by the sociologists. What has not been said traditionally must be said in the way which has remained hidden so far. In a broader way, therefore, sociology is the interpretation of the hidden cultural practices of the proletariats. In other words, sociology is the social science of the study of counter-culture, a culture which is against the established culture. This counter-culture is also marginal to the official culture.

Yet another eminent philosopher who has currently defined sociology is Jacques Derrida. Derrida is a French philosopher who has also delivered lectures in sociology. Basically, he is known for his deconstruction philosophy. Derrida's deconstruction is almost exclusively some type of phenomenology. In its development deconstruction has gone beyond the limits of philosophical gates. Although, first, it developed as philosophy, it has spread not only into literally, art, and film criticism and theory, but also into psycho-analytic, pedagogical and social theory.

Deconstruction also relates to culture and aspects of sociology. Sociology has its texts about society. It has texts of founding-fathers; it has texts of mythology; it has texts of history. But these texts are not always the profiles of social reality. This reality need not be the real one. By deconstruction what Derrida means is that what is given in textual reading does not give us the hidden sight of society. Deconstruction accounts for analysing the texts in their implicit meanings. Derrida observes:

> It means that deconstruction accounts for how a text's explicit formulations undermine its implicit or non-explicit aspects. It brings out what the text excludes by showing what it includes. It highlights what remains indecidable and what operates as an indecidable in the texts itself.

What Derrida has said in the definition of sociology is that sociology uses the theoretical framework of deconstruction. It is the deconstruction of great and little texts which is amply available in art, culture and philosophy. These texts have definite explicit meanings. But, behind explicit meanings, there are also implicit meanings in these texts. And then, the explicit meanings could also be wrong. In such a situation the task of sociologist is to analytically look into the narratives with the perspective of explicit and implicit analysis.

We have argued earlier that rural sociology employs the perspectives of sociology. These perspectives which are basically sociological have been discussed by us in our attempt to define sociology. In a nutshell, the sociological perspective is characterised as below:

1. Sociology is scientific in nature and, therefore, analyses societal activities from the point of view of interactions.
2. The basic unit of study in sociology is the social action taken up by the subject or actor.
3. Activities studied by sociology are those which construct a system.
4. Sociology tries to find out the hidden aspects of society. And, in addition to it, it also studies the counter-culture which is the culture of the proletariat.
5. Sociology does not accept anything as real which is given in our traditional texts. The explicit meanings of texts could be wrong; and in addition to it there might be explicit meanings, which have remained implicit. Deconstruction stresses on the implicit meanings of texts and criticises or rejects the explicit meanings of the texts. Deconstruction is the idiom of sociology.
6. Despite variations in the definitions of sociology, there is consensus that sociology studies the interaction patterns which emerge out of the relations among the people.

At this level of discussion we could safely say that rural sociology is a sub-discipline of sociology. But, with the changes in the conceptual framework of sociology, there is also a change in the formulations of rural sociology. If sociological perspectives undergo change as is evident from the contributions of Bourdieu and Derrida, the analysis of rural sociology also changes. There is mutuality between the two---sociology and rural sociology. The second dimension of rural sociology is the social anthropology. As a matter of fact, the nature of rural sociology is interdisciplinary. It borrows heavily from sociology and social anthropology. If rural sociology is a branch or sub-discipline of sociology, it is equally a branch of social anthropology. Let us, then, define social anthropology.

Social Anthropology

Tim Ingold once observed that anthropology is philosophy with the people in: anthropology is the science of the people. It has several variants---physical anthropology, social anthropology, cultural anthropology, ethnology and linguistics. Logically, social anthropology and for that matter anthropology itself is quite distinct and autonomous discipline differentiated from sociology. But, in India, historically it has become difficult to differentiate social anthropology from sociology. In the beginning sometime by the end of the 19th century, social anthropology was taken by British anthropologists, such as Risley, Russel, O'mella and Blunt. At a later stage, in the first quarter of 20th century, the sociologists also took to social anthropology as their major theme of discussion. If Risley and O'mella wrote about caste in India, equally G.S. Ghurye also dealt with the caste in system. The social anthropologists helped the British, in colonial countries including India and South Africa to exercise their hegemony over the natives. The British also used social anthropology to explore the local markets for the sale of their products. John Beattie (1964) described social anthropology as the social studies of other cultures. The study of other cultures was the study of pre-industrial colonial countries. The historical forces of this kind brought social anthropology and sociology quite closer. The closeness is so intimate that it has today become very difficult to differentiate sociology and social anthropology. If any formal or pedagogical differential has to be made it can be made without any difficulty. Surely, a professor of sociology is not a professor of social anthropology, but in their writing such a kind of differentiation can hardly be made.

We shall have to look into the meaning of anthropology in the long past. The origin of the discipline lies in the classic Greek historian Herodotos (484-420 B.C.) or in the geographer Strabo (64-32 B.C.). Both were significant pioneers regarding ethnographic description; they wrote detailed narratives about foreign peoples. The writings of both deal with foreigners whose customs, languages and peculiarities they describe in, as detailed a fashion, as possible, frequently without passing moral judgement.

Historically, the beginning of modern anthropology is sometimes traced back to 18th-19th century. David Hume and Immanuel Kant contributed empirical method of study to the study of anthropological problems. Kant argued that humans were born with certain formulas for thinking, from this idea, it follows that people all over the world would think in roughly the same way. Related notions about universal mental traits have formed an important focus for discussion in modern anthropology.

The traits of modern anthropology are also found in mid-19th century in the works of Herry Min's *Ancient Law* (1861) and Lewis Henry Morgan's books, including *Ancient Society* (1877). Both these authors developed theories of primitive society which were to wield influence far into the 20th century. Min, who had worked in India, proposed a distinction between status and contract societies, a conceptual pair which is reminiscent of many later distinctions between modern and traditional societies.

Morgan's most important contribution to early anthropology was undoubtedly his theory of social evolution. He distinguished between three main phases in the evolution of societies: savagery, barbarism and civilisation. Morgan's developmental scheme was only one of many evolutionist theories in the 19th century.

What we call contemporary or modern anthropology owes its emergence from the works of Franz Boas and Bronislaw Malinowski. They are said to be the first modern anthropologists. Boas was a German but migrated to US in the 1880s to study American Indians. He conducted intensive field study, nearly single-handedly. Alfred Kroebar, Ruth Benedict and Margaret Mead were the distinguished students of Boas. The theory of cultural relativism was developed by Boas. He gave the master idea that every culture must be understood according to its own logic. Cultural relativism is still indispensable as a methodological tool in social anthropology.

Malinowski was a Pole, but he immigrated to British in 1910. His most important work was the meticulous recording of social life in the Trobriand islands of New Guinea. He conducted his fieldwork between 1915 and 1918. He studied the interrelationships of various aspects of society and therefore held that long field studies were absolutely necessary.

Many other important influences on contemporary anthropological thought are due largely to Durkheim, and his nephew, Marcel Mauss. Mauss contributed substantially on the practice of gifts among the tribals. Sigmund Freud's *psycho-analytical theory* has also influenced American anthropology. Finally, Karl Marx, Ferdinand Tonnies, Max Weber and others, even today, continue to exert strong influence on contemporary social anthropological thinking.

Outline of Anthropology

The word 'anthropology' consists of the *two Greek words---- 'antropos' and 'logas'----which are translated as 'human' and 'reason', respectively.* Analysing the basic meaning of anthropology, T.H. Eriksen, in his recent (1995) work on *Small Places, Large Issues* observes:

> Social anthropology would mean knowledge about human in societies.

Anthropology frequently uses culture. The word 'culture' originates from the Latin 'colere' which means to cultivate. Again, in the words of Eriksen:

> Cultural anthropology, thus, means knowledge about cultivated humans; i.e., knowledge about those aspects of humanity which are not natural, but which are related to that which is acquired.

A short definition of anthropology as proposed by Eriksen reads thus:

> Anthropology is the comparative study of cultural and social life. Its most important method is participant observation, which consists in lengthy field work in a particular social setting.

It is really difficult to define social anthropology in definite words. This is because it has been defined with varying emphasis. Despite variations in definitions it is certain that anthropology tries to account for the social and cultural differentiation in the word. A substantial part of anthropological studies consists in conceptualising and understanding similarities between social systems and human relationships.

Emphasising the similarities in social system Claude Levi-Strauss observes:

> Anthropology has humanity as its object of research, but unlike the other human sciences, it tries to grasp its object through its most diverse manifestations.

In reality, anthropology is about how different people can be, but it also tries to find out in what sense it can be said that all humans have something in common. Quite like Levi-Strauss, Clifford Geertz expresses that anthropology essentially deals with the differences between humans and animals.

Though, social anthropology accounts for the different aspects of human existence and studies interrelationships at the local level, a village or a colony, it asks large questions. It gives insights from small places to the wider society. Malinowski's study of *Trobrianders* and Bourdieu's *Enquiry into Algerians*---quite local places, gave emergence to theories of functionalism and post-modernism. It is what Eriksen's title of book suggests: Small Places, Large Issues. *Some Variants of Anthropology: Shift in Emphasis.*

Anthropology is a diversified discipline. It includes a number of sub-disciplines. Its diversified nature has taken different emphases in different countries. Despite its diversity it retains its distinctive character everywhere. Identifying some of its traditions in different countries Eriksen writes: "Since the Second World War the core areas (of anthropology) have been Great Britain, the US, France and Australia. British anthropology, which is generally spoken of as social anthropology and which also enjoys a strong position in Scandinavia and India, emphasises the study of social processes and is, thus, close to sociology. The British social anthropologist Edmund Leach (1982) once characterised his subject as a 'comparative micro sociology'. In the US, we tend instead to speak of cultural anthropology, and in general the sociological underpinning characteristic of the British tradition has been less prominent there. Instead, linguistics and prehistory have informed American anthropology in different ways. Several important specialisations, such as cultural ecology, linguistic anthropology and various approaches in psychological and interpretive or hermeneutic anthropology, were developed in the US. French anthropology in the post-war period has been strongly associated with structuralism, notably with the names of Claude Levi-Strauss, Louis Dumont and the structural Marxist Maurice Godelier. In South America, Italy and the Iberian peninsula, and partly in Belgium and the Netherlands, the French orientation is strong."

Indian anthropology has two main sub-disciplines: social anthropology and physical anthropology. The tradition in social anthropology in our country is to study the caste, tribe and village. This tradition has linked social anthropology to sociology in the country. Those who study rural sociology should, therefore, also have knowledge about sociology and social anthropology. If anthropology in Great Britain is social anthropology, if anthropology in America is cultural anthropology, if anthropology in France is structuralism, anthropology in India is tribe, caste and village.

One very important point which differentiates social anthropology from sociology is that the former is strongly characterised by fieldwork. It is generally said that social anthropology has the methodology of residing in tents for conducting fieldwork. It studies the small places such as villages and highlands. Rural sociology shares this methodology and focusses on villages, tribal groups and caste clusters.

Social anthropology, thus, has the following major characteristics:

1. It studies similarities and dissimilarities between social systems and human relationships.
2. The humanity is its object of research.
3. It tries to understand both connection *within* societies and connection *between* societies.
4. It asks large questions but draws its insight from small places, such as villages and tribal hinterlands.
5. It studies *other cultures*.
6. It develops insight in the structure of the society.
7. Its basic agenda is culture. All its researches are oriented to cultural paradigms.

All said about anthropology and social anthropology, it is certain that discipline is one though, it has many specialisations and many diverse strands of thoughts. It is also certain that notwithstanding specialisations and different traditions, social anthropology in India is abundantly oriented to rural, caste and tribal studies. It would not be an exaggeration to observe that more than three-fourth of the research material in sociology and social anthropology in India is related to or falls in the domain of rural sociology.

Rural Sociology

Studies on rural sociology go back to the origin of society itself. Whatever advanced societies we see today, whether US or French, they originate from the village society. The general process is that rural society turns into a town society, then shifts to city, mega city and metropolitan community. However, the systematic origin of rural sociology goes back to 19th century. Generally, when the feudal society took to capitalism, it gave rise to the systematic study of rural sociology emphasising the impact of industrialisation and capitalism on rural economy and the subsequent need for studying rural society A.R. Desai observes:

> The impact of the capitalist-industrial civilisation upon the rural economy and the social structure in various parts of the world forced the attention of scholars to the study of the trends of rural social development. Research in the subject of the origin and the nature of village community which was undergoing transformation was launched.

Before rural sociology developed into a systematic sub-discipline of sociology, several scholars notably sociologists and social anthropologists dealt with the discourses on rural society; for instance, *The Systematic Source Book in Rural Sociology* (Vol. I) edited by Sorokin, Zimmerman and Galpin. The volume vividly shows that the earlier social thinkers paid due attention to the description of rural society but this, however, was not the formal beginning of rural sociology.

Origin and development of rural sociology: US and India

It is interesting to note that the sociology of rural Life in its systematic form originated in the US. It was sometime by the second quarter of the 20th century. "It originated from the report of the Country Life Commission (CLC) appointed by the American President, Theodore Roosevelt, in 1907. At that time there was mass poverty and economic crisis which affected the American rural life, as he feared that if nothing was done about it, the United States might face a deterioration in moral life too. Social problems of the rural United States has increased to a significant extent, and the CLC was to study these rural social problems and make recommendations for improvement of rural life."

The CLC made elaborated investigation, circulated about 5 lakh copies of questionnaire to farmers and rural people. This report provided benchmark data for rural sociology. The findings were referred to the members of American Sociological Society in its annual meeting held in 1912. This reference to US Sociological Society motivated sociologists to take up study of rural society in a massive way. Consequently, huge data on rural life was poured out in the form of research monographs and dissertations. "All these provided grounds for the emergence of rural sociology. John M. Gillette was the pioneer in writing a textbook on rural sociology in 1960. A journal entitled *Rural Sociology* was for the first time launched in USA in 1935."

Reputed sociologists, such as James Michel Williams, Warren H. Wilson, and Newell L. Sims contributed substantially to the study of American rural society. The early rural sociologists used statistical and historical data along with field interview to find out empirical reality of the US country life. Rural church life was elaborately studied by Warren Wilson. C. J. Galpin, likewise, made investigation into American rural life.

Evaluating the origin and growth of rural sociology in US, A.R. Desai observes:

> In the USA rural sociology, though, a new science and still in a state of immaturity, is commanding wider and wider interest among social thinkers to day. More than 800 professors and research workers are engaged in developing that science in that country.

Not only in US but in other parts of the world also increasing attention is being paid to study the rural life in a scientific way. The League of Nations, in its formative days, sponsored a large number of studies in the form of monographs. UNO, UNESCO, FAO and other world organisations have also contributed to the rapid development of rural sociology.

In India, the beginning of the study of rural society goes back to Sir Henry S. Maine. Maine brought out, among others, two significant books, viz., *Ancient Law* (1861) and *Ancient Society* (1877). Maine, though wrote about Indian villages and designated it as a *republic*, he had his own bias which was Euro-centric in its cognition and value terms. Dumont has criticised Maine for his European bias in analysing Indian rural society. Dumont observes: "Sir Henry Maine hardly ever looked at the Indian village in itself, but only as a counterpart to Tutonic, Slavonic or other institutions. India was to him little more than the the historical repository of veritable phenomena of ancient usage and ancient juridical thought."

Actually, the British administrators-turned ethnographers and anthropologists considered the village community as an autonomous sociological isolate. This is, particularly, reflected in the writings of Charles Metcalfe and other British administrators in India besides Henry Maine. Despite some of these weaknesses the fact remains that Maine made a beginning of a systematic study of rural life. It is he who for the first time theorised that kinship was the mainstay of India's rural society. However, the systematic growth of rural sociology started in India after the promulgation of Constitution of India and the implementation of Community Development Programmes. It was argued that when the British anthropologists consolidated their colonial empire in South Africa and India, why social anthropology could not be helpful in nation-building in the wake of development programmes. This gave rise to a number of rural studies.

Even, during the days of British East India Company, there were efforts made by sociologists and social anthropologists to find out the patterns of land tenure, customary laws and the functioning of peasants and artisans. For instance, Ramakrishna Mukherjee (1957) informed by scruitinising the source material on the nature of the village community from British Administrative Report of the Punjab (1852) and Marx's commentary on the Indian village community that there were discussions on the village communities.

Also, during the British period, researches or enquiries were made on the affairs of rural life. The recurrent famines in India provoked several studies. The report of the Royal Commission on Agriculture became a monumental work dealing with the problems faced by the countryside. A number of economists had begun studying village communities. Slater started the idea of economic survey of villagers as part of the activities of the University of Madras in 1916. These villages were resurveyed in 1936 and 1961.

All this is good but when did rural sociology emerge in its modern form? The ICSSR—an apex body of social scientists that carried out a survey of researches done in India for a period of 10 years, the first report taking into consideration the preceding 10 years came out in 1970. In the first volume entitled *A Survey of Research in Sociology and Social Anthropology* (Vol. I), the sub-discipline of rural sociology is discussed under the chapter 'Rural Studies'. The following report for the period 1969-1979 also analyses the development that took place in rural sociology under the heading 'Rural Studies'. The question is: Why does trend report not mention the chapter titled as 'Rural Sociology' instead of 'Rural Studies'. There is some ambiguity. It appears that sociologists suffer from the obsession of including rural sociology as a part of sociology. What is rural sociology is for sociologists only rural studies. The fact of the matter is that the rural studies included in both the volumes fall within the domain of rural sociology. This omission on the part of ICSSR has made the status of rural sociology quite vulnerable.

Rural sociology, in its own right and merit, occupies a qualified status. It has its subject matter, its scientific nature and above all methods and tools. By its nature it is interdisciplinary and draws freely from the sister disciplines of economics, political science, sociology and social anthropology. A.R. Desai has readily done a pioneering work in the field of Rural Sociology by editing *Rural Sociology in India*. The edited work was first published in 1969 and by now has gone into more than half a dozen editions.

A.R. Desai before defining rural sociology and delineating its scope rightly raises certain questions: Is rural sociology a distinct science or is it merely an application of the general principles of sociology? Should rural sociology restrict its scope merely to the life processes of rural society or should it also include as an integral part a study of rural and urban social life, comparative as well as in their mutual interconnection and interaction and further, include as its central concept, what Zimmerman describes as, "the mechanism and effects of urbanisation and ruralisation upon a population"?

Desai interrogates further: Should rural sociology only provide scientific knowledge about rural societies and laws governing its development or should it also serve as a guide and suggest practical programmes of reform or reconstruction of that society in the economic, social and cultural fields?

Many more questions could be raised about the definition and status of rural sociology in social sciences. Controversies are enough. Sociologists and social anthropologists have defined rural sociology in various ways. For instance, J.B. Chitambar defines rural sociology as below:

> What are the phenomena rural sociology studies?.... They are the phenomena resulting from rural man's reciprocal interaction with other rural people—behaviour relationships not *within* the individual but between individuals. Rural sociological phenomena are not

individuals but the interactions and interrelationships between individuals.

The argument put forward by Chitambar is that the interactions and interrelationship in the urban and rural segments are not the same as both the segments differ in their physical, social and cultural environments. It is this environmental differentiation which distinguishes rural sociology from urban sociology.

P.C. Deb has discussed the theme and subject matter of rural sociology. His definition runs as below:

> It can be stated that rural sociology is that branch of sociology which studies relationships of human beings living in villages of rural areas. In other words, rural sociology studies rural society. Just as in any other society, in rural society, specific kinds of social relationships are in existence. Major social institutions exist both in urban and rural society but they are always identical. Because of the noticeable differences in the nature of village social institutions from those of urban areas, and because a majority of the population in developing countries lives in rural areas, rural sociology is gradually being given the status of an independent discipline.

Some of the foreign sociologists have also defined rural sociology. For instance, Chapin F. Stuart defines it as:

> ...a study of rural population, rural social organisation and the rural social process operating in rural society.

According to Senderson:

> Rural sociology is the sociology of life in the rural environment.

Perhaps the definition of rural sociology given by A.R. Desai is more closer to Indian situation. He observes:

> Rural sociology or the science of the laws of development of rural society in general has come into being only in recent times. The basic task of rural sociology is to discover the laws of development to rural society.... The prime objective of the rural sociology is to make scientific, systematic and comprehensive study of the rural social organisation, of its structure, function, and objective tendencies of development and on the basis of such studies to discover the laws of its development.

The catalogue of definitions of rural sociology could be enhanced. There are variations in the definitions. But, notwithstanding the variations, it is argued by all the scholars that rural sociology is in no case an arm-chair discipline. By studying the rural life scientifically, rural sociologists should construct theoretical formulations which can be successfully applied for improving the lifestyle of the rural people. If the empirical generalisations made out of the study of rural society are not appropriate for the betterment of rural life, rural sociology has no right to exist. It is because of this shared understanding that rural sociology is basically a social science for the development of rural society. Some of the points shared by most of the rural sociologists, economists and social anthropologists are as under:

1. Social life all over the world is divided into two divisions: (i) rural division, and (ii) urban division. Though, there is interaction between the two divisions, each division has its identifiable traits.
2. It is further agreed that the social life in rural division is conditioned by the rural environment—physical, social and cultural. Rural life has a historicity, composition and interaction. This specificity and individuality makes the rural division highly distinct.
3. All the scholars share the view the prime objective of rural sociology should be to make a scientific, systematic and comprehensive study of the rural social organisation, of its structure, functions and objective tendencies of development and on the basis of such a study to discover the law of its development.
4. It is agreed that in the developing parts of the world, such as Latin America, Africa and Asia, a new significance of rural sociology has emerged. All the developing countries are engaged in the task of nation-building. Such an objective invariably includes the development of the people at the grassroot who are closer to the soil.

Some basic characteristics of rural sociology

Our preceding discussions about the origin, meaning and definition of rural sociology bring out some basic features as under:

1. **Rural sociology is multi-dimensional;** it has orientation to sociology and social anthropology. It has different traditions in US,

Europe and Asia. Rural sociology in Asia is more sociology and social anthropology than rural sociology. It draws subject matter, scientific nature and methodology from both sociology and social anthropology.

2. By design and functioning rural sociology, is interdisciplinary.
3. Sociology studies interactions and interaction systems. When this perspective is applied to the analysis of rural society it becomes rural sociology.
4. Rural sociology is the study of small places, such as villages and tribal habitations. The empirical abstractions made out of the little or small places help to construct theoretical constructions: the studies made by Levi-Strauss, Malinowski, Radcliffe-Brown, Boas and Bourdieu elaborately show that theories of repute have come out of the studies of grassroot people---people living in highlands, forests and small villages.

2 Nature, Subject Matter and Methods of Rural Sociology

Rural sociology is the sister discipline of sociology. Or, in other words, sociology is the big brother of rural sociology. In our country rural sociology is treated as a part of sociology, quite like, social demography, urbanisation, industrialisation or sociology of social stratification. The trend reports sponsored by the Indian Council of Social Science Research (ICSSR) indicate that for the social sciences sociology, social anthropology and rural sociology stand at par. As a matter of fact, the social scientists in country have agreed to put sociology and social anthropology together. They considered rural sociology as a part only of the broader domain of sociology and social anthropology. Thus viewed, the nature of rural sociology, in fact, is the nature of sociology.

Nature of Rural Sociology

Sociology is considered as a social science. Though, there are debates on the nature of sociology in international social sciences. By and large, sociology is a science. There are scholars like C. Wright Mills, Peter Berger and others who consider sociology as an 'imagination'—only as an art. The debate is not new. It starts from the period when social sciences parted their company with philosophy. In its earlier period, sociology was considered as positivistic science. At a later stage, it was realised that sociology could not be like any natural sciences because of its subject matter. Without entering into the debatable nature of sociology it could be observed that the nature of sociology is scientific. Pierre Bourdieu, in one of his discourses, observes that:

> Sociology seems to me to have all the properties that define as science....All sociologists worthy of the name agree on a common heritage of concepts, methods and verification procedures.

What characterises a science is that it has certain concepts, methods and verification. Sociology as certain theoretical formulations, it has logic of enquiry and above all it is subjected to verification. Despite this common agreement on the scientific nature of sociology it must be agreed that sociology is a diversified discipline. It is because of this nature that it is being divided into different realms. It studies different aspects of human society, such as demography, education, family, caste, tribe, village and a number of other segments of a society. Essentially, however, despite having a large number of 'specialities' it continues to remain a social science. Some of the reasons advanced for sociology being a science are as under:

1. *Empiricism*

Biology or physics had laboratory for precise experiments, measurement and verification. To some extent, the empirical method, i.e., fieldwork in sociology provides opportunity for experimentation, observation and verification. The research material available in the body of sociology clearly shows that many of its theoretical formulations have emerged out of the data generated from fieldwork.

2. *Accumulated Facts*

Science grows on the data accumulated from the field. Robert Merton very rightly observes that a sociologist stands on the shoulders of other sociologists. Whatever Talcott Parsons or for that matter, Marx, Durkheim or Weber did, was carried forward by the next generations.

3. *Objectivity*

Yet another characteristic of science is its objectivity. It means the willingness and ability to see things as they really are—to study facts in a given field of investigation as they exist—without personal bias, prejudices or feelings as to their desirability or undesirability. Personal values and desires are not involved in a scientific endeavour.

The objective nature of science is difficult to be applied in social sciences. The status of researcher in empirical investigation has been debatable in sociology and social anthropology right from the 18th century. Pareto argued that when subjectivity and objectivity coincide it becomes objectivity Max Weber, however, did not agree to this hypothesis. He said that in any activity the role of actor is decisive. He gave due place to subjectivity. In one of his recent works Bourdieu has taken up the issue of subjectivity and objectivity. Bourdieu takes up issues of epistemology and methodology for wider scrutiny. He says that subjectivity is important so that individual has his own consciousness but beyond that there is an objective social reality also. He observes:

> There is, therefore, more to social life than the subjective consciousness of the actors who move within it and produce it. There is, if you like, an objective social reality beyond the immediate interactional sphere and the self-conscious awareness of individuals.

What goes on in sociology about objectivity is that there should be a healthy negotiation between the subjective consciousness and the objective reality. The social scientist, therefore, in his research endeavour, should make a fine combination of his subjectivity, objective reality and the prevailing ideology.

4. *Precision and Accuracy*

Science is also characterised by accurate and precise observations. "When scientific observations are made it is extremely important that these describe situations or persons as they actually do exist at the time of observation—this is accuracy."

5. *Methodology*

Science must have a valid methodology. It should be valid in sense that other scientists could also employ the same method and reach to their findings. Such a rigorous methodology can yield dependable theoretical constructs.

6. *Reciprocity in Theory and Empirical Research*

Theory in science is constructed out of the experiments made in the laboratory. But approach to laboratory is through the media of theoretical constructs and hypotheses. Generally, in scientific research, we move from theory to empiricism or from empiricism to theory. In any case there is both-way interaction between theory and empirical research. There is a healthy interaction in the domain of science between laboratory investigation and theoretical formulation. C. Wright Mills very emphatically observed that *theory without data is empty, but data without theory are blind*. Almost all the social anthropologists including the rural sociologists have done hard fieldwork. Malinowski, Radcliffe-Brown and others have done tremendous fieldwork before constructing their theories.

Rural sociology precisely is a specialised field of sociology and social anthropology. Its nature is scientific as it borrows heavily from these social sciences. Those who have conducted rural studies in the field of caste, family, agrarian relations and land reforms have undergone fieldwork in the villages. Whatever theoretical constructs which we have in the field of rural sociology have grown out of the intensive fieldwork done by social scientists.

Subject Matter of Rural Sociology

The subject matter of rural sociology has never been static. In the earlier days of its development, during 18th and 19th centuries, it studied the society of aboriginals and primitive people. The colonial countries of south and central Africa along with India were the target countries for the study of primitive people. The British Raj along with its anthropologists approached these countries for discovering new markets and spreading Christianity. The British administrators turned to the study of primitive people.

We have in our country administrators-turned sociologists and anthropologists who studied the primitive people and the indigenous institutions of village, caste and culture. The initial subject matter of study for social anthropology and in this respect rural sociology was the life of village people and the forest dwellers. In fact, rural sociology remained restricted to the small places of the type of villages or clusters of neighbourhood. Henry Maine, the British administrator, was perhaps the first person to study an Indian village. He characterised an Indian village as a republic in itself. Theoretically, such a kind of portrait of village life can be criticised vehemently. Yogendra Singh (1986) provides a critique to such an understanding of village life because here Maine's emphasis was "on showing how each of these social entities (villages) affirmed the principles of segmentation and autonomy rather then being parts of an organic whole". Despite the criticism made on the republic character of village India, the fact remains that each village was self-sufficient and independent. At a later stage, Gandhiji also observed that our villages were self-reliant and had their local rule.

Thus, the subject matter of rural sociology during the colonial period in India remained confined to the study of hill and forest people—the tribals, the villages and a few of the traditional institutions such as family and caste which were pervasive in the small places. Soon after independence there was a sudden shift and emphasis in the subject matter of rural sociology. It was unhistorical for India to prepare a constitutional agenda for the development of more than its 5 lakh villages. The Constitution of India made it obligatory that the state shall spare no efforts for the development of villages. The Constitution also laid emphasis on the development of Panchayati Raj. It was in the year 1950 that the Constitution of India was promulgated. And then came in 1952 the five year plans and subsequently the community development and extension programmes. Now, in the real sense, the idiom of our development became the development of village. The government policy, thus implemented, created the need for the study of village life. With this context historically created in village development, there came a flood of village studies by the middle of 1950 to the end of 1960. The subject matter of rural sociology, thus, consisted of the study of tribal people, caste and village communities.

M.N. Srinivas (1955), in his edited work, *India's Villages* makes the point that in the context of development planning it was necessary to provide a portrait to the layman about the social life lived by village people. The subject matter of rural sociology, according to Srinivas, consisted to the unity of village, caste and other village institutions. The contributors to this work argued that the Indian village had a traditional unity. The villagers who lived in a restricted area at some distance from other similar groups, with extremely poor roads between them, a majority of them were engaged in agricultural activities. They closely depended upon each other—economically and otherwise. They shared a vast body of common experience and this fostered what is called as the unity of the village. It was the dominant caste in the village which supported and maintained the total village system.

However, the development programmes and the forces of technology, industrialisation, urbanisation, market, and a host of other factors brought about tremendous change in the community. This provided a new set of subject matter to the body of rural sociology. Land reforms, land ceiling, land tenure, and above all agrarian relations constituted new issues for intensive study. The process of democratisation, along with the emphasis on Panchayati Raj, created a new awakening among the people. Agricultural capitalism, as is manifest in green revolution, provided a new stratification pattern to the village society. The village peasantry witnessed widening social differentiation in the form of big or *kulak* farmers, small farmers, marginal farmers and landless labourers. The peasant struggles became more than frequent. There emerged rural leadership and rural conflicts. All these areas constituted a new discourse on subject matter of rural sociology.

Beyond the new subject matter, rural sociology has begun to study the role of village people at the state and national level politics. There is a distinct village lobby working in national politics. The village politics is yet another theme forming part of rural sociology.

To conclude this section on the subject matter of rural sociology, one could put down the following themes as the substantial areas for the study of rural sociology:

1. Rural sociology consists of the study of tribal, forest and village people. It provides a discourse on the study of the social life of these people.
2. Rural sociology is concerned with the problems and structure related to land and agriculture. In other words, it dwells heavily on the themes related to agrarian relations.
3. Village development programmes have been new additions to the subject matter of rural sociology. The objective of these programmes, on one hand, is to improve the life-standard of the people and, on the other hand, make them participants in the task of nation-building.
4. Rural sociology also studies the stratification pattern which has emerged from the working of developmental programmes.
5. It also analyses the impact of technology on the rural life.
6. And finally, the subject matter of rural sociology also includes environmental decay and erosion of ecology.

Methods and Tools of Rural Sociology

Methods

There is a fundamental difference in methods and tools of study. *Method* is the basic of enquiry whereas *tools* are the instruments by means of which data are generated from the field. In social sciences, when we talk about methodology, we include both the logic and the tools of data collection. The methods of structural-functional, structural, structural-historical and historical-materialist or Marxist, broadly, constitute the logic of enquiry. Fieldwork, comparison, observation, administration of schedule and case studies form the tools of data generation.

In the case of the methodology of rural sociology, one could ask the question: From whom does rural sociology borrow its methodological kit? Obviously, it borrows its approaches to the study of rural communities primarily from social anthropology and sociology. It also draws heavily from economics and political science so far the village economy and Panchayati Raj are concerned.

At the outset, it must be observed that it is the need of the rural society which constitutes its subject matter and finally it is the subject matter which determines its methodology. Yogendra Singh, in the *Survey of Research in Sociology and Social Anthropology* (1969-1979) (1985), observes that "during the fifties there was dominance of the structural-functional theory" as a major theoretical orientation in sociology and social anthropology. Towards the end of this decade structuralist, structural-historical and historical-materialist or Marxist approaches came to be employed by sociologists and social anthropologists. However, during 1970s and onwards, village studies became infrequent or out of academic endeavour. Structuralists, structural-historical and Marxist orientations became out of vogue in rural studies. Though, conflict became a method of study. In these studies, the emphasis was to consider conflict as adaptive tensions resulting from the structures out side of it.

Yet another method employed for village studies has been comparative method. This method has remained popular with the social anthropologists since 18th century. The comparative method employed in village studies has been based on systemic comparison. The third method, generally used by rural sociologists, has been intensive fieldwork. In the following section we discuss all the three methods or approaches employed in the study of rural life:

1. structural-functional method
2. systemic comparison
3. fieldwork

1. *Structural-functional method*

The structural-functional studies of village India implied a systemic 'teleology' based on the Brahminic or hierarchical model of caste society, assumption of harmony or consensus as the system state from which status of mobility, differentiation or roles of power structure and of factional ties, and processes of fusion and fission in the caste structure, were studied. The village studies, thus, were micro-structural. In these studies, the expressions of conflict in the affairs of the village or for that matter in polity and economy were considered as deviant but manageable expressions. Mobility within the caste was interpreted often through a reference group theory which itself was deeply anchored in consensual ideology.

A stock-taking of village studies undertaken by Indian and foreign sociologists shows that the villages are considered as small and self-sufficient. In the paraphrase of Robert Redfield, the villages are, in fact, little communities. M.N. Srinivas argues that a social anthropologist selects a small community as he wants to obtain an idea of the way in which all the parts of a society hang together. The structural-functional method is appropriate for the holistic study of village life.

The Marxist approach, however, has not been employed in the rural studies conducted during 1950s to 1970s. The weaknesses, which are found in structural-functional method, are also found in these studies. The method suffers from the fact that it does not take into consideration the mode of production, production relations and, in fact, the total kit of Marxian terminology.

2. *Systemic Comparison*

Rural sociology is quite ambitious in its study. It has the whole of human society as its field of interests, and tries to understand the connections between the various aspects of our existence. For instance, when we study the economic system of a village, say, Rampura or Kishangarhi, we simultaneously try to find out, how their economy is connected with other aspects of their society and finally compare it with other village studies. If comparative method had not been the mainstay of rural studies, there was no need to study only one tiny village or tribe. When the mankind is concerned with the study of vast masses of people, the knowledge gained by the study of one village can hardly be a reliable guide. It is in this context that M.N. Srinivas (1962) lays emphasis on systematic comparison. He observes:

> But then, systematic comparison is considered to be of the essence of the method of social anthropology. For instance, no anthropologist would dare to speak of Indian villages as a whole until a sufficient number of villages in the different cultural areas had been studied...In addition it provides the anthropologist with some insight into rural social life all over the country. Of course, such insight is not knowledge, and once this distinction is clearly made, even a single village study enables the anthropologist to say a good deal about rural social life in India as a whole.

There are several illustrations of the application of comparative method in rural studies. T.S. Epstein, in her study on *Economic Development and Social Change* (1962) in two of the villages of south India, makes a comparative study of dry and wet communities. She comes out with the finding that the villagers belonging to wet village, i.e., village having irrigation from canal water, are progressive and forward-looking compared to the villagers from dry village.

Comparative method of study has been a reliable logic of enquiry in rural studies. The concepts of dominant caste, sanskritisation and great and little traditions have stood the taste of comparative method. There is sufficient evidence of the usefulness of dominant caste in a variety of village studies.

3. *Fieldwork*

It may be reiterated that the methods employed in rural sociology are largely those which are in vogue in social anthropology. It is because of the fact that social anthropology is concerned with the study of tribal groups and villages. In the field of methodology, sociology has little to impart to rural studies. In India, sociology is concerned with the complex communities or groups. Because of this, its methods are not considered to be useful for the study of village life.

Among all the social sciences, social anthropology distinguishes itself from the other social sciences through the great emphasis on the fieldwork as the most important source of new knowledge about society and culture. Describing the importance of fieldwork in anthropological studies T.H. Eriksen (1995) observes:

> A field study may last far between a few months to two years or longer, and it aims at developing as intimate and understanding as possible of the phenomena investigated. Although, there are differences in field methods between different anthropological schools, it is generally agreed that the anthropologist ought to stay in the field long enough for his or her presence to be considered more or less 'natural' by the permanent residents, although he or she will always to some extent remain stranger.

Most of the valuable theoretical formulations in social anthropology have been constructed out of fieldwork carried on for a protracted period. For instance, Malinowski worked among the Trobriand islanders for years together. Similarly, Radcliffe-Brown worked among the Andaman islanders and Australian tribes. Recently, Pierre Bourdeau, who is known for his contribution to habitus and structuralism (Richard Jenkins, 1992), worked in Algeria for a long period and conducted fieldwork. It is certain that a sociologist who is trained in fieldwork carries to his credit substantial work in social anthropology. As a matter of fact, fieldwork is very demanding, much time-consuming, in terms of professional expertise and human relationships. Eriksen very rightly observes that fieldwork is highly troublesome for an anthropologist when he writes:

> The tidy, systematic and well-rounded texts written by anthropologists are more often than not the end-product of long periods in the field characterised by boredom, illness, personnel privations, disappointments and frustrations....

M.N. Srinivas who is credited to have worked in Rampura village and among the Coorgs of south India has considerable experience of working in the villages. In his book *The Remembered Village* (1976), Srinivas gives vivid description about his familiarity with the people of Rampura. He describes the appropriate time for conducting fieldwork:

The field worker records practically everything he sees even when, for instance, his aim is only to make an analysis of the kinship system of the people he is studying. He will try to collect as much information as he can. In the 12-18 months at his disposal, about the other activities of people, such as agriculture, house building, commercial activities, manners, morals, law and religion.

In Indian context, thus, a social anthropologist should devote a year for conducting fieldwork even for a tiny village. Many of the village studies included in Srinivas' *India's Villages* and Mackim Marriot's *Village India* show that the field work for a single study took about six months to more than a year.

Requirements in fieldwork

It is expected of a researcher to take part in local life of the village in as much as possible way. When he is in the field, looking to the kind of fieldwork, he applies several tools of data generation. The tools include structured interviews, observation, case study, statistical sampling and other techniques. Most of the fieldwork depends on a combination of formal techniques and unstructured participant observation. We shall have detailed description about the field techniques or tools employed in the field.

While in the field, the researcher keeps with his person a note book or diary as it is called for regarding what he observes in the field in all possible details. He would even note down the things for which he is not concerned. It is due to his overdeveloped sense of curiosity, and partly to his awareness that the various aspects of a society form a closely woven mesh, and that the particular aspect he is studying might influence and be influenced by every other aspects of social life. The field worker will have obtained, by the time he has completed his study, an intimate and all-round knowledge of the village or tribe he has been with.

The social anthropologist when in the field actually takes the role of a clown. He speaks strangely with a flawed local dialect; he asks surprising and sometimes tactless questions, and tends to break many rules regarding how things ought to be done. He would not hesitate to dress in the style of the people of his village—putting on a turban or taking food on leaves. Such a role of a researcher is essential to establish rapport and proximity with the people. The beginning of fieldwork in such a way is an excellent starting point.

The field researcher has to move very cautiously in his village of study. A little flaw on his part might defeat his objective of enquiry. He might run the risk of encountering suspicion and the hospitality. Andre Beteille had to encounter hostility from the village of a study, Sripuram of Tanjore district in south India. In his book, *Caste, Class and Power* (1971), he gives details of his fieldwork experiences. What happened with him is that in the beginning of his visit to the village he stayed with a Brahmin family. It was really a privilege given to him. Actually he was "the only non-Brahmin ever to have sat and eaten with the Brahmin in Sripuram on ceremonial occasions. I was identified with the Brahmin by my dress, my appearance and the fact that I lived in one of their houses". Beteille recollects his field experiences further and says that his identification with the Brahmin caste made him suspect in the eyes of the non-Brahmins and Adi-Dravidas, who at first regarded him as just another Brahmin from north India. Such a suspicious social environment of the field, according to Beteille, influenced the quality of his fieldwork. He writes:

> Consequently my data for the Adi-Dravidas and also, to some extent for the non-Brahmins are of a poorer quality than for the Brahmins. But it has to be realised that there was, in fact, very little choice.

It is also required of a researcher for rural studies that he should employ informal field methods for generating data, whether or not it is supplemented with other techniques. The objective of employing informal field method is to enter as deeply as possible into the social and cultural field to the village life. In such situations, the researcher neither belongs to the host community nor to his parent community. Evans-Pritchard makes a very remarkable observation on this account:

> The researcher in practice becomes doubly marginal person, in a sense suspended between one's own society and the society under investigation.

A recipe for doing fieldwork

I have many ways of conducting fieldwork, and it is impossible to provide a clear recipe for how to carry it out. For one thing it is certain that the researcher studying the rural life is himself the most important 'scientific instrument'. He invests a great deal of his/her own personality in the process. He must tailor his methods to fill the requirements of the particular village where he is doing fieldwork. Evans-Pritchard once recalled his first attempts to learn about fieldwork in the early 1920 (1983, 1937). "He had asked a number of renowned anthropologists how to do it and he received various answers. First, he asked the famous Finnish ethnologist Westermark, who said: "Don't converse with an informant for more than twenty minutes because if you aren't bored by that time he will be." Evans-Pritchard comments: "Very good advice, if somewhat inadequate." Alfred Haddon said: "...that it was really all quite simple; one should always behave as a gentleman." Evans Pritchard's teacher, Charles Saligman told: "...to take 10 grams of quinine every night and to keep off women." Finally, Malinowski himself told the new researcher, "not to be a bloody fool". Evans-Pritchard himself emphasises, later in the same account, that facts are themselves meaningless; in other words, one must know precisely what one wants to know," and then fashion a suitable methodology from the available techniques. There is—alas—no simple recipe for fieldwork. It is a method where the researcher's most important "scientific instrument is him".

Fieldwork does not have to be either capital-intensive or labour-intensive. As a research process, it is cheap, since the only scientific instruments involved are the fieldworkers themselves and possibly a few assistants. Eriksen has the following to observe in this regard:

> However, and this is perhaps the main point about fieldwork as a scientific method, it is time-intensive. Ideally, one should stay in the field long enough to be able to see the world as the local see it. Even if this may be impossible, among other reasons because one cannot entirely get rid of one's own cultural background, it can be a worthwhile aim to pursue. The strength of the anthropologist's knowledge can thus be said to lie in his or her mastery of both the local culture and a different culture (his or her own), and of tools of analysis, making it possible to give an analytical, comparative account of both.

It may be recalled that any rural study—large or small village—is ultimately related to theory. Empirical material is fundamental in all empirical sciences including sociology, social anthropology and rural sociology. No science can rely on theory alone, and if it does so it becomes pure mathematics or philosophy. In other words, research has an inductive and a deductive dimension. "Induction consists of going out there, watching and wandering, collecting information about what people say and do. Deduction consists of attempts to account for facts by means of a general hypothesis or theory. Suppose I work to explore the hypothesis that the position of women in society is proportional to their contribution to the economy, working deductively, I would develop an argument showing why this made sense. In the actual research process, however, I would have to shift to an inductive mode, exploring the relationship between the position of women and the economy in a number of existing societies. As soon as I came across one or several societies where there was no apparent relationship between the contribution to the economy and the relative rank of women, I would have to modify my initial hypothesis."

Actually, the researcher has to develop a general insight through the processes of observation of facts and theoretical reasoning. Where new facts modify the theory and modified theory accounts for the fact, the research exercise is worthwhile. Each time one shifts from theory to description of empirical process and back, one's insight has become a little bit mare accurate.

In social anthropology and sociology, fieldwork has become much more common since the 1950s. However, one argument sometimes used against fieldwork in one's own society is that the overall aim of the discipline is to account for cultural variation. It is in this context that when we take up rural studies one should study people who seem culturally remote. What is particular about our villages in India is that they are increasingly coming closer to the urban life. Communication facilities including the forces of market and consumerism have made amazing changes in the rural life. Despite all this, there is a marked cultural variation in the rural life. So far this continues fieldwork is a reliable method of enquiry in the rural life.

Tools of Data Generation

Data in the field are generated through the administration of a wide variety of tools. *The Survey of Research in Sociology and Social Anthropology* enumerates a few of the tools employed by government development agencies, social science research institutions, census and sociologists and anthropologists. A catalogue of such tools is given as under:

1. Rural Survey
2. Village Monographs
3. Observation
4. Interview
5. Structured Schedule
6. Case Studies

1. *Rural Survey*

Surveys are holistic in nature. The totality of village life in all its dimensions is presented through the tool of social survey. The Ministry of Agriculture of the Government of India financed many surveys since independence through the agro-economic research centres, associated with various universities in the country. Its objectives were to conduct village studies to monitor changes in the structure and functioning of the village economy due to external stimulus, government plans or other inputs. These studies were thus problem-oriented.

2. *Village Monographs*

The Department of Census, Government of India has regularly—every decade—brought out village monographs. These monographs present an overall picture of the village life. In these monographs a casual observation of the village life is made. The fieldwork in these monographs has always been casual---non-intensive. The researcher just steps in the village, meets knowledgeable people and goes out with a battery of data.

3. *Observation*

Observation is the fundamental method employed in village studies. Though, it is a vaguely defined research technique, it serves as a convenient blanket term to cancel both ethical and methodological shortcomings in the actual research process. Observation is two-fold: participant observation and non- participant observation. Participant observation refers to the informal field methods which form the basis for most fieldwork. It provides opportunity for coming closer to the subject of study.

Most of the village studies conducted after 1950s have used participant method for enquiry. The non-participant method is one wherein the researcher does not participate in the activities of the villagers. He only becomes a bystander. The difference in participant and non-participant observation is that, in the former, the researcher identifies himself with the village people. In his study of Rampura, M.N. Srinivas identified himself with the village people. He was even involved in setting the disputes of the village people.

4. *Interview*

It is difficult for village people to spell out about the activities which take place in their community. They also do not want to reveal the caste relations among the members. In such a situation protracted interviews reveal a lot of information. At the time of report writing, whatever is revealed through interviews is analyzed by the researcher and put in the form of conceptual formulations.

5. *Structured Schedule*

Illiteracy is a common phenomenon in India's villages. Though, the people have their moderate earnings, and levels of consumption, they do not have accounts for this. Such a life has been a way of living for them for centuries. The exploitation of the villagers for their illiteracy has become proverbial in India. Much of their indebtedness is due largely to their illiteracy. Such a situation denies the administration of questionnaires to the people. For factual data, however, structured schedule is administered by the researcher. Even the schedule is sometimes taken with suspicion by the people. It, therefore, has to be administered with caution.

6. *Case Studies*

Case study is a deep study. Some of the authors of village studies have profitably employed the technique of case studies. Generally, it is the supplementary data generated through case studies to provide insight to the main study. F.G. Bailey, in his work, *Cast and the Economic Frontier* (1958), has made some case studies to throw insight in the study of his field.

References

Bailey, F. G., *Caste and the Economic Frontier*, Oxford University Press, Bombay, 1958.

Beteille, Andre, *Caste, Class and Power*, University of California Press, London, 1971.

Bourdieu, Pierre , *Sociology in Question*, Translation by Richard Nice, Sage Publications, London, 1993.

Epstein,T.P., *Economic Development and Social Change*, New Delhi, 1962.

Eriksen,Thomas Hylland, *Small Places, Large Issues : An Introduction to Social and Cultural Anthropology*, Pluto Press, London, 1995.

Jenkins, Richard , *Key Sociologists: Pierre Bourdieu*, Routledge, London, 1992.

Marriott, McKim, *Village India*, Chicago University Press, 1955.

Radcliffe-Brown, A.R., *Structure and Function in Primitive Society*, Cohen and West, London, 1952.

Singh,Yogendra, *A Survey of Research in Sociology and Social Anthropology* (1969-1979), Satvaham Publications, New Delhi, 1985.

—, *Indian Sociology*, Sage Publications, New Delhi, 1986.

Srinivas, M.N. (ed.), *India's Villages*, Asia Publishing House, New Delhi, 1955.

—, *Caste in Modern India and Other Essays*, Asia Publishing House, New Delhi, 1962.

—, *The Remembered Village*, Oxford University Press, Delhi, 1976.

Wright Mills, C., *Sociological Imagination*.

3 Studies in Rural Sociology

Gandhiji often used to say that if the villages prosper, the country prospers; and if the villages ruin, who can save the country. Gandhiji advocated all through his life that all our efforts should be directed towards the development of our village. The main objective of village studies has been to know as much as possible about the village life. How do our millions of village people live their life? What are the reasons for their poverty and backwardness ? These questions have great relevance in our planning for the development. However, village studies in the form of administrative reports were made by the first quarter of the 19th century.

The British Raj, incidentally, brought out a systematic report about the village life. Ramakrishna Mukherjee was the first sociologist who analysed the social organisms of village communities when he had written the *Rise and Fall of the East India Company.* He informs that upto the advent of the British in India, the village community system had been noted by several authorities. He finds out that village social organisation was almost absent or rudimentary in the south-western extreme of the sub-continent, such as in the present-day state of Kerala, but in other parts of country village had been the dominant institution in society.

The British officers of the East India Company found out that there were village communities in India and on the basis of the exhaustive description the *British Parliamentary Papers* were prepared. This was perhaps the first effort made by the officers of the British Raj to bring out a document in the form of *Parliamentary Papers* on India's villages. It could, therefore, be said to be the beginning of village studies, though the nature of these studies was administrative.

If we analyse the village studies available to us from the period of British Raj to the present day, we could put the scholars or agencies working on village studies into three categories as under:

1. studies/reports brought out by administrators;
2. studies conducted by economists; and
3. studies prepared by sociologists and anthropologists.

Studies/Reports Brought out by Administrators

On the basis of the information complied by the findings of East India Company's official in the Madras presidency, at a later stage, Holt Mackenzie reported about the existence of village communities in northern India. Following Mackenzie, Sir Charles Metcalfe, a member of the Governor-General's Council brought out details about the Indian village life. In the same vein Elphinstone noted the presence of village communities in the Deccan in his report. Similarly, the first Punjab Administrative Report in 1852 after the consolidation of British power in that territory was brought out. The accounts given by Baden-Powell (1899) gave the impression, that "all land must have some landlord, with tenants under him". The *British Parliamentary Papers* recorded quite categorically that previously the jamindars (i.e., revenue farmers, who were turned into landlords during British rule) were essentially accountable managers and collectors of revenue, and not lords and proprietors of the lands, that the sale of land by auction or in any other way for realising arrears of land revenue, appears to have been unusual, if not unknown in all parts of India, before its introduction by the British government into the Company's domination, and that stresses still remained to show that the village community system existed also in this part of India.

If we go into the official records of East India Company, Ramakrishna Mukherjee concludes that village community system flourished practically all over India. It appears that the villages upto the advent of British India were autonomous. Jurisdiction of the village authorities extended over houses, streets, bazaars (markets), burning grounds, temples, wells, tanks, wastelands, forests, forests lands, that the village council looked after the village differences, settled village disputes, organised works of public utility, acted as a trustee for minors and collected the government revenue and paid them into the central treasury.

The village autonomy was also manifested in the decision-making process pertaining to a village. Each village had its representatives for decision-taking. Local executive officers were usually hereditary servants and not the members of the central bureaucracy; they usually sided with the local bodies in their tussel with the central government.

Perhaps, the pioneering work on village studies was done by Gilbert Slater (1918). Slater, while writing in his introduction to the study of some *South Indian Villages*, observes:

> Villages came before towns and even in the most industrialised countries, where all economic questions tend to be studied from an urban point of view, it is well to be reminded that the economic life of a town or city cannot be understood without reference to the lands which send its food and raw materials, and the villages from which it attracts young men and women. The importance of rural activities and of village life in India in view of the enormous preponderance of its agricultural population over that engaged in mining, manufacture, commerce and transport is not likely to be overlooked and last of all in southern India, which has no coal mines and no great industry like cotton manufacture in Bombay and jute in Bengal.

Studies Conducted by Economists

After the First World War it became clear to the British Raj and the Indian National Congress that there was a marked deterioration in India's rural economy. There was an abject poverty, squalor and disorganisation of village societies; the rumblings of rural discontent begin to reach the ears of the government and the educated public in towns and cities. Prior to the end of First World War, the Asian countries had become conscious about the writings on Asian Mode of Production (AMP) given by Karl Marx. This brought the intellectuals of the country aware about the plight of the Indian peasantry. The classic description given by Marx on the basis of the literature available to him runs as below:

> Those small and extremely ancient Indian communities, some of which have continued down to this day, are based on possession in common of the land on the blending of agriculture and handicrafts, and on an unalterable division of labour, which serves, whenever a new community is started, as a plan and scheme ready-cut and decide... The chief part of the production is destined for direct use by the community itself, and does not take the form of a commodity.

> Hence, production here is independent of that division of labour brought about in Indian society as a whole, by means of the exchange of commodities. It is the surplus alone that becomes a commodity, and a portion of even that, not until it has reached the hands of the state into whose hands from the time immemorial, certain quantity of these products has found its way in the shape of rent in kind. The constitution of these communities varies in different parts of India. In those of the simplest form, the land is tilled in common, and the produce divided among the members. At the same time, spinning and weaving is carried on, in each family as subsidiary industry. Side by Side, with the masses thus occupied with one and same work, we find the 'chief inhabitant', who is judge, police, and takes gatherer in one, the book-keeper who keeps the accounts of the village and registers everything relating thereto; another official, who prosecutes criminals strangers travelling through, and escorts them to the next village; the boundary man, who guards the boundaries against neighbouring communities; the water overseer, who distributes the water from the common tanks for irrigation; the Brahmin, who conducts the religious services; the school master, who on the sand teaches the children reading and writing; the calendar-Brahmin, or astrologer, who makes known the lucky or unlucky days for seed time and harvest, and for every other kind of agricultural work; a smith and a carpenter, who make and repair all the agricultural implements; the potter, who makes all the pottery of the village; the barber, the washerman, who washes clothes; the silversmiths, here and there the poet, who, in some communities replaces the silversmith, in other, the school master. This dozen of individuals is maintained at the expense of the whole community.

The British Raj, after the First World War, realised that agrarian crisis was eminent in the villages. It appointed the first Royal Commission on Agriculture in 1976. The Indian National Movement also took the economic crisis which the peasantry has to suffer. Commenting on the role of national movement in the economic crisis of the villages, Ramakrishna Mukherjee observes:

> Contextually, the Indian National Movement played a significant role for one of its fruitful bye-products was to create interest of social scientists in 'village studies'. The mass movement of 1920s, led by Gandhi and based essentially on the rural question, synchronised with series of village studies carried out in different parts of India.

S.J. Patel (1952) has described the nature of agrarian crisis almost all over India by the end of First World War. He observes:

> With the end of the First World War, the beginning of an agrarian crisis was accompanied by the entry of peasants into the political arena, as exemplified during the Champaran and Keira campaigns led by Gandhiji. As a result, the cultivator of the soil began to attract considerable attention from the students of Indian society.

G. Keatings and Harold Mann in Bombay, Gilbert Slater in Madras and E.V. Lucas in Punjab initiated intensive studies of particular villages and general agricultural problems. The results of these investigations evoked great interest and stressed the necessity still for the further study.

Historically, the origin of village studies with the economic perspective really goes back to the period beginning after First World War to the attainment of independence. During this long period, the condition of peasantry in the country as a whole was worse. There were famines, famine reports and the general poverty gripped with indebtedness. It was realised by the leaders of the struggle for independence to understand the reasons for the appalling poverty of the masses of villagers.

The Punjab Board of Economic Enquiry organised village surveys conducted by individual workers since 1920s. The Bengal Board of Economic Enquiry was set up in 1935 and it conducted village surveys. Again, in Bengal, Tagore's Visva Bharati took up village surveys around Shanti Niketan. J.C. Kumarappa was a Gandhian economist. He developed Gandhian economic perspective by conducting surveys in the villages. Writing introduction to Kumarappa's book, *An Economic Survey of Matar Taluka* (1931), Kalelkar wrote:

> If there is one thing that characterises the educated man in India and distinguishes him from his confrere elsewhere, it is his abysmal ignorance of the actual rural conditions in his own country. There are some people who are anxious to see India industrialised. But neither of them have secured the bedrock of statistics collected from the mouths of the peasants themselves. The present survey is unique in this respect.

Even during 1940s decade social scientists in India showed considerable interest in village studies. Only it could be noticed that henceforth the social scientists began to launch extensive enquiries by covering large tracts in the light of the picture of rural society already built up by means of the ever increasing numbers of isolated 'village studies'. Concurrently, they were often found to concentrate on specific aspects of the rural problem in a particular area.

If we critically examine the village studies made by economists, voluntary agencies and commissions, we would find that the focus of enquiry invariably was economic status of the village people. Poor status of agriculture, drought and famine indebtedness were the major thrust of rural studies. Commenting on the status of village studies largely during the period after First World War till independence. Ramakrishna Mukherjee writes:

> Economic and material well-being of the rural folks had thus become the pre-occupation with those undertaking village studies as the situation dictated...This course of development and outcome of village studies meet evidently an important need of the country and the government. So it may not be fortuitous that from a different motive it was brought up by the British East India Company as early as 1689.

Actually, the interest of the British Raj in promoting the study of villages was to assess the revenue potential of the villagers. The British were interested to increase their trade and at the same time maintain their force. The renewed interest in village studies came after the attainment of independence and particularly the implementation of Indian Constitution. The government decided to take up the task of reconstruction of India's villages. It was argued by the social anthropologists and then rural sociologists that when rural studies cannot help the British Raj to consolidate their colonial reign in India, why could these studies be helpful. To build-up the new nation from the grassroots. This promoted the social scientists, particularly the social anthropologists, to take up village studies in a larger way.

Studies Prepared by Sociologists and Social Anthropologists

During the colonial period, the anthropologists were busy in studying the tribal communities. With the village development programmes in operation, the anthropologists found it obligatory to shift to the study of village communities. S.C. Dube (1958) explains this shift and observes:

> ...anthropologists are no longer concerned primarily, or even mainly,

> with the study of tribal cultures; in increasing numbers they are now operating nearer home in village communities where they have discovered challenging possibilities of theoretical and applied social science research.

It was convenient for social anthropologists to shift from tribal studies to village studies. They had been employing the fieldwork method in the study of tribal communities. This method was also suitable for the study of village communities. The concept of ideal folk society, developed by Redfield, was tried out in analysing the cultures of Latin America, but there it was found almost non-operative. While re-examining it Redfield thought that there was nothing wrong in the concept itself. The later studies proved that the folk societies tend to lose increasingly their basic traits when they come into contact with other advanced cultures. Folk societies, thus, gradually transform themselves into village communities and isolate themselves from the ideal types, say, the one constructed by Redfield. The culture contact gives rise to a continuum, technically known as the folk-urban continuum. The intermediate category between the two polar types presents the peasant societies or the village community.

Yogesh Atal (1969), while evaluating the rural studies conducted in India, observes:

> Thus, the processes of change initiated and accelerated by contact have opened new vistas of study. They presented new problems of analysis and research methodology. It was apparent that the holistic approach that could be successfully employed in the study of isolated and remotely situated small tribal communities was not possible here. The 'whole' of the village community was not complete. It was a part of a wider 'whole'—of a greater society. In order to apprehend the village in its totality, it was deemed essential to take cognizance of extraneous forces and factors that fact the life-ways and work-ways of the community.

The village studies which were conducted during the first quarter of 1950s had an obvious advantage vis-a-vis survey research. The village surveys which were undertaken by government agencies, commissions and individual scholars were highly extensive. There surveys, however, did not rigorously confirm to the rigid texts of validity and reliability. By their nature the surveys could not explore the depth of rural life.

There are some social scientists who differentiate between rural sociology and rural anthropology. For both these social sciences, the field is common but the methods and techniques are different. Keeping this difference in view it could be said that rural sociology makes a generalised analysis on national level while rural anthropology makes intensive study of particular village communities. In India, however, such a kind of difference is not necessary. Here:

> ...both sociologists and anthropologists are jointly exploring the village community with a largely common methodology. Rural India provides a good meeting ground for the two disciplines. This effective communication is indeed a healthy trend and one should welcome this happy 'merging' (Atal, 1969).

Decade of the Flood of Village Studies

Social Background

If the village studies during the colonial times were made for consolidating the British Raj, in the post-independent era these were conducted for basically two reasons, namely, village development or reconstruction and Panchayati Raj. Village studies, thus, became an urgent task for nation-building.

Enumerating the flood of village studies which came in 1955 and afterwards, Yogesh Atal (1969) makes a stock-taking:

> The year 1955 was of immense significance for Indian anthropology and sociology (also rural sociology). In that year, for the first time, four books and several papers on Indian village were published. These studies were made by Indian as well as American and British social scientists. Dube's *Indian Village*, Majumdar's *Rural Profiles*, Marriott's *Village India*, and Srinivas' *India's Villages* were the major publications of the year. The same year a conference was also held under the chairmanship of Dr. (Mrs.) Irawati Karve at Madras in which Prof. Robert Redfield also participated. They much discussed the concept of *sanskritisation* proposed by Srinivas in *Religion and Society in Coorg*, reiterated by him who thought the discussion had reinforced his belief in its validity. The proceedings of the conference have been published in a book entitled *Society in India.* Later, *Twice Born* (Carstairs, 1957), *Indian Changing Villages* (Dube, 1958), *Caste and Communication in an Indian Village* (Majumdar, 1958), *Caste and*

the Economic Frontier (Bailey, 1957) and *Village Life in Northern India* (Lewis, 1958) were added to the library of Indian rural studies. Albert Mayer's book *Pilot Project India* (1958) summarises the main achievements of the Etawah project. And *Introduction to Rural sociology in India*, an anthology edited by A.R. Desai, appeared in a revised and enlarged version in the year 1959. Recently, Edrian Mayer's work *Caste and Kinship in Central India* (1960) has come out. Besides these major publications several research papers based on fieldwork in rural areas have appeared in various journals. The yearly sessions of the Indian Sociological Conference have also included discussions on varied and important problems of rural analysis. University departments of anthropology and sociology have been and are undertaking various projects for conducting researches in the rural areas. The Research Programme Committee of the Planning Commission, Government of India is also promoting rural research through such centres.

After the decade of 1950s, there has definitely been a thrust in the study of villages. Earlier, the anthropologists were engaged in the study of tribal communities. They also took to the study of castes found in different clusters of villages. The village studies included, largely, caste as a form of stratification. The economic aspect of the village more or less remained neglected. Actually, with the introduction of development plans, economists, sociologists and social anthropologists came together to provide a holistic profile of the village community. Analysing the status of village studies Ramakrishna Mukherjee very rightly observes:

> Thus, the frontiers of the three disciplines meet in the field of 'village study', and so scientists duly equipped to cross the no-man's land between the discipline should also be forthcoming.
>
> The question, therefore, does not bail down to which discipline should undertake the task or that it can be accomplished only by interdisciplinary research. Contrariwise the question throws up the challenge to create interest among those belonging to any one of the disciplines to assume the responsibility and equip themselves accordingly.

Some Issues Included in Village Studies

There are few studies which could be categorised as single village studies. In these studies, either the holistic nature of the village communities is discussed or certain specific aspects of rural life are focused. We propose to discuss some of single village studies in this section.

S.C. Dube's (1955) *Indian Village* is a traditional account of Shamirpeth. Shamirpeth is located in the Telangana region of Andhra Pradesh. Dube brings out details about the village and informs that despite there being more than a dozen castes, the village displays integration. The methodology employed in this study is interdisciplinary. Experts from different development departments have contributed towards the completion of study. It is a classic example of structural-functional method. The nature of study is holistic.

M.N. Srinivas' (1955) edited work *India's Villages* contains 17 village studies conducted by Indian, British and US anthropologists. Among the contributors are included M.N. Srinivas, David Mandelbaum, Eric J. Miller, Kathleen Gough, Mckim Marriott, S.C. Dube and others. These studies have taken into consideration the totality of the village life. However, some issues are raised in some of the studies. Some of the contributors have come out with certain conceptual constructs.

The problem of the unity of village has been a major concern of the contributors to *India's Villages*. For instance, the unity of village has been questioned by a number of scholars. Admittedly, a few people living in a small village, at some distance from other similar villages, with extremely poor roads between them and majority of them being engaged in agriculture activity, must display a strong sense of unity. The unity of the village, it is found, is based on the solidarity of caste. Caste is a strong unifying factor. The concept of 'dominant caste' has for the first time appeared in this edited book. It has been proposed by M.N. Srinivas in his study of Rampura. The methodology employed by the contributors has been structural-functional.

Marriott's *Village India* (1955), yet another edited work, also includes both foreign and Indian anthropologists. His emphasis in the editing of the work is to look at the Indian villages from the complexity of Indian civilisation. The methodology, however, is structural-functional. The contributors have re-examined the concept of caste. It has been the effort of the editor to make caste more precise, and less open textured. It is here that Marriott constructs the concepts of 'universalisation' and 'parochialisation'. These twin concepts have been explained with the concepts of great and little tradition. He argues that there is a constant interaction between the great and little tradition.

Quite close to the studies of Dube, Srinivas and Marriott, is the edited work of D.N. Majumdar, *Rural Profiles.* It includes contributors belonging to the disciplines of sociology and social anthropology. Some of the concepts developed by Srinivas, namely, 'sankritisation' and 'dominant castes' have been re-examined by the contributors of this edited work. For instance, through the concept of de-sanskritisation, Majumdar suggests a reverse process by which Brahmin castes also try to identify in some matters with other castes. Most of the studies included the work consisting of single village.

F.G. Bailey's (1957) study of two villages in Orissa brings out the problem of caste and class formation. He argues that at the local level economic formulations run across the caste ranking. Bailey employs structural-functional method and analyses the rural life in the context of changing agrarian structure.

D.N. Majumdar (1958), in the study of Mohana, a village in Uttar Pradesh, considers village as a concept, a way of life. He follows Redfield's concept of 'little community' and applies four specific characters of Redfield's little community. Majumdar's conceptualisation of village runs as below:

> The study of a village as a whole, as an integrated way of living, thinking, feeling or as a constellation of parts, such as material culture, occupation, technology, kinship system all leading to a proper understanding of a little community, has its limitations, particularly, in Indian conditions.

The Indian village has a special kind of communication system characterised by caste relation. Majumdar observes:

> Here in Mohana live the high castes and the lower castes, here they share a similar pattern of life, here they feel a kind of consciousness of homogeneity, interdependence, and also a sense of security born of living together and sharing opportunities and crisis.

G.S. Ghurye (1960) made a new experiment in the village study, in his *After a Century and a Quarter.* The village of a study Lonikand or the town of Loni was earlier studied by Major Coats in 1819. The description given by Coats has served as a cutting point for Ghurye. He argues that the village is interwoven by pervasive role of religion.

The author has described the structure of the village community. Its social organisation and the changes brought in it during a period of a century and a more in the field of bio-social life of the people. The village pattern of living is brought through a description of representative families. Though, the author has not constructed any theoretical formulation, he very interestingly brings out changes in Lonikand from Coats to the present study. In fact, Lonikand is a study unfolding social and cultural change that took place during a long period of 100 years.

Andre Beteille's study of Sripuram is yet another village study which has acclaimed a high reputation in rural sociology. It is an intensive study of a multi-caste village in south India. Quite like Ghurye's Lonikand, Sripuram is a study of transformation. He observes that the social change in the village is in the direction of a more open social system. Until recently village social life was shaped by its division into three caste groups in Sripuram: The Brahmins, the middle-level non-Brahmins and the Adi-Dravida; the caste of a villager determined his position in the class system and power in hierarchy, and caste itself was acquired only by birth.

Beteille's work falls in the domain of rural stratification. On the strength of empirical data he generalises that in village India caste remains a major form of stratification. Class and power operate within the longer ethnic group of the caste. The work raises certain issues pertaining to caste, class and power.

Rural Sociology in India (1969) by A.R. Desai is a very interesting and refreshing work in the field of rural sociology. Desai has provided an interesting introduction to rural sociology in India in its first part. The remaining 16 parts contain village studies done by different anthropologists and sociologists. These parts are actually readings in rural sociology, which include a comprehensive narration and analysis in the domain of historical aspects of village life, Indian village community, rural stratification, agrarian unrest, land reforms, rural industries and institutions, Panchayati Raj, Bhoodan and Gramdan movements, village social change, village studies and theories of agrarian development.

Besides structural and historical aspects of rural sociology A.R. Desai has edited yet another giant work on *Peasant Struggles in India* (1979). The edited work provides a panoramic view of tribal and peasant struggles in India during the colonial period. In fact, it is a book of readings which gives an insight into various sources, some of which are rare documents, not easily available and have acquired the character of archival importance. This is a praiseworthy attempt to present an all-India picture of tribal and peasant struggles. It is precisely a work couched in Marxian scheme of interpretation.

Desai vehemently argues that some of the issues raised in the work are not "merely academic discussions". They determine strategies, shape polices, organise action and frame approaches towards different sections of the rural population.

There are dozens of village studies which could be included for our analysis. But, the fact remains that in sociology, social anthropology and rural sociology, study of village community has become an established tradition. The issues raised in these studies are several. Some of the issues have been critically debated.

Village studies have become very popular in social anthropology and sociology. Though, some of the issues concerning villages have been continuously raised, a few of the issues have been seriously contested. A few years back (in 1957) a strong protest about treating villages in India as sociological micro-cosms came from Louis Dumont. Dumont's comments are as below:

> To what extent, we are asked, is an Indian village a micro-cosm reflecting the macro-cosm of India civilisation? But India, sociologically speaking, is not made up of villages. It is true that the *idea* of the village is present in Indian literature and thought and can affect the unwary sociologists as much as the villager or the modern Indian politician. To pose the opposition of village to civilisation is at once to have given the village a sociological reality which similar groups may have elsewhere and to have been deceived by the appearances...the idea of the village in Indian civilisation, its reinforcement by Mahatma Gandhi, the pragmatic interest of early government officers and the influence of anthropological methods elsewhere in the world have created this fundamental supposition that the clue to an understanding of an Indian society lives in the village.

Yogendra Singh (1994) argues that a sociological analysis has to be cognitive-structural or in other words culturological. "It should focus upon the representation or ideas of reality rather then reality *per se.*" Yogendra Singh further analyses Dumont's methodological position and says that our understanding about social reality consists in replacing the simple in the complex, small in the great, in lighting up a restricted area by bringing it back to its environment, which common thought and often thought in general suppresses and if one could add "it also lies in understanding the objective realities of social phenomena in terms of systems of ideas, ideo-structures or representations".

Dumont's conception of Indian village as a micro-cosm makes it reality of Indian society. Commenting on Dumont, Yogendra Singh observes:

> In fact, villages in India demonstrate many elements of structural unity, such as, sentiment of territorial 'political' kinship and economic solidarity...the sense of village identity on many occasions cuts across caste loyalties which usually divide a village.

The authors concerned with the village studies have also raised the question of village unity. As we have seen above, the village unity becomes weakened by caste and political parties. In the villages of Rajasthan we have as elsewhere several evidence to show that the castes of Jat and Rajput very much divide the village organisation. One can very easily observe that a single village is divided into many by Jat and Rajput clusters. Viewed in this respect village cohesion or unity is an illusive phenomenon.

Yogendra Singh finds that there are several village institutions which have their network spread over to a number of villages. The inter-caste relations are characterised by reciprocity. For instance, the *jajmani* system unites a single village to a number of villages. The recent studies which we have in social anthropology show that the village unity today has become a fiction. *Jajmani* system is replaced by cash payment. In fact, in all regions of Indian villages are changing in respect of economic institutions, power structure, and inter-caste relationship. "A major source of economic change is land reform which has created great sociological impact on village social structure... Land reform in village has been introduced through: (i) abolition of intermediaries; (ii) tenancy reforms; (iii) ceiling on landholdings and redistribution of land; (iv) reconsolidation of holdings and prevention of holdings from deteriorating to uneconomic size; (v) emphasis on development of cooperative farming; and (vi) religio-economic movement for gift of surplus land by the rich to the poor as *bhoodan*. These measures have been implemented differently in different states but they have created some uniform sociological consequences."

It appears that the earlier kind of village unity has been replaced by on new form of unity consisting of land reforms. If we take a stock-taking of village studies in India, it could be said that villages have remained as a micro-structure since ancient period of history. What Metcalfe observed during the British period that "village communities are little republics, having nearly everything that they want within themselves, and almost independent of any foreign relations" has been reinforced by Mahatma Gandhi. In other words, Gandhiji observed that a village should be self-sufficient, and should be morally and economically integrated within the Indian society. Yogendra Singh, while emphasising the importance of village in contemporary observes:

> The village as a micro-structure has thus not only been recognised but has gradually become a vital aspect of national developmental planning and politico-cultural consciousness.

References

Atal, Yogesh, "Rural Studies: Indian Village", *The Eastern Anthropologist*, Vol. 14, 1959.

Baden-Powell, B.H., *The Origin and Growth of Village Communities in India*, Swan-Sonnesnsheir, London, 1899.

Bailey, F.G., *Caste and the Economic Frontier*, Oxford University Press, Bombay, 1957.

Carstairs, M., *The Twice Born*, The Hogarth Press, London, 1957.

Desai, A.R. (ed.), *Rural Sociology in India*, Popular Prakashan, Bombay, 1969.

—, *Peasant Struggles in India*, Oxford University Press, Bombay, 1979.

Dube, S.C.,Presidential Address to the Social Anthropological Section (1958), *The Study of Village Communities.*

Dumont, Louis, "Village Studies", *Contributions to Indian Sociology*, Vol. I, No. 1, April 1957.

Ghurye, G.S., *After a Century and a Quarter*, Popular Book Depot, Bombay, 1962.

Kumarappa, J.C., *An Economic Survey of Matar Taluka*, Ahmedabad, 1931.

Majumdar, D.N., *Caste and Communication in an Indian Village*, Asia Publishing House, Bombay, 1958.

Patel, S.J., *Agricultural Labourers in Modern India and Pakistan*, Current Book House, Bombay, 1952.

Singh, Yogendra, *Modernization of Indian Tradition*, Rawat Publication, Jaipur.

Slater, Gilbert, *Some South Indian Villages*, Madras University Economic Studies, No. 1, Madras, 1918.

4 Some Key Concepts of Rural Sociology

Any social science, may it be economics, political science or history, has a definite category of concepts. The formation of concept is a part of theory-building. The researcher starts with the observation of certain particular items. On the basis of these items he makes empirical generalisations. These generalisations then are given an abstract form. The abstract form is the concept. Concepts, thus are empirical, subject to verification. The rural studies which we have analysed in the preceding chapter have given certain concepts. It is hoped that in course of time when the concepts are multiplied, rural sociology may be successful to construct a single large facet theory of rural society. Such a comprehensive theory of rural society would require research work for a number of years. Before we get such a theory we shall have to satisfy ourselves with whatever concepts we have been able to make.

Relevance of rural studies has been criticised enough. For instance, it is alleged that the village studies are not the social fact which could give us the reality of India's village life. The findings of village studies that there is unity of village, there is solidarity of castes, there is extension of village into the outside world and the interpenetration of the wider world into the village, there are kinship networks and above all the village economy is influenced by the outside economy, have not much significance in the context of contemporary change. But whatever small concepts that have emerged out of these studies would help us in the long run to construct a general theory of rural society. It is with this significance of rural studies that we refer to a few of the concepts emerging from village studies.

Changing Language of Rural Sociology

If we make a cursory view of the present status of rural sociology in India we would quickly find a change in the language of the subject.

The terminology of rural sociology has generally become more influenced by economics, sociology and social anthropology. Words such as 'function' and 'social structure' have become less common. Those like 'class', 'contradiction' 'stratification', 'Panchayati Raj', 'agricultural capitalism', 'grassroots', 'subaltern' and 'activists' have become more frequent. Though the terminology in terms of concept framing is fast changing, no new concepts have come.

It should be admitted that the flood in rural studies which we witnessed till 1970s has now become very slow. Though, crores of rupees have been spent by way of village development, no serious evaluation of the rural society is made by rural sociology. Either the results of development programmes are considered to be not worth the investment or the rural sociologists have become unconcerned with all these changes. In absence of any noteworthy researches in rural sociology, one is content any by making interpretation of the earlier concepts.

Emergence of New Methodology

The earlier village studies of 1970s were made through structural-functional methodology. The studies were conducted by the method of positivism. In the present context of the theme of rural research, positivism has became outdated. What is required of a rural sociologist is to become both a researcher and an activist. On one hand, the researcher tries to understand the reality of society and on the other hand, he himself works as a variable. Between the two—the objective reality and the researcher—there comes the role of ideology. Thus, the reality, the researcher and the ideology constitute the total understanding of the rural society and for that matter any theme of enquiry. We would, therefore, find that in the present context of conducting research in rural sociology, the methodology and the language of concepts are fast changing. When we analyse the theoretical content, data and method of rural sociology, we should always keep our eye on the fast changing rural society.

Here, we will discuss a few of the concepts which have resulted from the rural studies. The usefulness of these concepts lies in the fact that they help us to analyse the social change witnessed in rural society.

Dominant Caste

The concept of 'dominant caste' was propounded by M.N. Srinivas. It was for the first time appeared in his essay on the social system of a Mysore village. While constructing the concept, perhaps Srinivas was unconsciously influenced by African studies on the dominant clan and dominant lineage. Srinivas developed the concept in his study of Rampura village which is a little away from Mysore city in Karnataka state. Srinivas, in fact, wanted to give a comprehensive study of Rampura. To write down the details of the village he had gone to Stanford for writing down a monograph on Rampura. But there "by a strange quirk of fate all the three copies of my fieldwork notes, processed over a period of eighteen years" were destroyed when a fire took place in his Stanford office. Everything was destroyed for Srinivas. Whatever he remembered about Rampura, later on came in the form of *The Remembered Village* (1976).

The definition of 'dominant caste' has undergone some change over a period of time. Srinivas worked in Rampura in 1948. His finding was first reported in 1955. He defined the concept as below:

> The concept of dominant caste which has emerged in recent sociological research is important in this connection. A caste is dominant when wields economic or political power and occupies a fairly high position in hierarchy (even in the traditional system of a caste which acquired economic and political power did succeed in improving its ritual status).

Srinivas says that the existence of dominant caste is not particular to Rampura only. It is found in other villages of the country also. For instance, in Mysore villages, Lingayat and Okkaliga; in Andhra Pradesh, Reddy and Kamma; in Tamilnadu, Gounder, Padayachi and Mudaliar; in Kerala, Nayar; in Maharashtra, Maratha; in Gujarat, Patidar; and in northern India, Rajput, Jat, Giyar and Ahir are dominant castes. Traditionally, numerically small castes owning land in rural areas or wielding political power or inheriting a literary tradition, were able to dominate the villages. Srinivas has provided historical reasons for the power exercised by the traditional higher castes. He says that the traditional high castes had influence because of western education and the benefits which they conferred.

Earlier, numerical strength of a caste was not much important.

But with the coming of adult suffrage and the reservation given to scheduled castes and scheduled tribes, numerical strength has assumed importance. Srinivas writes:

> Nowadays, with the coming of adult suffrage, numerical strength has become very important and the leaders of the dominant castes help the political parties to secure votes. But the traditional forms of dominance have not entirely disappeared and neither has dominance shifted fully to the numerically strongest caste, there is no doubt, however, that there is a shift and this traditional phase is marked by inter-group tensions. But what is significant from our point of view is that in many parts of India there are castes which are *decisively* dominant.

It was in 1962 that M.N. Srinivas specified the following three characteristics of a dominant caste:

1. A caste dominates when it wields economic and political power.
2. It has a high rank in caste hierarchy.
3. Numerical strength.

The earlier definition of dominant caste was reviewed by writers of several village studies. Srinivas also looked into the field and the comments made by the others. In 1966, he reviewed his earlier definition which runs below:

> For a caste to be dominant, it should own a sizable amount of the arable land locally available, have strength of numbers, and occupy a high place in the local hierarchy. When a caste has all the attributes of dominance, it may be said to enjoy a decisive dominance.

Characteristics

On the basis of the definitions of dominant caste given by Srinivas and the comments offered by other sociologists, a construct could be made which includes the ideal type of dominant caste.

1. *Economic and political power*

The power of a particular caste lies in the owning of land. The caste which has larger portion of the land in the village wields greater power. First, his agricultural income increases. The size of the land is also related to irrigation. In case of larger landowning and adequate irrigation facilities, naturally, the wields of the casteman increase. Second, the larger landowning caste also provides jobs to the landless farmers and marginal farmers. Such a situation renders the superordinated landless labourers as the 'servants' of the large landowning caste. These castes also apply modern techniques of agriculture such as chemical manure, improved implements and new patterns of cropping.

Yogendra Singh (1994) observes that the social anthropologists have found the presence of dominant castes in most of the south Indian villages. The basic determinant of a dominant caste is the superior economic status, especially in land. In the south Indian villages, for instance, Brahmin and Okkaliga are dominant castes. "The Havik Brahmins in village Toltagadde in Malaud area of Mysore and Smarth Brahmins in the Kumbapettai village in Tanjore (Tamilnadu) have been observed to be dominant castes. Okkaliga are dominant in the village Rampura, Wangala and Delana studied in Mysore."

Putting his analysis of dominant castes, Yogendra Singh observes:

> An interesting common factor which plays a very significant role in the dominance of these castes in the villages ... is their superior economic status, specially in land. Brahmins in Toltagadde have ownership of all cash crop land; Kumbapettai Brahmins traditionally controlled all land; Okkaligas in Wangala; and Delanas control more than 80 per cent of land; Rajputs in Senapur, eastern UP control 82 per cent of land in the village; and the Vaghela Rajputs in Cassandra village in Gujarat have control over all the land in the village. In all these villages the degree of dominance of these castes is high.

Higher education is also accepted by the big landowning castes. Administrative and income generated in urban areas have also given economic power to these caste groups. Besides economic power, namely, agriculture and jobs in administration, the big landowning castes have increased their prestige and power because of their role in Panchayati Raj. Srinivas says that "the introduction of adult franchise and Panchayati Raj has resulted in giving a new sense of self-respect to the villagers". Srinivas argues that the economic and political power which has come to the big landowning castes has thus enhanced their power status.

2. *High rank in caste hierarchy*

Normally, the caste which is traditionally higher in the caste hierarchy enjoys the status of dominance. The Brahmins and the Rajputs have traditionally been dominant in the villages. The Brahmins have at the top of the caste hierarchy and they officiate at the religious festivals and rituals of the village. The Rajputs have been the feudals-*thakurs* in the village. They have traditionally occupied larger portions of the village land. The economic and political power, thus, in the village has given the dominant status to the Brahmins and Rajputs.

Recently, the criterion, namely, economic and political power, has undergone a change. The reservations made for scheduled castes, scheduled tribes and women have given a new attribute to the concept of dominant caste. As a result provision power has passed into the hands of numerically large landowning peasant castes. Some of the scheduled castes, who are numerically strong and also take advantage of the new educational and other opportunities available to them, have also gained economic and political power. The high rank in the caste hierarchy has now gone in favour of those castes which have benefited from their reserved status. Now, the traditional higher status in the hierarchy no more remains an attribute of a dominant caste.

3. *Numerical strength*

Before the advent of modernisation and development, numerical strength did not have any strength of the dominance of a caste. Recently, numerical strength of a caste assumes importance because of the vote bank created by adult suffrage. The castes which have larger number of voters, naturally, determine the fate of a candidate contesting elections. What is called these days as caste-war is actually the importance of a caste to determine the fate of a candidate.

Now, a caste is dominant not only in single village. It extends to a cluster of villages. A caste group which has only a family or two in a particular village but which enjoys decisive dominance in the wider region, will still count locally because of the network of ties binding it to its dominant relatives. What is equally important is that others in the village will be aware of the existence of this network. Contrariwise, a caste which enjoys dominance in only one village will find that it has to reckon with the caste which enjoys regional dominance.

4. *A sizeable amount of the arable land*

Normally, in India's villages, smaller number of big landowners occupy larger portion of land. In other words, the caste which has larger portion of village land wields power. The big landowners, thus, are patrons of the bulk of the poor villagers. In villages, those castes which have larger portion of land, enjoy power and prestige. Srinivas says that landownership is a crucial factor in establishing a dominance. He observes:

> Landownership confers not only power but prestige, so much so that, individuals who have made good in any walk of life tend to invest in land. If landownership is not always an indispensable passport to high rank, it certainly facilitates upward mobility.

Criticism

The decades of 1950s and 1960s in the field of rural sociology witnessed a keen competition between those who preferred Redfield's approach to village studies and Radcliffe-Brown's analysis of functional analysis. Despite differences in their approach, both the camps focused on culture. Later on Louis Dumont stressed the importance of culture and caste as determining variables in the study of Indian civilisation as a whole.

The concept of 'dominant caste', it is argued, has emerged out of the African studies on dominant class. When Srinivas put forward the concept of dominant caste, it was seriously commented upon by sociologists and social anthropologists. As a matter of fact, during 1950s and 1960s, the academic environment in the country, in rural sociology and social anthropology, was charged by studies on caste and village communities. Some of the criticisms of the concept have relevance even today in our understanding of rural society. These criticisms are enumerated below:

1. *Dominant caste today is found only in traditional villages*

Srinivas has argued that a dominant caste has most of the power in the village within its fold. In fact, it is the dominant caste which runs the village; maintains the village system.

The empirical reality today has undergone vast transformation. Surely, in the past, the powerful families in the village were the big landowning families. The Brahmins and the Rajputs, in the earlier periods of history, got immense favour from the feudal lords and the British rulers. In order to keep these higher castes in favour of the ruling group land was given as gift. Those who received such favours included Brahmins, Rajputs and the Marathas. Viewed from this perspective admittedly, the Brahmins and the Rajputs became big landowning castes.

But, with the land reforms including land ceiling and abolition of *jamindari* and *jagirdari*, big landowning has ceased to be a determinant factor of dominant caste. In place of big landholding, political power has become a decisive factor in the formation of a dominant caste. Andre Beteille very rightly observes:

> The powerful families in the past were the big landowning families. These included the principal Brahmin families among non-Brahmins, the Maratha family. Today political power whether in the village or outside it is not as closely tied to ownership of land as it was in the past. New bases of power have emerged which are, to some extent, independent of both caste and class. Perhaps most important among these is the strength of numerical support.

D.N. Majumdar, who conducted the study of Monana village of Uttar Pradesh in 1958, observes that the Brahmin and the Thakur were the dominant castes in Mohana. But, at a later stage, he finds that the dominance of the Thakur group has begun to be shaken up, ever since the legal removal of its economic pillar—the *jamindari* system—which was the strong medium through which it held the various other castes in a position of economic subordination... But Majumdar also finds that with the abolition of *jamindari*, much of the economic power of the Thakur is retained. He says that "with their wide moneylending business they still are a powerful group".

If economic power is considered to be an important factor of the formation of a dominant caste, it is only limited to the traditional villages, such as, that of tribals which have not received the impact of modern political transformation.

2. *Dominant caste is not always numerically a preponderant caste*

Yet another criticism of dominant caste falls into two camps. One camp of scholars argues that in traditional villages it is not the numerical strength but secular power and ritual status that determine the status of a dominant caste. Among those who stand for this argument include D.N. Majumdar and others. However, the second group consisting of Andre Beteille, M.N. Srinivas and Yogendra Singh has advanced the idea of ritual and secular status of a caste as dominant. This group asserts an empirical evidence that nowadays "with the coming of adult suffrage, numerical strength has become very important and the scheduled castes and scheduled tribes have assumed a greater importance".

Majumdar does not consider numerical strength as a decisive factor in the formation of a dominant caste. Historically, "Indian villages probably never exercised majority rule or accepted majority verdict. The feudal India did not compromise with numerical strength. Besides, alone-Brahmin, a *sadhu*, a *jamindar*, alone social worker---each has exercised more influence than a numerically preponderant community in the village". Majumdar denies the idea that scheduled castes and scheduled tribes, though, having numerical strength may occupy a status of dominant caste. According to him, "the backward classes, scheduled castes preponderate in many villages, even a particular caste like the *Lodha* or the *Pasi* may be numerically the largest caste in a village, but authority and importance may attach to the few upper castes families, or to the *jamindar* family, i.e., the social matrix of India village".

Thus, on one hand, it is argued that numerical strength has ceased to be a factor in the making of a dominant caste while it is also held on the basis of empirical strength that the modern forces of democracy and development including the improvement of the status of scheduled groups have gone a long way in making a group dominant in a village.

3. *Dominant caste is a part of structuralist approach*

Most of the criticism labelled against the dominant caste is that of those theorists who oppose structuralist approach in the study of Indian society. Louis Dumont is the leader of this approach. M.N. Srinivas, while giving the concept of dominant caste, also follows the line of a structuralist. Srinivas stands far hierarchy, i.e., the opposition between pure and impure. He looks at the pure caste, namely, Brahmins and Rajputs as the higher castes in the caste system. he has taken upper caste view in the construction of dominant caste. This perspective of Srinivas has been criticised by Edmund Leach. In fact, Srinivas has overlooked the force of history when he writes:

> Historical data are neither as accurate nor as rich and detailed as the data collected by field anthropologists, and the study of certain existing processes in the past.

The making of a dominant caste, thus, is highly empirical and does not take into consideration the forces of history. A cursory view of the contemporary rural India would immediately show that much of the relevance of dominant caste has fallen into erosion. As a matter of fact, there has been sea-change in the social reality of Indian villages that much cannot be comprehended with the help of this concept. The reservation given to scheduled castes and scheduled tribes, the intensification of democratisation, and the introduction of Panchayati Raj through 73rd amendment to Indian Constitution have gone a long way in shrinking the influence of dominant caste. However, there are some politically dominant groups which have begun to exercise influence on the villagers.

Village Unity

Traditionally, it is argued that Indian villages all through its periods of history have maintained unity. There have been wars and attacks, ruling dynasties have come and gone, and neighbouring states have waged wars against one another, but there has not been any disturbance in the unity of the village. the collective consciousness among the villagers has been so strong that they have unbreakable ties among themselves which are manifested in the celebrations of village festivals, rituals and ceremonies. The *Panch Parmeshwar* has been the supreme body in the village life. A person is not much shy of remaining imprisoned than to be punished by the village panchayat.

The traditional unity of village has been explored by social anthropologists. It is said that the fabric of village life consists of caste and kin groups. The ties of castes and kin have always divided the villages into numerous factions. Andre Beteille's Sripuram is very clearly divided into the Brahmin households and the untouchables. Srinivas argues that though caste and kin have created cracks in the village unity, the village continues to enjoy a solidarity. Besides, the inroads made by transport and communication have not succeeded in jeopardising the village unity. Many of the village studies have made a point of the village unity. Srinivas, while taking a stock of the proverbial village unity, argues:

> Caste is even today an institution of great strength, and as marriage and dining are forbidden with members of other castes, the members of a caste living in a village have many important ties with their fellow castemen living in neighbouring villages. These ties are so powerful that a few anthropologists have been led into asserting that the unity of the village is a myth and that the only thing which counts is caste. Secondly, in spite of the fact, that communications between the villages are still poor and were even poorer in the past, they were far from being self-contained. Intimate links, economic, religious and social, existed between neighbouring villages.

Whether the caste solidarity or kin ties maintained the village unity, the significant point is that even today a village has its unity. Despite political party factions, transport and media, a person identifies himself with his village. Democratisation has further strengthened the village unity. It is common to observe that the people of a village or for that matter the people of the cluster of neighbouring villages immediately mobilise when their village is discriminated against by the village panchayat or the government authorities.

Characteristics

Following are some of the main characteristics of the village unity:

1. For the fulfilment of the several needs of the village, the unity is observed in many respects of village life. It is argued that the village self-sufficiency contributes to the maintenance of village unity. "Writers as different as Metcalfe, Maine and Marx believed that with the exception of a few commodities, such as, salt and metals, the traditional Indian village produced within itself all that it consumed." Surely, many of the day-to-day needs of the village are fulfilled by itself. Among artisans we find potters, carpenters, goldsmiths and blacksmiths. The village services are represented by barbers, washermen, pipers and several categories of priests. It is because of this traditional unity of village that Gandhiji has

talked about village self-sufficiency or *swaraj*.

2. Village unity is manifested in the collective celebration of festivals, fairs and ceremonies. Holi, Raksha Bandhan and Diwali have become the festivals of the whole village, notwithstanding the presence of Muslims and Christians.
3. Yet another expressive form of village unity is the identification of villagers to their community. In matters of political orientation the villagers may hold different ideologies but in social, cultural and economic life the village unity is well maintained. It is common to find a villager migrating to a city, draws his fellow men with no loss of time to his place of migration. In these days, when a large number of villagers seek migration to urban centres, the village unity is well illustrated.
4. Village unity does not mean that there are no factions in the villages. In present India, a few new forces have made their inroads in the village life. These forces tend to weaken village unity by promoting inequalities and dividing the society on class and reservation lines. Looking to it, one thinks that the future does not hold any optimism for village unity.

Sanskritisation

Caste system in theory is a closed system. Movement upwards or downwards within it is inadmissible, although there is some movement in practice. Despite this limitation of caste system, the concept of 'sanskritisation' helps to explain social change within the caste system. The term 'sanskritisation' was conceived by M.N. Srinivas. It helps to describe the process of cultural mobility in the traditional social structure of India. Srinivas found empirical evidence for constructing sanskritisation in his study of religion and society among Coorgs in Mysore. He found that "lower castes, in order to raise their position in the caste hierarchy, adopted some customs of the Brahmins and gave up some of their own, considered to be impure by the higher castes. For instance, they gave up meat-eating, consumption of liquor and animal sacrifice to their deities; they imitated the Brahmins in matters of dress, food and rituals. By doing this, within a generation or so, they could claim higher positions in the hierarchy of caste".

M.N. Srinivas, initially, defined sanskritisation to denote

Brahminisation. Later on, he replaced it by sanskritisation.

Brahminisation was limited in its scope and did not include other models of caste mobility. His findings of Coorgs, thus, were of a specific kind and did not include the other non-Brahmin castes who were twice-born. The concept of sanskritisation redefined by M.N. Srinivas runs as below:

> Sanskritisation is the process by which a 'low' Hindu caste or tribal or other group changes its customs, rituals, ideology and way of life in the direction of a 'high' and, frequently, 'twice-born' caste. Generally, such changes are followed by a claim to a higher position in the caste hierarchy than that traditionally conceded to the claimant caste by the local community. The claim is usually made over a period of time, in fact, a generation or two, before the 'arrival' is conceded.

Sanskritisation, in fact, is the process of cultural and social mobility within the framework of caste. In this case, the source of social change lies within the caste system. In other words, the source of social change is indigenous. In terms of general sociology it is a process of socialisation wherein the lower castes socialise themselves with the customs, rituals and ideology of the higher castes, i.e., the twice-born castes of Brahmins, Rajputs and Banias. The scope of sanskritisation also extends beyond the cast system. It includes non-caste groups also, such as tribals. For social change, the caste of a local place makes its model of imitation. This imitation model could be any twice-born caste. Yogendra Singh applies the redefined concept of sanskritisation to the 'varna' system. He says that the central idea of sanskritisation is that of hierarchy in caste system, theoretically represented by *varna*. There are four *varnas*, viz., the Brahmin, the Kshatriya, the Vaishya and the Shudra in the same hierarchical order, and all individual castes or sub-castes, with the exception of the untouchables, can be classified on the basis of *varna* into a hierarchical order. The untouchables have traditionally been outside the *varna* hierarchy and form the lowest rung of the caste stratification.

Characteristics

When the concept of sanskritisation emerged in sociological literature in 1952, it created much academic uproar among social anthropologists and sociologists. It was agreed that the concept is useful to analyse social change among villagers, specially in terms of culture change. Both Indian and foreign social anthropologists reacted to the usefulness of concept on the basis of whatever is available in sociological research material, we give below a few of the basic characteristics of sanskritisation:

1. *It is a cultural paradigm*

Ideas, beliefs, traditions, rituals and things of this kind constitute the culture of a caste. When there is a change in these aspects of social life, it is a change in cultural life. Thus, sanskritisation is a cultural change among the lower castes and non-caste groups.

2. *Sanskritisation is a change directed to twice-born castes*

Though, initially, sanskritisation meant Brahminisation, but later on, Srinivas included other models of higher castes for imitation. It was Milton Singer (1964) who had drawn attention of Srinivas by saying that there existed not one or two models of sanskritisation but three if not four. He said that the local version of sanskritic Hinduism may use the four labels—Brahmin, Kshatriya, Vaishya and Shudra—but the defining content of these labels varies with locality and needs to be empirically determined for any particular locality. For instance, a particular village may imitate Brahmins as their model of change but looking to the historicity and contextuality, another village may decide Kshatriya or Vaishya as their model. Brahmins not in all cases are homogeneous. Nor are the Kshatriyas. There are Brahmins, such as the Kashmiri, Bengali and Saraswat who are non-vegetarians. Similarly, there is variation among the Kshatriyas and Vaishyas. It is, therefore, the local history and the contexts which determine the sanskritic model for the lower castes. However, the Shudras do not make any model for imitation.

3. *Sanskritisation also applies to tribals or non-caste groups*

In his refined definition Srinivas has stated that sanskritisation is not confined to Hindu castes only but it also occurs among tribal and semi-tribal groups, such as the Bhils of western India, the Gonds and Oraons of central India, and the Pahadis of the Himalayas. These tribal groups claim to attain the status of a caste, i.e., to become a Hindu.

4. *Sanskritic values, ideology, beliefs belong to Indian tradition*

When Srinivas talks of sanskritisation of the lower castes, he has in his view the caste-Hindu traditions. Hinduism draws heavily from its scriptures, such as *Ramayana*, *Mahabharata*, *Upanishads* and *Brahmanas*. The values and beliefs held in these scriptures become the content material for the imitation of the lower castes. The Brahmins, i.e., the priestly caste, naturally interpret the traditions and, therefore, they become the model of imitation for the lower castes.

Surely, acquisition of wealth and power makes a group or person belonging to a caste, important. But, only wealth and power do not enhance the status of a caste. The improvement in the ritual status can only help the lower caste to improve their hierarchy in the caste system. The imitation of the customs and habits of the higher caste, therefore, goes a long way in imparting sanskritic status to the lower caste, if the later has wealth and power.

5. *Sanskritisation, in other words, also means teetotalism*

Srinivas, to be fair to him, has always refined and redefined his understanding of sanskritisation. At a later stage, he found that the lower castes in sanskritisation have a tendency to move higher in the caste hierarchy and in a generation or two they could improve their status in caste hierarchy by adopting vegetarianism and tee-totalism.

Empirically no researcher has reported that a lower caste has improved its rank in the hierarchy despite having three generations. Though, there is no improvement in the rank it must be said that the lower castes have taken to the prohibition of alcoholism and many of the evils which traditionally characterised their caste.

Criticism

It must be admitted that Srinivas has made a serious attempt to analyse social change not only in villages but in the wider society at large. Concepts are not theories, they are only formats of a theory. There is a possibility of a format to suffer from several weaknesses. Response of Srinivas' concept of sanskritisation has been much encouraging, notwithstanding its drawbacks. For instance, in 1965, the University of Chicago organised a seminar on 'Social Change in India'. The seminar was important in the sense that it was attended by Srinivas himself and a number of social anthropologists, such as Bernard S. Cohen, David G. Mandelbaum, McKim Marriott, Owen M. Lynch, Milton Singer and a few others. All these had rich experience of working in Indian villages. Sanskritisation was discussed thoroughly in this conference. Besides, some of the Indian sociologists also conducted intensive field studies to verify the concept. The critique which we give below is drawn from all these comments.

1. *Religion is sui generis for Srinivas*

Whether we consider dominant caste, sanskritisation on westernisation, in all these concepts the major thrust of Srinivas is caste. Caste is related to religion and, therefore, when Srinivas talks about caste he means religion. His fundamental assumption is that caste has originated from religion. It is the Brahma who created four *varnas* out of the different parts of his body. Religion and caste, therefore, for Srinivas, are the two sides of the same coin. Viewed from this perspective, the concept of sanskritisation is the concept of religion. And when he focuses on caste, he is concerned with hierarchy. K.L. Sharma (1986) rightly observes:

> Srinivas' study of the role of religion among the Coorgs is clearly an extension of Radcliffe-Brown's functionalism. Religion is sui generis for Srinivas. Caste and religion are intertwined. Hence religion becomes the basis of caste hierarchy (emphasis ours).

The weakness of the concept of sanskritisation is that it is only concerned with the culture. It would not be wrong to say that Srinivas is concerned only with the cultural and normative criteria which brings change in rural society. The economic and political parameters of change have largely been overlooked by him.

2. *Hierarchy is supreme*

The concept of sanskritisation is based on hierarchy. The idea in the process of sanskritisation is that the lower castes might rise to higher caste by imitating the sanskritic rights of the twice-born. Such a social change is hierarchical. When today, in contemporary India, democratisation has become a new value, hierarchical transformation is increasingly becoming weak.

Parvathamma brings out this weakness of sanskritisation when she observes:

In all the writings of Srinivas, the Brahmin non-Brahmin values are juxtapose, hierarchy remains basic to Srinivas.

3. *Social tensions and contradictions by-passed*

For Srinivas, the idea of India society is that of caste society. He altogether forgets that Indian society is a plural society; it does not discriminate individuals on the basis of caste. By giving the concept of sanskritisation he very rigidly adheres to caste model of Indian society. K.L. Sharma comments harshly on this weakness of Srinivas:

> A scholar of the eminence Srinivas does not take cognizance, perhaps inadvertently, of the continuity of 'social formation' of India society, and prefers to adhere to caste model of Indian society. He refers to 'rural caste' and 'urban caste', like some American scholars, such as Rosen and Marriott. Caste and class, theoretically speaking, are principles of social status determination, hence not concerned with 'rural' or 'urban' people as such. *'Rural' and 'urban' are patterns of living and not principles of ranking* (emphasis ours).

4. *Sanskritisation may lead to inter-class hostility*

Yogendra Singh has yet another weakness in the concept of sanskritisation given by Srinivas. His guess is that sometimes sanskritisation may manifest suppressed inter-class hostility. In support of his guess Yogendra Singh refers to the observation made by Harold Gould:

> One of the prime motives behind sanskritisation is this factor of repressed hostility which manifests itself not in the form of rejecting the caste system but in the form its victims trying to seize control of it and, thereby, expiate their frustrations on the same battlefield where they acquired them. Only then can there be a sense of satisfaction in something achieved, i.e., tangible, concrete, and relevant to past experience.

Not only Yogendra Singh but Srinivas himself has admitted that sanskritisation subsumes many meanings. Some of the meanings are mutually antagonistic.

5. *Sanskritisation is a limited concept*

Surely, one of the weaknesses of sanskritisation is its limited usefulness. It refers only to social change in the caste hierarchy. Caste hierarchy is basically ritual-cultural hierarchy. But beyond caste, i.e., in secular hierarchy sanskritisation ceases of exist. In any case the concept is not comprehensive enough in explaining social change.

6. *It is a process confined to little tradition only*

Admittedly, sanskritisation is a process of social change. Theoretically, "sanskritisation may represent changes in cultural structure, of the little as well as the great tradition. But most empirical observations of this process are confined to the little tradition". In other words, changes in the great tradition, i.e., in epics like *Puranas* can be made by a comprehensive cultural renaissance that can be effected at the local level. And, therefore, sanskritisation though wider in scope remains restricted to a few castes found in a specific regions. For instance, if there is a movement of sanskritisation among the potters, it does not necessarily mean that the movement would spread among the potters at national level. Obviously, a caste varies from place to place, region to region.

7. *Sanskritisation sometimes is a protest against the normative structure*

There are empirical observations in some parts of rural India that the lower castes have rebelled against the sanskritic values of the higher castes. Such protests have resulted out of the democratic values given by education, party ideology and idiom of equality. Emphasising this point Yogendra Singh observes:

> Looked at from an ideal-typical value frame, sanskritisation is a form of protest against the normative structure and principles laid down by the great tradition. It, amongst to a rejection of the Hindu theory of *karma* which integrates the various levels of role institutionalisation supposed to be ascribed by birth, is thus a process of usurpation of a position higher in *hierarchy* as defined by the great tradition, by rejection of fundamental principle of *hierarchy* (great tradition).

The protest against sanskritisation thus gets manifested in the denial of the *karmakanda* practised by Brahmins. The ritual status of Brahmin in this process gets eroded. Similarly, the former ruling class of Rajputs is also looked down by the rebels. And, therefore, it would be erroneous to understand that on all occasions sanskritisation is looked with favour.

8. *Weakening dominant caste also lowers sanskritisation*

The concept of dominant caste is a supplement to the concept of sanskritisation. In modern India, the construct of dominant caste is fast becoming irrelevant. No more are Brahmins a dominant caste in many of the villages. Dominance carries power, professional status and party association. Quite like the construct of dominant caste sanskritisation also suffers certain weaknesses. The developed villages now hardly consider dominant caste as their reference models for sanskritisation.

9. *Power acquisition and political participation are more important than cultural status*

Milton Singer has brought out a new empirical evidence (1968) to suggest that the contemporary upward mobile group has rejected sanskritisation for political participation. Singer, in this regard, refers to the studies of Owen M. Lynch and William Rowe. Lynch conducted a study among the Jatav of Agra. While rejecting Srinivas, Lynch observes:

> The concept of sanskritisation describes the social changes occurring in modern India in terms of sanskritisation and westernisation. The description is primarily in cultural and not in structural terms.

Lynch argues that in place of sanskritisation the process of 'elite emulation' applies well so far the Jatavas, i.e., Chamars are concerned. He says that the Jatavas have given up claims to a 'dominant' status of Kshatriya and sanskritic cultural behaviour, and have become antagonist of castes and caste system; in effect, they have reversed their old position against the Adi-Hindu movement. The reasons for rejection of sanskritisation, i.e., caste culturology, as given by Lynch, are:

> The change is due to the fact that sanskritisation is no longer as functional as is political participation for achieving a change in style of life and a rise in the Indian social system, now composed of both caste and class elements. The object of sanskritisation was ultimately to open and legitimise a place in the opportunity and power structures of the caste society. The same object can now be better achieved by

active political participation. It is no longer ascription based on caste status, but rather achievement based on citizenship status that, manifestly at least, is the recruitment principle for entrance into the power and opportunity structures.

For Lynch, Rowe, Singer and others sanskritisation is basically a concept of social mobility. Quite like these American scholars Y.B. Damle has also applied Merton's reference group reference group theory to analyse social change in rural India. It is argued that sanskritisation is very limited in its scope, whereas reference group theory is quite comprehensive.

Concluding our description on sanskritisation it could be said that the nature of sanskritisation is definitely empirical. It focuses on localised culture. It is concerned with the culture of the twice-born. Its weaknesses are several. The difficulty with the concept is that rural India is changing fast and the concept has not received any corresponding change. It is well known in theory that concepts commit their own suicide when they do not interact with the reality. This is exactly what has happened with the concept of sanskritisation. Some of the youngsters even belonging to the dalit castes raise their heads and say: Who cares for the twice-born? We have our own dignity. We have our legitimate rights. Who can deny it?

Westernisation

Quite like sanskritisation the concept of westernisation is also employed for evaluating social change in rural India and elsewhere in the country. The concept was also constructed by M.N. Srinivas to describe the the process of social and cultural mobility in the traditional social structure of India. It has also emerged, in Srinivas' study of the Coorgs of south India. The author has defined westernisation as:

> ...the change brought about in Indian society and culture as a result of over 150 years of British rule, the term subsuming changes occurring at different levels...technology, institutions, ideology and values (Srinivas, 1962).

The emphasis given by Srinivas on westernisation basically included humanitarianism and rationalism. Commenting on the broader dimensions of westernisation, Yogendra Singh (1994) writes:

Emphasis on humanitarianism and rationalism is a part of westernisation which led to a series of institutional and social reforms in India. Establishment of scientific, technological and educational institutions, rise of nationalism, new political culture and leadership in the country, are all by-products of westernisation.

Srinivas argues that the acceleration in westernisation does not slow down the process of sanskritisation. As a matter of fact, both the processes go hand in hand. It is found that sometimes increase in westernisation also boosts the process of sanskritisation. A cursory view of the impact of westernisation including communication and transport facilities has modernised the sanskritic institutions, such as pilgrimages and caste associations. It is a common observation that in the last three or four decades new religious celebrations have emerged. The deities which were oblivious have now become target of popular celebrations. The caste associations have received better organisation. At empirical plane it is found that with the increase in westernisation sanskritic ties have also got solidarity.

Origin

Srinivas has given details about the development of westernisation in India. He traces it from the period of British Raj. Surely, the colonial rule brought with it exploitation and suppression of the masses of people both at the rural and urban levels. At the same time, it also brought certain radical changes in Indian society and culture. The British rule initiated a period of new technology, institutions, knowledge, beliefs and values. The colonial rule, thus, integrated the different segments of Indian society. The modern state actually got its beginning from this period. The land was surveyed, revenue was settled, a new bureaucracy emerged, and army, police and law courts were established. The British rule also developed communications, railways, post and telegraph and also started schools and colleges. "One obvious result was that books and journals, along with schools, made possible the transmission of modern, as well as traditional knowledge to large numbers of Indians—knowledge which could no longer be the privilege of a few hereditary groups—while the newspapers made people in different parts of the far-flung country realise that they had common bonds, and the events happening in the world outside, influenced their lives for good or ill."

Yet another force released by the British rule was the working of Christian missionary. The Christian missionaries worked in the different parts of the country, particularly in those which were backward and inhabited by tribals and untouchables. This brought the weaker sections closer to westernisation.

In contemporary India, when we talk about westernisation, a tremendous change has come in rural India. The impact of five year plans has brought the village people in the wider network of communication and modernisation. The democratic institutions such as Panchayati Raj and massive spread of education have brought the villagers to come closer to westernisation.

What is interesting in the concepts of sanskritisation and westernisation is that in the former, is observed within the caste structure while in the latter, is observed beyond the caste system.

Characteristics

Srinivas has commented on westernisation from time to time. These comments have come as a result of the academic responses given by other Indian and foreign sociologists. Some of the important characteristics of westernisation included by Srinivas are discussed below:

1. *Humanitarianism*

Westernisation is loaded with certain value preferences. "A most important value, which in turn subsumes several other values, is what may be broadly characterised as humanitarianism, by which is meant an active concern for the welfare of all human beings, irrespective of caste, economic position, religion, age and sex." Srinivas has argued that the term 'humanitarianism' is quite comprehensive. It is inclusive of a large number of other values, the important being the welfare of all.

2. *Equalitarianism*

Westernisation has another value of equalitarianism. It is a democratic value and stands for minimising inequality, removal of poverty and liberty to all. The humanitarianism, as a characteristic of westernisation, stands for a society which could be called as a socialist society in the long run.

3. *Secularisation*

Both the British rule and at a later stage the Constitution of India introduced a new value of secularisation. Secular India is conceived as a nation charged by the idiom of a rational and bureaucratic society. Accordingly, the state is required to have respect for all the religions of the society. It also includes the value of scientific ethics.

4. *Initiation of social reforms*

The idea of westernisation which was propagated by the British rule struck hard on social evils which eroded the Indian society. The introduction of British law put an end to certain inequalities that were part of Hindu and Islamic jurisprudence. The evil institutions of *sati*, untouchability and *purdah* got condemnation from the spread of the notions of equalitarianism and secularisation.

5. *Predominance of science and technology*

The British rule also introduced science and technology in Indian society. This brought railways, steam engines and technology. As a result of this, the Indian society moved towards industrialisation. Though, science and technology came as a setback to village industries and local arts and artifacts, the industrial growth increased. This also gave encouragement to urban development. Migration from village to town and city also increased.

There was a take-off from tradition to modernity during this period. Industrialisation and urbanisation also introduced new values in society. Many of the traditional institutions like untouchability and caste received new interpretation.

Clearly, the concept of westernisation introduced by M.N. Srinivas is meant to measure the social change which came in India during the British period. In post-independent India westernisation got accelerated. The Indian society came in contact with other countries also. The United States had a profound impact on our society. At a later stage Srinivas was suggested to review the concept looking to the new impact of modernisation. For instance, Daniel Lerner, after considering the suitability of 'westernisation' as well as 'modernisation', has opted for the later. Modernisation also includes urbanisation. If also enhances media exposure and wider economic participation. "Mod ernisation also implies social mobility. A mobile society has to encourage rationality for the calculus of choice which shapes individual behaviour and conditions it rewards. People come to see the social future as manipulable rather than ordained and their prospects in terms of achievement rather than heritage."

If we examine M.N. Srinivas' concepts of sanskritisation and westernisation, we will be able to find out that in the assessment of rural change westernisation is not much significant. Both the concepts are loaded with sanskritic and western values. The concepts also carry certain ideologies. Yogendra Singh argues that the use of the term 'westernisation' is pejorative for Indian elites. In place of westernisation, modernisation appears to be a better term. He observes:

> ...modernisation in India cannot be adequately accounted for by a term like westernisation. Moreover, for many new elite in India as also in the new states of Asia, the term westernisation has a pejorative connotation because of its association with former colonial domination of these countries by the West. It is, therefore, more value-loaded than the term modernisation, which to us appears as a better substitute.

Little and Great Traditions

In the preceding pages we have discussed a few of the concepts which have emerged from the village studies made during 1950s and are considered to be significant for analysing change in rural society. Many of these concepts are cultural in nature and from caste in rural India. The concepts of little and great traditions also stand for change in rural caste system. Both these concepts are constructed by Milton Singer and Mckim Marriott.

The origin of little and great traditions is from Robert Redfield, who conducted his studies in Mexican communities. It was Redfield who talked about little community. For him little community was a village that had smaller size, self-sufficient and relatively isolated. Redfield did not mention anything about traditions or great traditions. Singer and Marriott who were influenced by studies made by Redfield conducted their intensive study in Indian villages. They elaborated the original model of Redfield in the light of data generated from India villages. Yogendra Singh has commented upon the construction of little and great traditions in Indian villages by these two anthropologists.

He writes:

> Influenced by this model (of Robert Redfield), Milton Singer and Mckim Marriott had conducted some studies on social change in India utilising this conceptual framework. The basic ideas in this approach are 'civilisation', and 'social organisation of tradition'. It is based on the evolutionary view that civilisation or the structure of tradition (which consists of both cultural and social structures) grows in two stages: first, through orthogenetic or indigenous evolution, and second, through heterogenetic encounters or contacts with other cultures or civilisations.

The Indian social structure, in a broader way, is stratified into two divisions: (1) the folks or the unlettered peasantry, and (2) the elites. The folks and peasantry follow the little tradition, i.e., the village tradition. The second division of elites follow the great tradition. The great tradition consists of the traditions contained in epics, *Puranas*, *Brahmanas* and other classical sanskritic works. The roles and statuses of Sita and Draupadi constitute the parts of great tradition. The little tradition, on the other hand, is local tradition of great tradition tailored according to the regional and village conditions.

The great tradition is found clearly in twice-born castes, specially, priests, ritual leaders of one kind or other. Some of these corporate groups follow the traits of civilisation and the great tradition. The carriers of little tradition include folk artists, medicine men, tellers of riddles, proverbs and stories, poets and dancers, etc.

Little and great traditions help to analyse social change in rural India. The nature of this change is basically cultural. There is a constant interaction between great tradition and little tradition. The interaction between the two traditions brings about change in rural society. Yogendra Singh explains this interaction as below:

> Changes in the cultural system follow through the interaction between the two traditions in the orthogenetic or heterogenetic process of individual growth. The pattern of change, however, is generally from orthogenetic to heterogenetic forms of differentiation or change in the cultural structure of traditions.

Both Singer and Marriott argue on the strength of data generated from the villages of their study that the cultural content of social structure at the level of little tradition in a village witnesses changes. First, there is change in village culture due to the internal growth of village. In other words, the little tradition witnesses changes due to its own internal growth. Second, the little tradition also undergoes change due to its contact with great tradition and other parts of the wider civilisation. "The direction of this change presumably is from folk or peasant to urban cultural structure and social organisation." The great tradition, i.e., the epic tradition also witnesses universalised pattern of culture resulting from its interaction with the village or little tradition.

Singer has made certain statements about cultural change in rural India. His observations are as under:

1. The Indian civilisation has evolved out of pre-existing folk and regional cultures. This aspect of civilisation constructed the great tradition—*Ramayana*, *Mahabharata* and other religious scriptures. This great tradition maintained its continuity in India's diverse regions, villages, castes and tribes.
2. The cultural continuity of great tradition is based on the idea that people share common cultural consciousness throughout the country.
3. The common cultural consciousness is formed through the consensus held in common about sacred books and sacred objects.
4. In India cultural continuity with the past is so great that even the acceptance of modernising and progress ideologies does not result in linear form of social and cultural change but may result in the traditionalising of apparently modern innovations.

To conclude it could be safely said that there is one cultural approach out of several to explain rural social change in India. In simple words, one could say that a villager borrows norms and values from the great traditions of country's civilisation. In this borrowing he makes changes according to his village's local conditions and history. The villages vary from region to region and, therefore, the little tradition also continues to remain diverse. On the other hand, the great tradition, i.e., the sacred books, also receives a uniform pattern. The concepts, therefore, explain the cultural change both at regional and national levels.

Parochialisation and Universalisation

Parochialisation and universalisation are supplementary to the concepts of little and great traditions. These are processes of cultural change. When the great tradition, i.e., the tradition of epics and sacred books undergoes change at the local or village level, it is parochialisation or localisation of great tradition or civilisation. Parochialisation, therefore, is the cultural change made at the village level.

Universalisation, on the other hand, is a cultural change from little tradition to great tradition. Both these processes are related to the interaction between little tradition and great tradition. Interpreting the process of universalisation, Yogendra Singh observes that when the little tradition moves upward to the great tradition, it is the process of universalisation. And, when the great tradition moves downward to the local or village level, it is parochialisation. His interpretation runs as below:

> Elements of the little tradition, indigenous customs, duties and rites circulate upward to the level of the great tradition and are identified with its legitimate forms. This process Marriott calls 'universalisation'. Likewise, some elements of the great tradition also circulate downward to become organic past of the little tradition, and lose much of their original form in the process. He (McKim Marriott) used the term 'parochialisation' to denote this kind of transaction between the two traditions.

In the process of parochialisation, obviously, there is some loss of the elements of great tradition. Whatever is laid down as elements of great tradition is reduced at village level or interpreted differently by local leaders of priestly castes. In this process there is de-sanskritisation.

References

Beteille, Andre, *Caste, Class and Power,* University of California Press, Berkeley, 1971.

Majumdar, D.N., *Caste and Communication in an Indian Village,* Asia Publishing House, Bombay, 1958.

Sharma, K.L., *Caste, Class and Social Movement*, Rawat Publications, Jaipur, 1986.

Singer, Milton, "The Social Organisation of India Civilization", *Diogenes*, Vol. 45, Winter, 1964.

Singer, Milton and Bernard S. Cohen (eds.), *Structure and Change in Indian Society*, Aldine Publishing Co., Chicago, 1968.

Singh, Yogendra, *Modernisation of Indian Tradition*, Rawat Publications, Jaipur, 1994.

Srinivas, M.N., "The Social System of a Mysore Village" in McKim Marriott (ed.), *Village India*, Chicago University Press, 1955.

—, *The Remembered Village*, Oxford University Press, Delhi, 1976.

—, *Caste in Modern India and Other Essays*, Asia Publishing House, Bombay, 1962.

—, *Social Change in Modern India*, Orient Longmans, New Delhi, 1966.

5 Sociology of Rural Life

Admittedly, rural sociology is a specialised application of sociology. It is, therefore, imperative to study rural life from this perspective. When the economists study rural life, naturally, they focus on activities related to production, distribution, exchange and consumption. Similarly, when a historian enquires about the village life, his approach definitely, is to identify the conditions which have constructed the village. Each of these disciplines deals more or less exclusively with its own perspective.

When a sociologist approaches rural life he is concerned with the human relationships taking place among the village people. It would not be wrong to say that no other discipline focusses attention primarily on human relationships *per se.* It is here that sociology differs from all other social sciences. In other words, the sociologist interests himself in human relationships simply because they are social in nature and not because they are related to economic, political, religious and other types of activities. It must further be stressed that sociology does not study the unique. The study and exposition of the unique and particular are left to other sciences which have a special interest in such phenomena.

Rural sociology studies human relationships. But these relationships pertain only to rural, physical social and cultural environment. In definite terms it should be said that rural sociology analyses social relationships which take place within the boundaries of rural society. Long back, in 1958, Alvin Bertrand, while defining rural sociology, wrote:

> In its broadest definition, rural sociology is the study of human relationships in the rural environment. This definition correctly implies that it is no more nor less than the sociology of life in rural setting... The systematised knowledge of rural social relationships could more aptly be called the sociology of rural life.[1]

The social relationships which take place in what we call rural society are manifested in family, caste, class, economy, i.e., agriculture, politics, religion, etc. These social relationships are found in production relations, party politics and other institutions. Surely, family, caste and class are not found only in villages. These are also found in urban communities including the metropolitan cities. But, the operation of family, caste and class that we find in village communities is characteristically different from urban communities. For instance, inter-caste marriage in villages immediately gets contempt from the community. However, in urban life, such an affair largely goes unnoticed. What we want to argue is that several of the social institutions that we find in rural communities are specific to the communities so far their functioning or operation is concerned. It is with this locality approach that rural society is analysed in this chapter. In other words, we critically look at the web of social relationships found in the village communities from sociological perspective. The rural social relationships found in social institutions becomes the focus of our analysis.

What is Rural?

We, very often, talk about the term 'rural' without having any scientific definition in mind. The presumption is that everyone understands the meaning of the term. In a broader way, it could be said that a village is one which people call a village. But this, however, does not provide us any precise meaning of rural. However, in formal records, there has always been a need to define 'rural' in specific connotation. All over the world, the governments have defined 'rural' in statutory terms. For instance, the US government has adopted the following definition for rural habitations:

> ...all persons living in (a) places of 1,500 or more incorporated cities, boroughs and villages, (b) incorporated towns of 2,500 inhabitants or more except in New Inland, New York and Wisconsin, where 'towns' are simply minor civil divisions of countries, (c) the densely settled urban fringe including both incorporated and incorporated areas, around cities of 50,000 or more, and (d) un-incorporated places of 2,500 inhabitants or more outside any urban fringe.

The US Bureau of the Census, thus, defines rural community on the basis of population size, incorporation and density. Though, such an arbitrary definition of rural community may be subjected to criticism, it serves the purpose of the government. In our country also similar effort has been made. For purpose of government functioning, the term 'rural' is d-fined in terms of revenue. On population size, for the Indian government, the village means a revenue village. It might include one big village or a cluster of small villages. However, for Census Commission, a village is that which is identified by its name having definite boundaries. The Census of India has defined a village as under:

> The basic unit for rural areas is the revenue village which has definite surveyed boundaries. The revenue village may comprise several hemlets but the entire village has been treated as one unit for presentation of census data. In unsurveyed areas, like villages within forest areas, each habitation area with locally recognised boundaries within each forest range officer's beat, was treated as one unit.

India has a large number of villages. It is because of this that the country is proverbially called as the 'nation of villages'. According to 1991 census India had 5,58,088 villages. The number of cities and towns in the same census Year was 3,018. In terms of population size, out of India's total population, 74.3 per cent people reside in villages, the remaining 25.7 per cent being urban dwellers. Earlier, in the 1901 Census, 89.2 per cent resided in villages and remaining in cities.

The size of village has always varied. However, a large number of villages are medium sized. Details of village size and their percentage to the total number of villages, according to 1991 census, are given below:

Population Size	*Percentage to Total Number of Villages*
Less than 500	26.5
Between 500-2000	48.8
Between 2000-5000	19.4

Obviously, medium size villages constitute about half of the number of total villages. Besides population size, the number of villages found in different states also varies. For instance, the largest number of villages, i.e., 1,12,566, are found in Uttar Pradesh, followed by 71,352 in Madhya Pradesh, 67,546 in Bihar, 46,553 in Orissa, and

39,354 in Maharashtra. In terms of smallest villages having minimum number of persons are the states of Sikkim (440) and Nagaland (1,112). It is interesting to know that people settled in villages where they could fulfil their minimum needs of survival. There should be some land for cultivation, some source for drinking water and more or less a friendly physical environment.

Rural People

In Indian context it must be said that whether there are urban communities, metropolis or rural communities, they are all parts of the larger Indian civilisation. Despite the civilisational unities, the rural and urban communities differ among themselves on the bases of physical and socio-cultural environment, way of life, norms and values, and a large number of other factors such as density of population, birth and death rates, economic activities, poverty, caste and class, family and religion. These are some of the vital social organisations which characterise a rural community and differentiate it from an urban community. We shall discuss some of the social and cultural aspects of India's rural communities. We would reiterate that the sociology, i.e., the web of social relations, which is found among the people of rural communities, makes it specific for rural habitation.

Determinants of Rural Social Formations

On a broader plane if we look at the general characteristics of rural communities as are found in contemporary India, we would find in most of the rural life that there is not much differentiation from its counterpart, the urban communities. In the wake of development planning we would find that much advancement is observed in villages. A large number of them has received electricity; in a few villagers water supply has also been provided; there is an increasing network of roads and transport and above all some facilities of education and health are also provided to the village people. The difference in rural and urban life in the contemporary context thus has much reduced.

As a matter of fact, it is dangerous to define rural community and the way of life in rural India in terms of the introduction of modernisation. The way of rural life as is found today is considerably specific to a number of historical, physical, social and cultural factors. In the present chapter we would make an effort to delineate the characteristics of rural social life as are specific to India's villages.

Rural sociologists have argued that rural social life or rural way of life is the result of the interplay of a few factors. These factors have determined the social formation of village life. Whether caste, kin, clan, polity or economy, all these have been determined by a set of factors which are specific to the village habitation. We would discuss the sociological characteristics of India's rural life within the frame of these determinants. They are as under:

1. Geographic Environment
   (a) Location
   (b) Climate
   (c) Topography
   (d) Natural resources
   (e) Isolation
2. Social Environment
   (a) Predominance of primary group contacts
   (b) Social differentiation
   (c) Social stratification
   (d) Migration and mobility
3. Cultural Environment
   (a) Simplicity of cultural expression
   (b) Social control
   (c) Rural knowledge and skills
   (d) Levels and standards of living

It is fashion in the study of rural social life to argue that the rural life can hardly be differentiated from urban life. The general principles of caste and class are not specific to rural and urban life. They have a comprehensive spread to all over the country. Quite like these formations the polity and economy in the present context of globalisation and liberalisation can hardly be differentiated in terms of rural and urban settings. On the other hand, there is a controversy among rural sociologists as to whether rural-urban differences occur in dichotomous fashion along a continuum. Those who hold the view argue that differences between the two communities are categoric in nature and in direct opposition to one another. In other words, the dichotomy stands for contrast in both the communities. On the other hand, the proponents of the continuum theory feel that rural-urban differences only occur in relative degrees in a range extending between the two polar extremes—rural and urban.

The continuum theory has recently got support from sociologists who put the argument that instead of talking about the continuity of village life to urban life—a specific kind of evolution, we should emphasise on the nexus found between the two communities. Those who stand for rural-urban nexus, proposed that historically the two communities have never remained isolates. There has always been a close contact between the rural way of life and urban way of life.

The nexus theorists, in a recently held seminar at New Delhi, have brought the fact that historically both the communities have had economic and socio-cultural exchanges.

Notwithstanding the continuum or the nexus between the rural and urban communities, it must be stressed that geographically, population-wise in terms of density and physical facilities, the rural communities display a social life which is characteristically different from the political life. Our objective here is not to differentiate the rural and urban life that we propose to give in next chapter. What concerns us here is to focus on the rural life, the rural social formation in terms of caste, class and polity with reference to the above mentioned three determinants.

Geographic Environment

Geography is the study of location, climate, topography and natural resources. These aspects of geography vary from place to place and region to region. The topography of the states of Punjab, Maharashtra and Gujarat, for example, is such that it is suitable for cultivation and irrigation facilities. On the other hand, the topography of hilly regions, such as the states of north-east, is difficult and is not conducive for cultivation. It is, therefore, the strength and weakness of geography which determines the way of life of the communities inhabiting a particular geography. It is in this context that we look at the way of life of the rural people.

(a) *Physical Setting*

Location has a vital influence on the structural and cultural differences that are found in a rural society. For this purpose one has only to contrast the inhabitants of hot, humid climates with the residents of arctic regions, or the people who live on gentle, rolling planes, with the inhabitants of mountainous regions, and to see how the physical setting accounts for differences in human society.

In the case of India's rural physical setting one could easily observe that the village location which is in the plains and valleys is prone to take easy cultivation. On the other hand, where the physical setting is uncomfortable, neither there are industries nor any cultivation. Life found in such communities revolves round home industries, crafts and arts.

Surely, it must be admitted that location may also be unsuitable and unfriendly for the urban communities too. But, in these communities, due to the role of technology, much of the physical setting is modified. In urban communities, the hazards of climate are modified by the use of technology. As a result of technological efforts made by the urban people, the rural communities tend to develop 'customs' and 'personal traits' compatible with the struggle against nature. As a matter of fact, the urbanite seldom comes face to face with the extremes of physical environment. The villager generally works outdoors and has very little to protect himself. It must be admitted that location is not a strong determining force to differentiate between the rural and urban life. But it does set limits beyond which man cannot go. Within these limits the rural life develops its own way of earning and living.

(b) *Climate*

Rural people are basically agriculturists. It is because a substantial part of their income is drawn from agriculture. And we all know agriculture depends on climate. The peasant in the village is dependent on the *vicissitudes* of weather. His personality has an in-built element of uncertainty. He must expect, upon occasion, to see much of his year's work wiped out by a cloudburst, a hailstorm, or a plague of grasshoppers. He knows that sometimes it will rain when he needs sunshine, whereas at other times the sun will shine day-in and day-out until it burns up his crops. The peasant is no stranger to late freezes and early frosts. And, in areas of relatively high technology, he attempts to protect his tender plants and fruits with pots and fire.

The rural climate turns out a villager as a practical man. This is quite in contrast to the urban dweller. The rural personality, therefore, is largely fatalist. This is specific to rural way of life, conditioned by climate.

(c) *Topography*

The peasant is always in close contact with his land. It is the land which survives him. Historically, for India's peasant land is the hope and glory of the rural people. Describing the close communion of rural people with nature, Bertrand very rightly observes:

> The close contact of the ruralite with the soil tends to make him view land as the most precious of possession. This is another way in which his close communion with nature tends to set him apart. In this regard, the farmer is quite frequently at a loss to understand the real estate dealer's attitude toward his land as having only an impersonal value. *All in all, there are many personality traits of the farmers which can be traced to his close association with nature.*[2]

(d) *Natural resources*

Since the rural life is much dependent on natural resources, it is interesting to look at the social formations resulting from natural resources. These resources include water and irrigation, fisheries, forest and mineral wealth. These resources are potential forces to give a specific way of life to the rural people. The villages which have a river and stream system to construct small or major dams provide a new way of life to the inhabitants. It is found that the villages which have tank and canal irrigation tend to prosper in agriculture income. The villages having irrigation facilities normally develop a way of life which is characterised by capitalism and sophisticated technology. In our country, the villages inhabited within the network of canal irrigation facilities have got most of the facilities of modern life. Villages in Punjab, Karnataka, Tamilnadu and Maharashtra have developed a higher level of rural life. These villages are facilitated by the amenities of electricity, adequate water supply and a moderate system of education.

Mineral wealth and forestry are also strong determinants of the way of rural life. If the forests are rich, a substantial part of rural economy tends to depend on forest wood and forest produce. Similarly, the mineral wealth also affects the lifestyle of the people. Recently, the mining of copper and marble has given a boost to the social life of the people. It would be wrong to say that the contemporary Indian village today is replica of the proverbial traditional Indian villages. The fact of the matter is that the villages which have the potential of forests and mineral wealth have a way of life quite closer to an urban way of life.

Here, it must be observed that it is not the availability of modern amenities that makes a village closer to the city. The rural way of life is not solely dependent on modern amenities. It is the sociological factor—the way the people interact—which gives specificity to the village life. Notwithstanding the modern and technological facilities, the rural way of life continues to retain social formations. It is in this realm that rural sociology has to make a breakthrough for enquiry.

(e) *Isolation*

One of the most obvious features of rural life is its low density of population. Although, this factor in itself does not constitute a geographic influence, it is included here because the nature of agriculture forces, a low, man-to-land ratio. Agriculture requires invariably low density percentage in the villages. This has greater ramification on rural life. The density of population affects production and distribution and also generates social reactions which greatly influence the total life of society. The density of population further affects the level of standard of the people.

The official data (India, 1995) show that the population density of the country has gone up from 216 in 1981 to 267 in 1991. There are no data officially available for density of population at rural level, however, it is found that out of the total population of the country 74.3 per cent people live in villages as against 25.7 per cent in urban areas.

The people at the rural level relatively live in isolation. Surely, the present development in transportation has relatively improved the rural isolation. In the succeeding development plans new roads have been constructed and transport facilities are made available. Despite the modernising inroads made in the isolated villages, the fact is that there are a large number of villages that continue even today to live in isolation.

The isolation of the rural habitations tends to affect the personality and culture of the village people. Actually, the relative isolation of India's villages has two facts. The first concerns the availability of means of communication. Until recently, the great distances between rural habitations, especially in hilly regions, and unfriendly geographic environment, has made it impractical to introduce good roads and telephonic service. And, although, these facilities are now available in some areas, a large number of ruralites are deprived of these.

Yet, another impact of low density of population in rural life concerns the many services that can be supported only by fairly large population aggregates. For instance, the opening of hospitals and colleges is almost denied to the village people because of the lack of required people in these areas. One of the basic characteristics of the rural life, therefore, is that the rural person is more self-reliant compared to his urban counterpart. Distance also accounts in part for the fact that village people participate less in educational and social activities, and it keeps their outlook somewhat local in nature. As a result of relative isolation of villages, the total result is that several of the benefits of development and modernisation go in favour of the rural people. Thus, the isolation ends up in an increasing hiatus between the rural and urban life.

If population data pertaining to fertility and mortality rates are analysed in terms of rural birth and death rates, it could be found both the birth and death rates are alarmingly high in the villages.

Social Environment

Social anthropologists have elaborately worked among the tribals. We have enough data about the life of the tribals living in India. What is reported about them is that the tribal life is woven with the clan and kinship network of relations. It clearly shows that in the tribal villages it is the clan and kinship which determine the way of life of the people. If we look to the general lifestyle of the village people it, would be obvious that there is predominance of primary groups in the villages. The individual villager's life is moulded by the patterns of behaviour required in his family, kin, clan and fellow-neighbourhood. It is here that the villager learns loyalty, devotion, sympathy, respect and cooperation.

(a) *Predominance of primary group contacts*

The importance of primary groups in the village community assumes vital significance in the patterns of interaction. It is quite interesting to know that in village India the individual is identified by his belonging to a particular village. Primarily, the individual identifies himself with his village. Second, his identification refers to his kin, clan and caste. Class is no mark of identification for a villager.

There is reason for a villager's identification to his village because he is constantly in association with the village primary groups. Writing about the importance of primary group for the village people Bertrand observes:

> It is easy to see how the person whose associations are usually with primary groups might experience less loneliness and frustration, and perhaps even develop a better integrated personality than the person whose contacts were mainly with secondary groups. On the other hand, the person who is active in secondary groups will probably be less narrow and localised in his outlook on life.[3]

Rural sociologists have discussed the sociology of rural life in the studies largely conducted during 1950s. They have discussed village unity as a characteristic mark of India's villages. But, the recent social change which has taken place in our villages has weakened the predominance of primary groups in the villages. With the migration of urban groups to villages, either for trade, government service or a gentleman farmer has affected the unity of the village. Add to it the role of inroads made by the political parties in the traditional village unity. The present Indian village gives a portrait of heterogeneity rather than homogeneity. The secondary groups which were almost absent in the villages have now begun to occupy a determining role.

(b) *Social differentiation*

There is not much social differentiation in the village. The collective life of the people revolves round the agricultural calendar. Activities like sowing, weeding, harvesting and marketing engage most of the people all through the year. Most of the cultural activities of the village people, therefore, run parallel to agriculture calendar. The degree of social differentiation in these villages is, thus, greatly minimised.

(c) *Social stratification*

Although, the principles of caste and class are the same for both rural and urban life, they are the parts of same civilisation. There are a great many differences in the operation of these principles in the two communities. There are generally fewer strata or classes in rural society. The landholdings are more or less the same with little variation. The class differentiation in the villages, therefore, is not conspicuous. Secondly, generally speaking, social streams are greater in cities than in rural areas. In rural community, if there are sky-scrappers, there are slums also. In rural communities, it is exceptional to find persons owning large holdings. What is common in the village is that the rural classes tend to be intermediate, or middle classes. In other words, the stratification in village life does not assume any extreme.

The caste situations in the rural community traditionally has not been complex. Inter-caste relations are generally guided by village traditions. If the village is found in turmoil, the caste leaders normally find out a solution. However, in the wake of the implementation of development plans and the working of political parties, the caste equations have gone wrong. On the one hand, the village middle classes, who have cornered some development benefits and, on the other hand, the political party ideology have created schisms in the caste relations. The earlier observations of the rural sociologists that the village community was homogeneous, now stands rejected.

(d) *Migration and social mobility*

The way of the life of rural people is partly also shaped by the processes of migration and mobility. Mobility tends to circulate people within a given strata or from one social strata to another. The village people who were said to be immobile have now taken to different occupations. The caste-bound occupations have been replaced by secular occupations. Even the concept of 'purity and pollution' with respect to occupations has undergone change.

Migration has also become common with the village people. There was a time when the villager did not leave his village for earning a livelihood. With the narrowing of available land for cultivation and population pressure on land, the rate of migration has increased. When the migrants return from their place of work to the place of origin, they bring with them the traits of urban culture. Both in-migration and out-migration in village India have landed the people to a transitional stage. Consequently, this has brought about a characteristic change in the process of socialisation. What is the outcome of such a new process of socialisation? MacIver and Page have observed a characteristic remark on this account:

> The great difference in socialisation brought about by these different degrees of social mobility has created change in the way of rural life. With greater mobility comes greater uncertainty and this in turn makes the city a place where the individual's career is less foreordained than in the country. This fact helps to explain why ruralites take a rather stoical view of life and are less venturesome in most ways than urbanites.[4]

The social environment, which is found in villages, largely determines the way of life. In traditional India villages, the social environment consisting of family, kin, clan and caste was more or less rigid. And, consequently, decade after decade, the villages continued to remain sterile. But, the introduction of modernising forces and the politicisation of village life, the people are at a transitional stage of development. There way of life, therefore, stands at the crossroads of traditionalism and modernity.

Cultural Environment

In the earlier section we have discussed the influence of social environment on the formation of rural society in India. Even the development of personality of the individuals in the rural society has been discussed. The cultural environment is little different from social environment. The basis for differentiation, however, is that only individuals are cultural bearers. Thus, a distinction can be made between those socialisation factors that exist purely because of differences in the composition of society and those that come about because of differences in actual orientation. As a matter of fact culture patterns establish definite limits to the behaviour-norms or expected behaviour patterns. In this way each society indirectly selects the type of personality that will be most successful in it.

It is important in this context to realise that in spite of the uniform influence of culture, no two persons have exactly the same personality, even though, they may live in the same society. The reason for this phenomenon lies in the fact that every person participates differentially in his culture.

Despite certain universal features that exert a more or less uniform influence, each person has a certain areas of experience which are unique to him, because no culture is ever transmitted in its entirety. The more complex the society, the greater are the chance for personality differences. With these facts in mind, we may examine some of the different cultural influences in rural areas.

(a) *Simplicity of cultural expressions*

Village society is a simple society. It is simple because it is closer to nature. The people are bound up with the agricultural routine. Their festivals, fairs, folk-songs and folk-tales have all resemblance to their agriculture. All over the world the folk-literature pertaining to rural life is very rich. In India, the rural folk-literature is the treasure house of village traditions and culture. The folk-songs of *Alha-Udal* and the *Pandwani* of Chhatisgarh region of Madhya Pradesh are indicators of the village traditions and culture. The simple nature of village folks gets manifestations in folk-literature.

The tribal villages also give expression to folk-songs and folk-dances. Anthropologists, particularly Verrier Elwin, has brought out many instances of the simplicity of tribal expressions. Playing on flute, dancing and drinking liquor for the whole night is the festive expression of village life. These folk-songs and dances, though do not exhibit any sophistication, are excellent examples of village performing art. It also shows the characteristic feature of the rural life.

(b) *Social control*

In rural India, the police force which exercises control over the people lives far apart from the village site. Control in the village society is exercised by informal methods. Thus, neighbourhood gossip and other devices come into play when a member of a rural society violates a code. When the less violent means of control do not suffice, law courts are said to give more serious punishment. It is the rural public opinion which sets the society in order.

Admittedly, the village social control even today is exercised by the dominant castes and village leaders. Sometimes, the caste influence is so strong that the erring person is subject to the punishment given by the caste association. However, the punishment in any case is not corporal. The influence of education and mass media is fast increasing among the villages and more often than not. They refer their cases to the law court.

(c) *Rural knowledge and skills*

In the present context of rural society, when agriculture has become capitalistic, farming requires a great variety of knowledge and skills, and the successful farmer must be a jack-of-all trades. Not only he must understand the operation and care of machinery and equipment, but also have some knowledge of the requirements of soils, plants and animals and the prevention of plant and animal diseases. He must be an expert in farm management and marketing. These requirements make the farmer closely acquainted with many aspects of material culture.

The peasantry, as we find today in India, is not homogeneous. The peasants are categorised into divisions. The big farmers who are sometimes labelled as *Kulak* have large patches of land under their possession. Their agriculture is capitalistic. The small farmers do not have much skills in farming. Neither do they have threshers nor tractors. They are required either to borrow it on rent or have to satisfy with manual labour. They hardly take records to insecticides and other plant protection measures. Their agricultural practices are largely traditional. The marginal farmers and the landless labourers are far away from the mainstream of rural life. Their identity as a peasantry depends on the big and small farmers.

(d) *Levels and standards of living*

Cultural usage is reflected to a large extent in the home. The absence or presence of certain items, such as cycle, motor cycle, electricity, irrigation, engine, tractor, thresher and motor lorry, determines both the level of living and the degree of participation in the culture. Anthropologists and rural sociologists who have conducted rural studies in the field of standard of living pointed out two things. The first is that rural areas enjoy a lower level of living. Most of the villagers, who are found below the poverty line, live a sub-standard life. The second is the different emphasis on cultural items as a result of different needs or values. For instance, a big farmer may not be shy of putting on trousers and asking for elaborate marriage preparations. On the other hand, the marginal farmer would find it very difficult even to have aluminium utensils for cooking the food. In other words, the levels and standards of living correspond to the level of agriculture and income resource.

Concluding Observations

Whatever is the level of life found in the village, it is determined by the structure of rural society. It must be stressed that in a larger way rural social structure is largely influenced by geographical and physical environments. Though, much change has come in the modification of natural environment, but much requires to be done for the unfriendly rural environment. Lack of irrigation facilities, power supply, undulating topography and above all lack of cultivable land have not much influenced the specific characteristics of rural life. Despite the development done in rural India it is not difficult indeed to identify a member belonging to rural society. We have argued throughout the chapter that the availability of modern amenities in terms of electric power supply, road transport, medical and educational facilities does not render a village to the status of an urban community. Modern facilities are helpful to the people but the habits of the people, the village traditions, economic resources, caste rigidity and above all the local history give a specific shape to the rural way of life. And this is what we call sociology of rural life.

Notes

1. Alvin Bertrand (ed.), *Rural Sociology*, McGraw Hill Book Co., New York, 1958.
2. Ibid., p. 27.
3. Ibid., p. 28.
4. R.M. MacIver and C.H. Page, *Society : An Introductory Analysis*, New York, 1949.

6 Agrarian Social Structure

Land is the hope and glory of village India. A villager is tied to land for his sustenance. He survives on land and, therefore, he is emotionally attached to it. Even, during the past, particularly during the medieval India when there were constant wars, the villagers continued to work on their fields. The wars did not intervene in their cultivation. Gandhiji very rightly observed that if villages live who can perish India; and if villages perish, who can save India. As a matter of fact, the agrarian social structure is linked with the survival of the nation when the teachers and students of rural sociology are concerned with the development of villages, they are obliged to discuss the land and land problem of village India.

Study of Agrarian Structure

Andre Beteille[1] has written long essays pertaining to India's agrarian social structure and the problems related to land. Surely, agrarian structure is the central theme of rural sociology. Beteille observed that this problem was not seriously discussed by sociologists. The anthropologists had a long tradition in India of studying the material culture of the society. But this kind of approach was abandoned by the middle of present century. The anthropologists found it useful to study the agrarian system. Beteille's comments run as under:

> An area of research which holds much promise but has so far been little explored by anthropologists in India is what may broadly be described as the study of agrarian systems. The meaning of the phrase may not be immediately clear but what is implied is something more specific than the study of peasant societies and cultures as this is generally understood by anthropologists.

Land problem has also been studied recently by economists. As a matter of fact land is the source of state income. Then, land problem also agitates the state. If poverty removal is one of the objectives of rural development, naturally, land problem has to be solved. Perhaps, it was P.C. Joshi who in a systematic way analysed the problem of land reforms in India.[2] Joshi has focused on the land reforms in terms of trends and perspectives. He has also analysed some of the agrarian studies which were conducted in post-independent India.

Land problem or agrarian social structure has also been taken for intensive study by A.R. Desai. Desai, in fact, has brought out an edited work on the different aspects of agrarian social structure. What is interesting to mention in this respect is that the study of agrarian social structure has employed both functional and Marxian methodologies. There are some other sociologists also who have discussed the problem of rural agrarian system from the perspective of changing rural stratification. Among these may be included Yogendra Singh and K.L. Sharma. Anthropologists, sociologists and economists have stressed the aspects of rural agrarian structure with a focus on land tenure system, land ceiling, land reforms, land control and land management. These studies have also included the problems of peasantry and the peasant struggles. In the present chapter, we intend to deal with several of these aspects which are related to land, land tenure, agrarian stratification, green revolution, etc. We are convinced that without studying the agrarian social structure, it is almost very difficult for us to develop any insight in India's rural society. There is yet another reason for putting emphasis on land studies. A general observation in the realm of land reforms would immediately show that all over the country the agitations related to land demand for reforms pertaining to land, water and forests. The tribals generally raise this problem: *jamin* (land), *jal* (water) and *jungle* (forests). It amply shows that the village people can hardly afford to wait any further for the solution of land tenure and land relations.

What is Agrarian Social Structure?

The dictionary meaning of 'agrarian' means anything related to land, its management or distribution. Related to land distribution is also the aspect of 'equitable division of land'. It refers to the political movement in favour of change in conditions of propriety in land. It is called 'agrarianism'. The agrarian problem also dwells on a new ground wherein a movement has been started in some of the Asian countries which stands for the ownership of land in favour of women. Agrarian system also includes land tenure system.

Beteille has defined agrarian social structure. To him agrarian system does not mean only peasantry. He observes:

> The meaning of the phrase (agrarian system) may not be immediately clear but what is implied is something more specific than the study of peasant societies and cultures, as this is generally understood by anthropologists... The term 'peasantry' has variety of referents. But it is most meaningfully used to describe a more or less homogeneous and undifferentiated community of families characterised by small holdings operated mainly by family labour.

The study of agrarian system has been taken up as mentioned earlier by anthropologists, sociologists and economists. On a broader plane, the agrarian system as is conceived by social scientists in general, has been related to (i) land and its utilisation; and (ii) productive purposes. He observes:

> The study of agrarian systems will centre round the problem of land and its utilisation for productive purposes. In a land-based social and economic system the significance of this kind of study hardly requires emphasis.

Beteille, to refer to him again, it would be said that the land problem in India and for that matter the study of agrarian social structure revolves round two major issues as under:

1. technological arrangements, and
2. social arrangements.

Technological arrangement means the management of land. It includes landownership, control and use of land. Technological arrangement is discussed in relation to variations in ecological conditions. In other words, land is looked in terms of the geography which surrounds the land. The ecological setting of agriculture in India is highly variable. The diverse nature of ecological conditions in India has been described by Beteille as under:

> There are areas of heavy rainfall and areas with hardly any rainfall. There are irrigated and unirrigated areas. Irrigated areas themselves differ according to the dependability of irrigation. ... The different re-

gions show different patterns of diurnal and seasonal variations in humidity, temperature and sunlight. All these factors have a direct bearing on the kinds of crops that can be cultivated and the technology employed in their cultivation.

The technological arrangements, thus, include ecological conditions along with the new agriculture technology, such as water pumps, thresher, chemical manure, improved seeds, etc.

Another aspect of agrarian system is that of social management. It includes land control and landownership. It is found that the Indian agricultural communities have recently been highly stratified. It shows that there is close relationship between the system of stratification and the division of work. For instance, the census figures show that in Punjab and Haryana the proportion of agricultural labourers in the total agricultural population is relatively low, whereas in West Bengal, Tamilnadu and Kerala, it is high. In the three states the prevalence of sharecropping is also high, but this fact is not easily recorded in the censuses and large-scale surveys.

K.L. Sharma[3] has discussed the problem of agrarian stratification and argues that agrarian structures in India have always been uneven. He observes that despite the abolition of intermediaries not much substantive change in agrarian relations has come. The uneven structures of landholdings have also resulted in 'diverse land tenure systems'. The land tenure system, according to Sharma, has greatly affected the social structure. He writes:

> The variations in the relationship between land tenure system and social structure created an uneven feudal order in the pre-British and British periods. The shadow of the colonial and feudal inequality is still seen by us in various aspects of society.

Sociologists and anthropologists, who have recently studied agrarian system, have very strongly argued that changes in land relations have affected the stratification pattern of villages. The crucial aspect of agrarian structure is the control over land. It is the basis of agrarian stratification. When agrarian social structure is discussed invariably we refer to landownership, land control and use of land. Such an approach to land helps us to find out agrarian hierarchy. What has happened so far is that the dominant castes who have control over major portions of land, suppress and exploit the subordinated classes.

Oliver Mendelsohn and Marika Vicziany[4], who have discussed the rural land reform with reference to untouchables, argue that the subordinated people have gained nothing out of land reforms. The present social stratification of the village is due to our failure to settle land reforms. The authors observe as under:

> Land control is the basis of the agrarian hierarchy and, therefore, the means by which the dominants have subordinated untouchables the village. Small resources like a home site of one's own and even a very small plot of productive land can effect a powerful liberation of the subordinate untouchables from total and arbitrary dependence on their oppressor.

Yet, another aspect of rural stratification is the pattern of cultivation adopted by the peasantry. If the cultivators take to crops which require hard labour, naturally it would require larger number of agriculture labourers. In the states of Punjab and Bihar where paddy is grown, larger number of labourers are hired. Even landless labourers migrate from Bihar to Punjab for transplanting paddy. The agrarian hierarchy, therefore, is the resultant of the crops grown by the peasantry.

Beteille has discussed the rural stratification pattern in terms of land control and land management. The productive organisation of land consists of three main patterns: the first is based on family labour, the second on hired labour and the third on tenancy conceived in a broad sense. The three patterns of production have several variants. And it is interesting to note that the production which requires hard manual labour such as that of transplanting paddy the pattern may change. Beteille has categorised the peasantry on the basis of production system. He observes:

> For in talking about production based on family labour, wage labour and tenancy, we are talking also about landlords, owner-cultivators, tenants, sharecroppers and the agricultural labourers. These categories and their mutual relations constitute the heart of what may be described as the agrarian hierarchy... the most crucial features of India's rural social system and unless we understand its nature and forms, our understanding of caste itself will remain incomplete.

The rural India's basic problem today is the understanding of agrarian system. Control over land determines the rural hierarchy.

What is interesting is that the state does not impose any income-tax on the far production. As a result of this state policy, those who control larger portions of land, benefit the most. The rural agrarian hierarchy has today become more complicated owing to the land policy adopted by the state. But the state land policy, as we have in India today, has not evolved overnight. It is the result of the colonial land policy which we have inherited and have carved it in post-independent India in such a way that it has taken a capitalistic mode of production instead of minimising the hiatus between the big farmer and landless labourer. We have intensified the social inequality. We now trace the land policy adopted by the colonial rulers and later, the nationalist government.

History of the Study of Agrarian Structure

Colonial Land Policy

It is argued by economists and sociologists that the present agrarian problem of rural India is the outcome of the colonial policy adopted by British in pre-independent India. P.C. Joshi traces the history of land policy from pre-mutiny period of British rule in India. As a matter of fact, he says that the agrarian policy which India had in pre-mutiny period was not the gift of social science but was the result of the interplay of political factors. He observes:

> Thus, in India, agrarian research was not the gift of social science; social scientific enquiry was itself initiated and propelled by the chain of momentous development in the political sphere during the eighteenth and nineteenth centuries. Political factors also played a primary role in bringing about a shift in the focus of intellectual enquiry, even during the later period of British rule.

The most significant example of this shift was the report of the Royal Commission on Agriculture that was appointed in 1928 to make recommendations for the improvement of agriculture and to promote the welfare and prosperity of the rural people. The scope of the Commission's enquiry was, however, circumscribed by its terms of reference which directed the Commission not to make recommendations regarding the existing system of landownership and tenancy or of assessment of land revenue and irrigation charges.

What is interesting in the terms of reference to the Commission is that the crucial areas of landownership, land tenancy, and assessment of land revenue and irrigation charges were deliberately left out of the scope of Commission. It was during the pre-mutiny period. In fact, during this period, as is apparent, the colonial rulers were not seriously concerned with the agrarian system. A number of official reports of the Famine Commission only showed lip sympathy to the agrarian problem. It was after the post-mutiny period that the colonial problem raised its head. The emergence of colonial problem was due largely to the nationalist approach to this problem. As a response to nationalist approach to land, the British constituted their own land policy which Gunnar Myrdal called "the colonial theory of poverty and economic backwardness". This theory tried to explain India's poverty and backwardness without any reference to the economic and social framework created under British rule. Commenting on the British colonial theory on rural poverty and agricultural backwardness, P.C. Joshi writes:

> In particular, the British explained rural poverty and agricultural backwardness without reference to the agrarian structure created under British rule. Repeated in Nehru's words, the colonial theory simply amounted to saying: "If India is poor that is the fault of her social customs, her *banias* and moneylenders and above all her enormous population.

The British rule in India took for its guidance this policy of colonial theory. A few of the Indian scholars, particularly Vera Anstey, reacted to the British colonial theory. Anstey argued that the Indian agriculture was backward and did not take to commercial farming. However, she suggested that no radical land reform could be implemented in India by a foreign government as politically it was impossible. Other social scientists also explained the agricultural problem of India as an offshoot of population, pressure of land and retrograde social institutions like caste and joint family. The peasantry also lacked capital required for scientific farming.

Nationalist Policy

The colonial theory of land control, including revenue system, was contested by Indian nationalists. This approach is labelled as institutional approach. The nationalists' point of view was strongly put forward by Ranade. Ranade, besides being an economist, was a reformist. He argued that the Indian political economy would only be explained by adopting an institutional approach. He questioned the view that "the truths of economic science... are absolutely and demonstrably true and must be accepted as guides of conduct for all time and place, whatever might be the stage of national advance.

Ranade's observations assume importance because he contested the very methodology on which the colonial theory was based. He was himself in search of a new methodology, a new premise so as to contribute an alternative land policy. From the premise and assumptions of the colonial theory, Ranade makes a break in two important respects in explaining the backwardness of Indian agriculture. The colonial theorists underplayed, if not ignored, the question of the institutional structure. Even when they adopted an institutional approach, they avoided reference to the hardcore of the institutional structure, namely, the land relations which had a direct bearing on economic backwardness and whose restructuring required drastic state intervention. The colonial theorists drew attention to only such elements of the institutional structure, for example, religion and caste, as influenced the economy in an indirect way. In fact, the role of retrograde land system in buttressing retrograde social relations was always overlooked.

Ranade argued at length that the backwardness of Indian agriculture was largely due to the inadequate approach to institutional set up of the villages. In fact, the land relations during the British period were erroneous. The state became the super power in agricultural relations and gave no opportunity to landlords, jagirdars and jamindars to take any opportunity to provide technology and improved agricultural input to farming.

Besides Ranade, there were a few others, notably among them are R.C. Dutta, who provided a critique to colonial theory. Dutta contributed insights into the inter-connections and interactions between different elements of the institutional framework. He also indicated the scope as well as the limits of a land policy in tackling the evils of the institutional framework. In concrete terms he also showed how lack of industrialisation accentuated basic evils of the agrarian structure including preponderance of tenancy and small-sized holdings.

Admittedly, the nationalist writers like Ranade, Dutta and Anstey criticised the colonial theory of rural poverty and economic backwardness. But these writers failed to give any alternate theory based on institutionalism for ameliorating the land status of the village people.

Gandhi's Approach to Land Problem

Gandhiji was sensitive to the rural land problem. His theory started within the premise that to improve the life style of rural people, it is necessary to make drastic changes in the policy of land distribution and farm production. He argued that land should ultimately belong to the people. In fact, land, forest and water are the natural resources over which the people should have their control. Though, Gandhiji was concerned with the agrarian relations, he did not make any full-fledged agenda for land reform. However, whatever he thought about the land system on different occasions has a great bearing in the formulation of any land policy. P.C. Joshi, in his discourse on political genesis of agrarian studies, has made a precise note which indicates the importance of Gandhian ideology relating to land tenure, land ceiling and land relations.

Joshi's summary of Gandhian concern for land is given below:

1. *Village is the backbone of Indian society*: It is proverbial for Gandhi to say that real India resides in villages. India, in other words, is identified with rural India. It is in this context that Gandhiji talked about '*swaraj*', i.e., village India independent from the state intervention. Land in this respect assumes importance. There should be nexus between agriculture and cottage industries.
2. *Rural-urban nexus:* It was the policy of colonial rule and also the feudal rule in native states that urban society is the super-ordinate community which has a hegemony over the rural community. Even today, the present government considers the village India as the subaltern India. In its zeal of wooing the urban community, all modern facilities, viz., water supply, electricity, transport, education, government offices, communication centres, fuel supply and many other things are located in urban communities.

   Gandhiji disapproved such a kind of step-motherly treatment given to the rural community. It should never be thought that the rural economy is the hinterland of urban economy.
3. *New type of approach to town-village relationship:* Gandhiji all

through his life showed his concern for village autonomy. He stood for the notion that the urban communities are largely dependent on rural community. The relations between these two communities should be mutual both way. He argued for the emergence of a new pattern of interaction between the urban and rural communities.

4. *Multi-pronged approach to rural uplift:* The agrarian social structure is a comprehensive phenomenon. It is not only agricultural production, agricultural relations and land tenure which make the rural social structure. It is inclusive of many other factors, such as village industry, agriculture, education, Panchayati Raj and politics. Gandhiji stood for a rural society which was multi-pronged including economic, technological, social, political and cultural innovations.
5. *Emphasis on the human relations and human resource development:* As human beings, the villagers, the peasants, are store-houses of power. They possess skills in cottage industry, artifacts and agriculture. Any land policy which is designed for the rural development should focus on rural human resource development. They should be mobilised for their own development.

If we analyse the Gandhian outline of agrarian system, we would immediately find that Gandhiji was a staunch critique of colonial land policy. Gandhi's notions about land policy, thus, were in full confrontation with the colonial theory. His outline further argues that the state should take all steps towards rural development. It is said that when the draft of Indian Constitution was ready, it was shown to Gandhiji. He quickly found that the draft did not have any promising future for the village people. The village traditional institution of panchayat did not have any place of importance in the draft. Gandhiji immediately tore off the draft and commented that he did not like any constitution which did not provide any autonomy in terms of land, agriculture, forests and water to the people. The local people should be given all power to exercise their control over the local resources.

Notes

1. Andre Beteille, *Studies in Agrarian Social Structure,* Oxford University Press, Delhi, 1979.
2. P.C. Joshi, *Land Reforms in India*, Allied Publishers Ltd., Bombay, 1976.
3. K.L. Sharma, *Caste, Class and Social Movements*, Rawat Publication, Jaipur, 1986.
4. Oliver Mendelsohn and Marika Vicziany, "The Untouchables", in Oliver Mendelsohn and Upendra Baxi, *The Rights of Subordinated Peoples,* Oxford University Press, Delhi, 1994.
5. Mahadev Govind Ranade, *Essays on Indian Economics*, Third Ed., G.A. Nateson & Co., Madras, 1916.

7 Land Tenure System and Land Reforms

Whenever we talk of rural sociology we are concerned with the agrarian social system. The importance of land, landholding and land relations, including its control and management, assumes significant meaning in rural India. It is because of the fact that a large number of people at the countryside earn their livelihood from land. The village people depend on land directly or indirectly. The word 'land' includes all the characteristics and qualities of the earth. Land may take many physical forms, viz., plains, swamps, hills, mountains or valleys. It may have many kinds of vegetation and it may also have one of many kinds of climate, from hot to cold, from humid to dry.

Land is useful to man in many ways; e.g., as a source of food, for wood for many purposes, for hunting, as a place to live, and as a place to work. As a matter of fact land means many different things to different people. Generally, it is a part of natural environment. It is a factor of production in economic processes. All over the world land is considered as property, with legal connotation as to rights of ownership of individuals and rights and responsibilities of ownership and sovereignty of governments.

In our country, before the beginning of colonial rule, village land was owned by the community as a whole. It became a private property when the first land settlement was made. The British regime introduced a new revenue system by superseding the traditional right of the village community over the village land. The British Raj, thus, created two forms of property in land, i.e., landlordism in some parts of the country and the individual peasant proprietorship in others. Commenting on the introduction of private property in land A.R. Desai observes:

> It was Lord Carnwallis who, during his term of office, created the first group of landlords in India by introducing the Permanent Land

Settlement for Bengal, Bihar and Orissa in 1793. These landlords were created out of the tax farmers in the provinces who had been appointed by the political predecessors of the British rulers to collect revenue from these provinces on a commission basis. The Permanent Land Settlement converted these revenue collectors into too many landlords. Under the terms of the settlement, they had, henceforth, to make a fixed payment to the government of the East India Company.[1]

Thus, for the first time, land ceased to be owned by the community. Second, it became a part of private property. Third, there emerged an intermediary in the form of *jagirdar* between the tenant and the government. This was a watershed in the history of agrarian system.

Areas under Agrarian System

It is very common for students of rural sociology to talk about agrarian social structure, agrarian relations, agrarian hierarchy and many other things, such as agrarian unrest for problems related to land. In this chapter, when we analyse the components or aspects of agrarian social system, we tend to include the following areas related to land, land control and land organisation:

1. land tenure system,
2. irrigation system,
3. technology,
4. agricultural modernisation including green revolution,
5. agrarian stratification, landholdings, land distribution and agrarian classes,
6. land alienation, and
7. rural migration.

Land Tenure System

Land is held all over the world under different tenure situations. Holding of land depends on different reasons. Ownership or exclusive control by an individual is not the only concept under which land is held and used. If we look from Indian point of view, ownership of land is a western idea. As discussed above, in our country, ownership of land, before the Permanent Land Settlement, always rested with the community. However, in western world, individual ownership of land was recognised both by the state and the community.

Land as a Factor of Production

Theoretically speaking, notwithstanding India or any other country, land is viewed as a traditional economic factor of production including labour and capital. In this broad classification, land is defined to include all natural properties but to exclude invested capital. Capital is unrealistic: same capital is so firmly blended with land that it is impossible to separate the two. The important fact to bear in mind is that no factor is productive alone, each requires some or the others in order to be productive.

Land alone is not productive. It includes a number of other inputs. In contemporary times science and technology have resulted in the vast array of new production functions, which have largely transformed the productivity and use of land. It is this general conception of land tenure system that we have included technology and improved agricultural inputs for an all-round analysis of agriculture.

Peasant Proprietors and Tenants

It is the land which constitutes the major source of livelihood for the village people. But all the peasants who live in villages do not own their individual land. According to one estimate nearly three-fifths of world people derive their livelihood from agriculture. Out of this, most do not own land on which they live and work. The reality is that many of the peasants purchase rights of cultivation and occupancy from others. In return, from hired rights in land, these people pay the landowners or their intermediaries a share of the produce, a fixed amount of the produce or personal services or some combinations of these. Those people are the *tenants*. It is said that throughout the world tenants and their families probably constitute as many as two-fifths of the population engaged in agriculture.

Most of the tenants aspire to ownership of their lands. Therefore, tenancy may well be appraised in terms of how well it provides tenants with opportunities to gain experience, acquire capital and make decisions in the process of acquiring landownership. On the other hand, many tenants are not likely to become owners in the foreseeable future.

Emergence of Tenants during the British Period

A tenant is one who cultivates the land on certain conditions. Most of the agriculturists in our country are tenants. The emergence of tenant goes back to the British period when in 1793 the Permanent Land Settlement was made. The *jamindari* system which emerged from land settlement was an intermediary system. The system created the class of tenants who suffered from operation at the hands of the *jamindars*. It was a historical emergence found for the first time in Indian agrarian history. In the native states, also known as princely states, the jagirdar worked as an intermediary between the tenant and the central princely rule. In these states *jagirdar* was the counterpart of *jamindar*. The status of tenant in pre-independent India was highly deplorable. A.R. Desai very aptly sketches the oppressive condition of tenants during this period:

> In course of time, a series of intermediaries developed between the *jamindar* and the cultivating tenant, whose condition, thereby, increasingly deteriorated. The Bengal Tenancy Acts of 1859 and 1885 aimed at ameliorating the position of the tenant. However, the legislation did not accomplish much. The mass of tenants continued to live in an increasingly worsening condition.

Desai very sympathetically traces the conditions of the peasant proprietors in India. The peasant proprietors were actually the landowners. Their condition also worsened during the British period. The landowners were sub-divided into upper landowners, middle landowners and the lower strata of landowners. All these categories of landowners or peasant proprietors, quiet like the tenants, suffered considerably during the colonial period. The observations made by A.R. Desai run as below:

> As a result of the operation of factors like heavy land tax, small holdings, fragmentation of plots, growing heavy indebtedness, this class had been increasingly impoverished since it came into existence. It had been in a state of permanent disintegration.

The woes of the peasant proprietors during this period were altogether new. These land proprietors suffered from their disintegration.

However, a few of them who owned larger patches of land rose to the level of rich peasants while a large number of them were reduced to the status of poor peasants, tenants of absentee landlords or land labcurers. This process of differentiation of the peasant proprietors grew at an accelerated rate since the rate of impoverishment of the peasantry increased. The colonial period witnessed, on one hand, the impoverishment of the tenants and, on the other hand, differentiation and disintegration of the peasant proprietors. As a result of this process, there emerged, in rural India, the class of absentee landlords, on one hand, and the lower peasantry and agricultural labourers, on the other.

The post-independent India, thus, found a tenancy highly settled and disintegrated.

Variations in Tenancy

It must be observed that in India the agricultural sector, constitutionally, is the subject of the state. Land taxation, thus, is determined by the state government. Because of this statutory position, there is much variation in agricultural tenancy in the country. Yet another important aspect of tenancy in India is that it is shaped by the historical and cultural forces of a particular region or part of the country. For instance, we have certain castes which are actually agricultural castes; e.g., Patidars of Gujarat, Jats of Haryana and Sikhs of Punjab. This is purely a cultural phenomenon. It also affects the size and pattern of agricultural practices.

Historically, variation in tenancy could be explained by the fact that the colonial forces in British India and feudal forces in princely states also determined the form and extent of tenancy. However, at a broader plane, it could be said that there are five variations of tenants in the country:

1. *Cash tenants*: They pay a fixed cash rent for the use and occupancy of their land.
2. *Share-cash tenants*: They pay part of their rent in cash and part in the share of crops.
3. *Crop-share tenants:* They pay a share of the crops only.
4. *Croppers*: They pay a share of the crops but usually work under the close supervision of landlord or his agent.

5. Other and unspecified tenants.

We have argued that there is much variation in agricultural tenancy. The classes of tenants which we have given above are not exhaustive. As a matter of fact, the sharecropper is both a tenant and also landowner of a patch of land. K.L. Sharma, who has worked on the problem of feudalism and peasant movements in Rajasthan, argues that there has been much variation in the realm of tenancy in Rajasthan itself.[2] He says that all through the country the number of tenants has been increasing. Leaving aside a some, in Kerala, the agricultural labourers have increased over the last two decades.

The inter-state variations in regard to types of tenancy have been elaborately examined by Laxmi Narayan and Tyagi.[3] They have put forward the following questions which help us to understand the tenancy variations:

1. Who leases out land and who leases in land?
2. It is true that people who take land on lease are farmers with small holding?
3. What are the different types of tenancies?
4. What types of changes are taking place in different types of tenancies?
5. Is it true that crop-sharing tenancy continues to grow an importance?
6. What are the factors which explain inter-state variations in different types of tenancies?

K.L. Sharma has commented on the above questions raised by Laxmi Narayan and Tyagi. His observations in this regard run as below:

> It is not true that large farmers lease out land and the small farmers lease in land. In fact, it is quite the other way also. NSS data as given by Laxmi Narayan and Tyagi show that 38.7 per cent of the large farmers took the land on lease, and only 36.8 per cent of the small farmers cultivated leased land. Small land holders also leased out their lands for a variety of reasons. Commercial farmers take land on lease particularly in Gujarat and Rajasthan. Both crop-sharing tenancy and cash-rent tenancy are found in various states. A third type of tenancy, namely, the fixed product or fixed kind rent tenancy is found in

some states. About 53 per cent of tenancy in Rajasthan is found under some other forms, other than these three tenancies.

On a broader plane Laxmi Narayan, Tyagi and Sharma find four kinds of tenancies in different parts of the country. These types may be categorized as below:

1. crop-sharing tenants,
2. paying cash-rent tenants,
3. paying fixed product or kind tenants, and
4. unspecified tenants other than the above three.

A.R. Desai has studied, historically, the rise of new social classes of peasantry in India. His approach to the study of tenancy or tenants is based an Marxian perspective. He has taken into consideration the tenancy variations in India on a broader plane. Historically, as a result of the creation of *jamindari* and *ryotwari* system a new class of peasant proprietors emerged in India. While the *jamindari* system was a link between the tenant and the state, the *ryotwari* system included the peasant proprietors who were themselves owners of the land. Desai has made three divisions of the class of peasant proprietors:

1. *Upper class landowners* having big patches of land.
2. *Middle class landowners* having landownership at the intermediate level.
3. *Lower strata* including marginal and small farmers.

With the passage of time, the number of lower classes of peasantry increased. A large number of them were reduced to the status of agricultural labourers and paupers. What is important here is that tenancy variation is not new to rural India. It has been in operation since the period of Mughal Empire.

The issue of tenancy variation in contemporary times could be seen from the empirical studies made by Jan Breman, Andre Beteille, Denial Thorner, and others.

Jan Breman[4] has worked in Surat district of Gujarat. He has made intensive study of three talukas, namely, Bardoly, Palsana and Valod of Surat district. His focus is on the landowners, tenants and sharecroppers. He observes that the agrarian population has three categories of tenancy as under:

1. Marginal and small farmers (owning less than 5 acres of land)
2. Middle farmers (owning 5.15 acres of land and below 15 acres)
3. Large farmers (owning more than 15 acres of land)

The tenancy variations found in Surat district are not exclusive. They are only factual because at empirical plane there is much variation in the access to land. Pointing to this elaborate variation Breman observes:

> The limitations imposed on classification by this three-way division—still retained in much of the literature, nevertheless—are rather arbitrary given the great variation in access to land, soil fertility, intensity of cropping, availability of labour power and other factors of agronomic or social-economic nature which influence farming productivity.

Breman has drawn attention to the fact that tenancy variation should not be considered on the size of landholding only. In any scheme of tenancy variation we should also take into consideration the nature of soil, its productivity, irrigation facilities and infrastructure for marketing. Given all the productivity of land, the absence of marketing also puts the landowner or tenant to a perpetual loss.

Andre Beteille[5] has worked authoritatively on the problem of agrarian society. He dwells at length on landowners, tenants and agricultural labourers. Andre restricts his study to Sripuram village which is situated in south India (Tamilnadu state). He finds that in Sripuram the agricultural population is divided into two classes of peasants: (i) owners of land or peasant proprietors, and (ii) non-owners of land.

In the village Sripuram majority of people are non-owners of land who are engaged in agricultural work. They actually work on land owned by others. And this constitutes the basis of economic and social ties between the different classes of people in the village. His observation is that landowners and tenants constitute distinct entities only as conceptual categories, and not as concrete groups of individual. He writes:

> One and the same person may be, and not infrequently is, both an owner of land and a tenant on somebody else's land.

The variations in tenancy as given by Breman, Sharma, Beteille and others could be summarised in some categories. For instance, tenancy on a broader plane has two divisions. And more or less it includes most parts of the country. These two divisions are: (i) owners of land, and (ii) non-owners of land. The sub-divisions of owners of land consist of (i) large landowners, (ii) middle landowners, and (iii) lower landowners. This third sub-division is further divisioned into (i) small landowners, and (ii) marginal landowners. The second division of tenancy, i.e., non-owners of land, do not have any land in their possession. In this category too there are further sub-divisions, such as (i) share-cash tenants, (ii) crop-share tenants, (iii) cash tenants, and (iv) agricultural labourers.

Thus, the tenancy as a whole is divided into two divisions, which are further divided into several sub-divisions. It very clearly shows variations in agricultural tenancy. The divisions and sub-divisions are shown in the following chart:

Variations in Tenancy

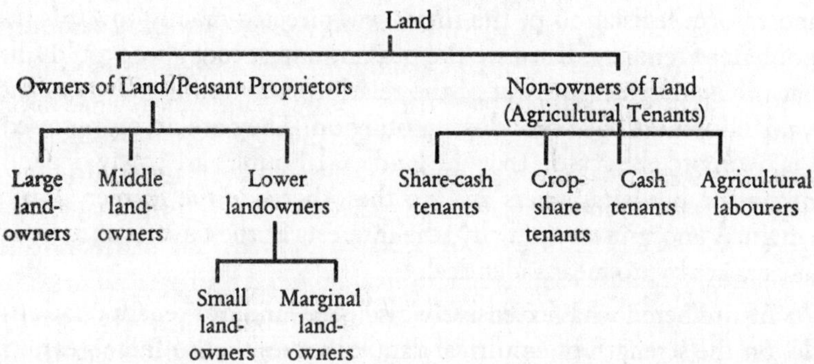

We have argued in the preceding pages that a majority of peasants in agricultural India are tenant peasants. Tenancy had its beginning during the colonial period when the British Raj introduced Permanent Land Settlement. Tenants constitute a heterogeneous group. Interestingly enough, some of the tenants are also landowners. Actually, there are variations among the tenants. We now propose to discuss the relations between the landowners and the tenants.

Landlord-Tenant Relations

Social anthropologists and sociologists have dealt with the problem of relations between landowners and landless peasants or tenants. H torically, the relations between the two assumed seriousness all over India after independence. The problem of tenancy was taken up as an agenda for land reforms. Tenancy has two aspects: (i) landlord-tenant relations; and (ii) landlord-agricultural labourers relations. In the case of labourers the problem of wages assumed importance. Commenting on the relations between tenants and wage labourers Andre Beteille observes:

> Although, tenants and wage labourers were both landless, their interests were by no means always identical, and where tenants themselves employed wage labourers they would even become contradictory.

Actually, the relations between landowners and tenants are three-fold: (i) landowner and tenant; (ii) landowner and agricultural labour; and (iii) tenant and agricultural labour. The issues relating to this relationship were raised by left-wing political parties in the fifties. The agitations of the peasant associations also centred round this issue. The land reform legislation of the fifties was directed mainly towards the problem of tenancy. If we see the peasant unrest today we would find that the issues emerging out of the relations between landowners and non-landowners have been lost in oblivion. They are no more raised. It is owing to the reason that the landless labourers are solely dependent on the big landowners and on the other side the former always remained unorgnised. Actually, the interests of the tenants and the labourers are by no means identical.

Andre Beteille has extensively discussed landlord-tenant relations. He, on the strength of empirical data, observes that in India's eastern and southern parts sharecropping is not uncommon, despite the legislation on land reforms. He estimates that in most parts of the country the class of landless labourers sometime constitutes as much as one-third of village. He further observes that in larger parts of the country the landowner continues to be known as *malik* or *manib*. These words denote 'owner' or 'master' and by tradition the *malik* has mastery not only over the land but also over the men who work on it. It should be emphasised that land reforms and economic change notwithstanding, these traditions are a part of the living reality in many villages in India. One aspect of this difference is reflected in the huge support. Such landowners are often able to master in national elections even after they have lost their estates.

Referring to the situation of landowners and tenants in north India, Daniel Thorner[6] informs that in western Uttar Pradesh large areas of land for long had been under peasant proprietorship. Thorner had the following observations to make after the abolition of feudal states:

> At the top are the *bhumidars*,, below them the *sirdars* and still further down the *asamis*. At the bottom of the heap remain the mass of sharecroppers and landless labourers.

Caste Context in the Landowner-Tenant Relations

When we look at the relations between landowners and tenants in agriculture we tend to look at the caste relations between the two classes. Empirical data available on this account and generated by K.L. Sharma, Jan Breman and Andre Beteille indicate that most of the landowners belong to the Brahmin and the Rajput castes. Beteille, on the strength of his data generated in Sripuram, says that landowners in the village are Brahmins. The Brahmin *mirasdars*, ritually, are prohibited to use the plough and, therefore, cultivation has to be done by the tenants and agricultural labourers who generally belong to lower castes. The cultivation of paddy everywhere in the country requires arduous work. And, therefore, both the Brahmin and non-Brahmin non-owners try to get the rough and heavy work done by others whenever they can afford to.

Beteille's finding is that in Tamilnadu there was much leasing out of land among the Brahmins. There are reasons for this. Normally, the educated members of a Brahmin family when get settled in cities for taking up professional jobs, such as lawyer, engineer or doctor, they lease out the land to lower castes. It all indicates that, by and large, the landowners belong to higher castes and the tenants and agricultural labourers generally belong to lower castes.

The caste system is also found operating in regard to the relations with the agricultural labourers. For labourers, sharecroppers and even petty cultivators the landlord is the *malik* par excellence, but the pattern of difference is also extended to others, notably to government officials. To conclude, the relations of tenants, sharecroppers and agricultural labourers to the landowners it could be said that the status of non-owners of land all over agricultural India is that of subordination.

Tenancy and Agricultural Backwardness

To what extent the relations between landowners and tenants are responsible for India's agricultural backwardness. The question has been examined by social anthropologists and sociologists. Actually, Laxmi Narayan and Tyagi pinpointed the issue when they ask as to who leases in the land and who leases out the land. This explains the situation of tenancy in India. It is found that in most of the cases tenancy arrangement discourages tenants from making investment in improving production in agriculture. The bargaining position between tenants and landlord is generally such that additional productivity flows to the landlord. And even if the tenant has some entrepreneurial zeal, he hardly has any operating capital.

Agricultural empiricists have given some data to explain the lease out land to the tenants. In Sripuram, according to Andre Beteille, some of the landowners find it difficult to be in touch with the land, they find the city life more involving and, therefore, they lease out the land to the tenants. The tenants on their part do not do anything substantial for increasing the productivity. In the village Sripuram the leasing out of land took three phases. The explanation provided by Beteille runs below:

> The first phase was one in which it (the landowning class) was tied more or less firmly to the village and relations between landlords and tenants were of a fairly close and durable character. In the second phase, which commenced towards the beginning of the first century, the old landowners began to look beyond the frontiers of rural society and many of them moved out, becoming absentee landlords. A third phase, seems to have set in recently, in which the old landowning families, already much depleted, have become keenly aware of their insecure position and are gradually beginning to dispose of their land.

The above three phases of leasing out land by landowners clearly show that the issue of agricultural production has fully been left to the efforts of tenants.

The study of rural sociology, in fact, is the study of agrarian social system. The social and cultural life of a village is largely determined by the relations of people to the land. It is in this broader context that we have discussed the tenancy system prevalent in our country. In doing so we have examined the status of landowners, their types and the status of tenants including their variations. On a broader plane it should be said that a larger portion of land is cultivated by tenants who are not the owners of land. The relations between landowners, tenants and labour are crucial in the process of production from the farm. The reality is that agriculture is the main source of employment and income in rural society.

Much depends on the production achieved in agriculture. Rural sociology basically studies the relations between the landowner, share-cropper, labourer and above all the market system where the farm produce is exchanged. Ironically, the land owned by the people is not in equal size for all the cultivators. The land size varies from peasant to peasant. There are peasants who own larger chunks of land, and at the same time there are peasants who are marginal only. In other words, land in not equally distributed. The unequal distribution of land creates sharp stratification in the rural society. Gunnar Myrdal very rightly observes in *Asian Drama*:

> Inequality among individuals is largely a question of landownership. Rural income has been functionally related to landholdings, the poor are more likely to be landless than owning land.[7]

In a rural society, land is the prime productive asset which determines the income, employment, status and authority of a person. In any discussion of rural sociology land tenure system and land reforms constitute an important part of study. In the next section of this chapter we shall discuss some of the measures taken for land reforms in India.

Land Reforms

At the outset it must be observed that land constitutes the Concurrent List of the Constitution of India. It is within the state power to legislate for land reforms. Normally, the central government does not intervene in the control, revenue and management of the land in the state. It is because of this constitutional division that each state in the country has its own agenda of land reforms. This also prohibits us to make any comparative study of land reforms.

The history of land reforms in India goes back to the period when the nation was involved in its struggle for independence. Our national leaders were struck by the unequal distribution of land. Land is the gift of god; it is a part of nature. Nobody can distribute water, neither can anybody distribute air. Vinoba Bhave argued that land belongs to god and, therefore, it has to be distributed equally. Nehruji always pronounced that when India will get freedom, land would be justifiably distributed. Other freedom fighters also had the perception that British colonialism was the sole cause of the poverty of the Indian peasants.

When India got independence, the government decided to abolish the systems of *jamindari* and *jagirdari*, in order to remove the intermediaries between the state and the peasants. This was the first legislation taken by almost all the states in the early 1950s and is known as Abolition of Jagirdari/Jamindari System Act. The land reforms made or legislated by the state governments thus had an objective to make a justifiable distribution of land and removal of all the intermediaries. Land reforms, thus, have the following objectives:

1. To make a redistribution of land to achieve a socialistic pattern of society. Such an effort will reduce inequalities in ownership of land.
2. To enforce land ceiling and take away the surplus land to be distributed among the marginal and landless peasants.
3. To legitimise the tenancy with the ceiling limit.
4. To register all tenancy arrangements with the Village Panchayat.
5. To establish relationship between ceiling and tenancy.

Land reforms thus constitute our national legacy. Admittedly, it was easy for the state governments to have abolition of *jagirdars* and *jamindars*, but when the question of imposing ceiling laws arose it became very difficult for them to enforce these laws. The basic objective of land ceiling is to remove the land inequality. And, this is always contested by the big farmers.

Our experience of the last four decades in the field of land reforms shows that except in states like Karnataka in the 1970s and West Bengal in the 1980s, very little success has been achieved in land redistribution. Even the Five Year Plan documents have acknowledged the failure of most states to achieve the objective of reducing inequalities in landownership. Inequalities seem to have increased with the concentration of land holding on the one hand and fragmentation on the other. The latter renders the holdings of the poor economically non-viable. Besides, the amendments to the Karnataka Land Reforms Act in 1995 and similar government orders in Gujarat indicate that even states that have implemented them in the past are going back on their commitment, in order to attract investment. This failure is attributed to factors like lack of political will, loopholes in the law, delays caused by litigation and the growing political clout for the peasants.

Access to Land Reforms

We must reiterate that land reforms is the subject of state government. Each state in the union has made its own efforts to implement land reforms. P.C. Joshi has suggested three approaches to land reforms.[8] These are: (1) The Gandhian approach, (2) the radical nationalist approach, and (3) the Marxist approach. "The Gandhian view does not bring out directly the contradictions of the Indian rural society in regard to its land relations." However, Vinoba Bhave started a movement which is known as *Gramdan*. This movement approached the landlords to part away with their surplus land as a donation to give to those who were landless peasants. In the initial stages, response to this movement was satisfactory. At a later stage the movement cooled down.

The second approach is that of radical nationalist did not work satisfactorily. It turned out to be a formal approach generally adopted by the state governments. The Marxist approach takes into consideration the peasant movements and other non-legal lines and action.

Taking into consideration the three approaches mentioned above, it is clear that in order to reduce the sharp class differences, land reforms have to be implemented. In a seminar organized by Centre for Agrarian Studies held in 1991 it was suggested by T. Haque that for the development of a socialist society it is essential in India to enforce land reforms in all the states. Haque observed:

> There is role of land reform as an engine of socio-economic transformation and rural development, and outlined the need for a re-examination of the direction in land reform in the light of the New Economic Policy.[9]

Before we examine the land reforms adopted by different states we must bring out some of the common features accepted by all the states in the country. Admittedly, some states have emphasised a particular perspective and the other have taken different perspectives.

Despite this variation in the attributes of land reforms, there are a few which have been stressed by all the states. Here we discuss some of the attributes of land reforms.

Some Common Attributes of Land Reforms

Soon after the adoption of Constitution, various states have taken certain measures for land reforms. These measures are as under:

1. *Abolition of intermediaries*

Before the attainment of independence we had four tenancy systems in the country, viz., (i) *ryotwari*, (ii) *mahalwari*, (iii) *jamindari*, and (iv) *jagirdari*.

(i) Ryotwari: This kind of land tenancy was first introduced by the British in Madras in 1772. Later on it was extended to Bombay presidency. Under this tenancy system every registered holder of land was recognised as its proprietor. He paid revenue directly to the government. He was at liberty to sublet his property or to transfer it by gift, sale or mortgage. He could not be ejected from his land till he paid the revenue.

Absence of sub-infeudation and the cultivator's direct relation with the government was the main advantage of this tenancy system. Yet another advantage of this system was that the proprietor of the land took all interest for improving the land and its irrigation facilities. But the inherent drawback of the system was that the land was sublet to the landless peasants. In the long run the *ryotwari* system created a group of peasants who were subordinate to the proprietor of the land.

The *ryotwari* system was abolished by the land reform measures.

(ii) Mahalwari: This kind of tenancy was introduced during the British rule. It was first started in Agra and Audh and was later on extended to Punjab. Under this system, land was held jointly by co-sharing bodies of village communities. This body was treated as "jointly and severally liable for the land revenue". A typical example of the *mahalwari* tenancy system was widely prevalent in Punjab. It was a kind of

joint landlordism and distinguished from individual landlordism under *zamindari* system.

In a typical joint village the owners were themselves cultivators. In some cases, land was cultivated by tenants who paid rent either in cash or in kind. Best results of cultivation were obtained when a peasant proprietor possessed enough land to cultivate with the help of his family.

The *mahalwari* system of intermediaries was abolished as a part of land reforms taken up in fifties.

(iii) Jamindari: It is yet another system of tenancy which prevailed in Bengal, Uttar Pradesh, Bombay presidency and Tamilnadu. Under this system one or more persons owned a village and were responsible for the payment of revenue. This system, also created by the British, was highly exploitative. It also encouraged absentee landlords who more than often enhanced the rate of land rent. The actual tiller of land was always in fear of his ejection from land because he was not the owner of the land. No land development efforts were made. The *jamindar* was interested to realise the land rent from the tiller. Prem Chand, the noted Hindi novelist and story writer, has very emphatically brought out the miserable condition of the tiller under the *jamindari* system. Hori, the hero of his novel *Godan*, very much exemplifies the plight of the peasantry under the *jamindari* system.

As a part of land reform programmes *jamindari* system has also been abolished by the various state governments in the country.

(iv) Jagirdari: The *jagirdari* tenancy system was found mainly in the former princely states of Rajasthan. Under this system, *jagirs* were granted to certain military commanders, ministers and courtiers, who took the revenue for their own support or for the military force which they were obliged to maintain. The *jagirdari* system thus created a class of unproductive mass of people by granting them *jagir* lands. K.L. Sharma[10] informs that the *jagirdars* "extorted and extracted as many as 175 taxes and cases. *Thikandars* and *jagirdars* levied these taxes not only to maintain the feudal set up, but also to meet expenses of individual members of the royal family, and on cultural,

religious and other miscellaneous activities."

The Rajasthan Jagir Abolition Act was passed in February 1952 and implemented in 1954. This put an end to *jagirdari* tenancy system in Rajasthan and elsewhere in other parts of the states of the union.

The abolition of intermediaries in the various tenancy systems as discussed above brought out many land reforms as under:

(1) The powerful landlords such as *jamindar* and *jagirdar* became extinct.
(2) The abolition of the intermediaries gave relief to the tillers. Their exploitation ceased to exist.
(3) Transfer of the land of intermediaries to the tillers reduced land inequalities to some extent.
(4) The new proprietorship of land, resulting from the abolition of intermediaries, provided opportunities for land improvement and land production.
(5) The ex-landlords or the *jamindars* and *jagirdars* withdrew their status and took to new occupations, thereby contributing the the growth of national economy.
(6) The rents received from the new owners of the land, as a result of abolition of intermediaries, gave additional revenue to the state government. This money is utilised for the development of agricultural input and general rural development.

2. *Land ceiling*

The basic objective of land reforms was to remove or minimise the unequal distribution of land. The position today is that a large number of people have minimum land in their possession; and a small number of people have maximum land in their possession. Such a kind of land distribution is against any principle of social justice. During our struggle for independence, the national leaders, time and again, stressed that in free India land would be distributed on the basis of social justice. The land reforms thus are the result of our historical commitment to the masses of peasants for equitable distribution of land.

Land ceiling is one of the measures to take away surplus land from those who cross the limit of land possession beyond a certain point. Ceiling limit on land was imposed on the following groups:

1. *Land is a source of income:* In rural India land provides employment opportunities. And, therefore, the agricultural labourers, marginal farmers and small farmers should be given some land for their livelihood. Land ceiling limit, therefore, should apply to only those groups who have more land to their requirement.
2. *Land ceiling should be imposed on all variety of lands*: The land possessed by the peasants is of different kinds: (1) fallow, (2) uncultivable, (3) cultivable, and (4) irrigated. Ceiling should apply to all these categories of lands.
3. *Ceiling on irrigated and two crops a year land:* Though the limit of ceiling on two crops a year and irrigated land varies from state to state, on a broader plane 18 acres has been the limit for possessing this kind of land. It means that a peasant having more than 18 acres of land which is irrigated and two crops will be declared as a peasant having surplus land.
4. *Assured irrigation and one crop land:* A peasant having up to 27 acres of land with irrigation and one crop a year does not come in the ceiling law. But any land above the 27 acres is declared surplus and taken over by the state government.
5. *Ceiling up to 54 acres:* In case of owners of holdings consisting of different types of land, the total holdings after the best categories of land into lowest category is up to 54 acres.

These limits of ceilings are subject to variation from state to state. The Ceiling Acts also take into consideration the family size which is dependent on the size of the landholdings. For the purpose of Act (1) a family of five members has been taken as a unit, including husband and wife and three minor children. Provision has been kept for the additional members of the family, but not exceeding twice the ceiling limit; (2) where both husband and wife hold land in their own names, the two will have the right in the properties within the ceilings in proportion to the value of the land held by each before the application of ceiling; and, (3) each major child is treated as a separate unit for the purpose of application of ceiling.

Some exemptions

The Ceiling Acts have also certain exemptions. These are as below:

(1) There are exemptions in favour of plantations of tea, coffee, rubber and cocoa.

(2) Exemption is also given for the land held by industrial and commercial undertakings.

(3) As a measure of exemption the sugarcane factories are permitted to own land up to 100 acres.

We would reiterate that the ceiling laws vary from state to state. For instance, in the state of Andhra Pradesh, the ceiling limit for irrigated land is 10-18 acres. In West Bengal it is 12.4 acres, whereas in Haryana it is 17.9 acres and in Karnataka 10.13 acres.

3. *Land possession and social power*

The agenda of land reforms as discussed earlier is quite comprehensive. Besides the abolition of intermediaries and land ceiling, it is also being increasingly realised that land is not only a source of production, it is also a source of power. Expressing this new dimension on landownership Walter Fernandes very rightly observes:

> An aspect that needs to be borne in mind in order to understand this apparent contradiction is that land is not merely a source of cultivation or of building, as it is made out to be in most legislation. Its ownership pattern in an agrarian economy is a sign of a person's social status.[11]

Quite supporting the point of view of Fernandes, Morley Mohan Lal also makes the following observation:

> The ownership of land...reflects social class and class relations, as they represent on array of legal, contractual or customary arrangements whereby people engaged in cultivation gain access to productive opportunities linked with land and thereby income.[12]

The objective of land reform legislation is also to bring social change in the society. Actually landownership pattern, besides bringing equal distribution of land, also symbolises social change. It is in this context that one has to study the land reforms and changes in the landownership pattern in the country.

4. *Legitimisation of tenancy within the ceiling limit*

The land reform legislation does not end with the enforcement of land ceiling. It also functions to regularise the land tenure records. The Indian rural society has a tradition to transfer the land from one generation to another. It does not take the form of a document. This comes in the way of getting a sanction for development loans. It is, therefore, also the objective of land reform legislation to enforce registration of all tenancy arrangements with the Village Panchayats.

5. *Land as private property*

The history of land legislation goes back to the British rule. It was for the first time that Lord Cornwalles in 1793 introduced the Permanent Land Settlement in Bihar, Orissa and Bengal. The land settlement system was important so far land revenue and land tenancy are concerned but it was also important that land for the first time became a private property of the landholder. Earlier settlement of land, all over the country was held by the community. There was no ownership of land on individual basis.

The land reforms legislations also try to strengthen the idea that land should be made legally a part of individual's property. It is in this respect that there should be proper codification of land and documents prepared thereof.

Failure of land reforms

Land reforms legislation has become controversial today. Its meaning also has become erroneous. Actually the term means reform of the basic relations between man and land, and between tillers of the land and other beneficiaries from the land-tiller interaction like landlords, moneylenders and village merchants. While discussing land reforms we must keep in mind that in a country like India where 70 per cent of the population is dependent on land, relations between various categories of people like big farmers, sharecroppers and agricultural labourers on the one hand, and the nature of their respective control over land on the other, is of paramount interest. It must also be admitted that any strategy for increasing agricultural production cannot overlook these structural questions, just as rural poverty and agricultural backwardness cannot be understood without reference to the agrarian structure.

When the land reforms were introduced it was understood that the discrepancy between the ownership of land and operation of land must be regarded as one of the basic maladies of our agrarian structure. If we look at the result of the operation of different land reforms legislations it appears that some of them have failed. However, the failure rate varies from state to state. We give below some of the areas of agriculture, that is, tenancy relations where the land reforms legislations have failed.

(1) *Increasing land inequality:* The basic objective of land reforms was to establish land equity among various categories of peasants. This objective has not been achieved because of constant change in definitions, it is difficult to compare the landownership data of different years. But one can see a trend of deteriorating land relations. Whatever aggregate data that we can get, shows that there have been inequalities in landownership. For instance, in 1961 a little over 19 million rural households were landless and the total number of landholdings was 64 millions. In other words, 19.01 per cent owned 0.49 acre or less or an average of 0.09 acre of land. This data of 1961 can be compared with the data of 1971. Such a comparison shows that 51 per cent of the total peasants were marginal farmers who occupy 9 per cent of the area. The percentage of small farmers has risen to 18.9. At the other extreme end, those owning more than 20 acres of land, a bare 1 per cent of the total occupied, 13.4 per cent of the operational area. These are the official data pertaining to the year 1971.

Walter Fernandes has another set of data to conclude that there has been a marked inequity in the landowning. He observes:

> By 1981 the percentage of marginal and small farmers was 56.5 and 12.2 per cent respectively. The semi-medium farmers were 14 per cent, the medium farmers 9.1 per cent and big farmers 2.4 per cent. According to the estimates of the Planning Commission in the mid-1980s, two-thirds of the rural households were made up of small and marginal farmers. The estimated surplus over the ceiling was 5.36 million hectares but only 2.10 million hectares had been taken over till the mid-1980s and 1.29 million hectares distributed.

The Reserve Bank of India survey data, given in 1981, show that "the poorest 10 per cent owned only 0.4 per cent of the total assets in the rural areas and 0.1 per cent in the urban areas. On the other hand, the top 10 per cent owned 49.5 per cent of the rural assets and 58.7 per cent of the urban assets. The trend continued till the late 1980s (Government of India, 1988) and is also true today."

Fernandes concludes in categorical words that the unequal system reflected in the landownership figures may also explain that the legislation on land ceiling, has been implemented half-heartedly even in states where the Zamindari Abolition Acts have been taken more seriously. Nalcalm Adiseshiah[13] makes a review of Five Year Plans with the perspective of land reforms and concludes that there is failure in implementing the land reforms legislations. Not only this, but whatever land reforms have been made, these have increased inequalities in the country as a whole.

(2) *State side with the big farmers:* N.C. Saxena[14] has analysed, elaborately, the failure of land reforms legislations in different states of the country. He says that the state governments which control the land operations have always moved favourably towards the big farmers. As a result of such a kind of prejudicial intervention of state governments, the small farmers have always suffered.

(3) *Big farmers corner the land of marginal farmers:* As a result of the transfer of surplus land to the landless labourers, marginal farmers and small farmers, the big farmers have increased the size of their land. Smaller patches of land cannot be operated upon by new technology. And, the small farmers find it difficult to operate upon their agriculture, manually. As a result their farm yields economically become costlier. Finally, the benefit of land ceiling goes in the favour of big farmers.

(4) *Surplus land is fallow and uncultivable land:* The surplus land got out of land ceiling is usually uncultivable. The holders of surplus land manipulate the land data in such a way that the land in excess in their possession is usually barren and uncultivable. Such a surplus land is of no benefit to the landless peasants. This renders the land reform legislations null and void.

(5) *Benami transactions:* The land ceiling legislations, in most of the cases, have proved to be fraud. The land possessed in excess to the land ceiling limit is adjusted against *benami* persons. Such *benami* transactions do not make any change in the operational aspect of agriculture.

(6) *Lack of political will:* The political parties are not without their

vested interests. It is because of the lack of political will that we find the failure of land legislations. Besides the political parties, the former *jagirdars* and *jamindars* are also responsible for non-implementation of land reforms. The Bihar Acquisition of Surplus Act of 1961 and the subsequent amendments could not correct the earlier deficiencies of Land Reform Act due to the influence of former intermediaries. It is reported that in Bihar big landowners who held much more than the ceiling area had been increasing their holdings. In a recent seminar (NIRD, 1991) it was concluded that in Bihar the impact of land reform measures was very little. Quite like Bihar the impact of land reforms in the Andhra Pradesh, Gujarat, Orissa, Madhya Pradesh, Uttar Pradesh and Haryana has not been striking. This can be explained by the fact that the politicians have little will to implement the reform measures.

However, if there is a political will, the reforms can be demonstrable. In the case of West Bengal much of the success of land legislations is attributed to political will and committed administration. If the political parties and the bureaucracy show their willingness, land equalisation can be attained to some degree.

Concluding Observations

It is through the land in rural India that employment and income are generated. Besides this, land possession also gives status and power. It is only recently that women have started in some parts of the country a movement which demands that the names of women should also be included in the land documents, i.e., *patta*. Such a kind of movement is basically a gender problem. What would happen to this demand is a guess today. However, what is important is that the land tenure system, land reforms and the problems associated with this cannot be postponed any longer. The issues and problems are urgent and immediate. The state governments will soon have to implement some of the important measures of tenancy and land reforms. Before the process of peasant pauperisation completes its course, land reforms have to be enforced.

Notes

1. A.R. Desai, *Social Background of Indian Nationalism,* Popular Prakashan, Bombay, 1981 (Reprint).
2. K.L. Sharma, *Caste, Class and Social Movements,* Rawat Publications, Jaipur, 1986.
3. H. Laxmi Narayan and S.A.Tyagi, "Inter-state Variations in Types of Tenancy", *Economic and Political Weekly* 12, 39, 1977, p. A. 77.
4. Jan Breman, *Of Peasants, Migrants and Paupers,* Oxford University Press, New Delhi, 1985.
5. Andre Beteille. Besides studies in agrarian social structure the author has initially made an intensive study of a village Sripuram situated in Tanjore, south India. The book is entitled *Caste,Class and Power*, University of California Press, London, 1971.
6. Daniel Thorner, *The Agrarian Prospect in India*, Delhi, 1955.
7. Gunnar Myrdal, , *Asian Drama: An Inquiry into the Poverty of Nations,* The Penguin Press, London, 1968, Vols. I-III.
8. P.C. Joshi, *Land Reforms in India*, Allied Publishers, Bombay, 1965.
9. *Economic and Political Weakly,* February, 22, 1992, p. 395.
10. K.L. Sharma, *Rural Society in India,* Rawat Publications, Jaipur, 1997, p. 112.
11. Walter Fernandes, "Ownership Pattern and Alienation of Tribal Livelihood", *Social Action*, October-December 1996, Vol. 46, No. 4, p. 430.
12. Mohan Lal, Morley, *Poverty Alleviation: The Indian Experience,* Himalayas Publishing House, Delhi, 1988, p. 386.
13. Malcolm Adiseshiah, "The Perspectives", in Malcolm S. Adiseshiah (ed.), *Eighth Plan Perspectives,* Lancer International, New Delhi, pp. 12-20.
14. N.C. Saxena, "Land Reforms and Equity", *Seminar*, No. 418, June 1994.

8 Rural Social Stratification

Caste and Class

According to Sir Henry S. Maine, during the British period, the Indian villages were 'little republics'. Maine's description of village India is contested by contemporary Indian sociologists. Despite this criticism the fact remains that there was very little social stratification in rural India. It is only after independence and importantly after the implementation of Five Year Plans that there has emerged a striking social differentiation in India's villages. Now, the Indian agriculture has become capitalistic. The number of marginal peasants has increased, rural people have come within the network of audio-visual development. Education in agriculture has increased. In fact, the process of modernisation including development in agriculture technology has changed the face of rural society.

We have enough studies on Indian villages which very clearly show that the villages have witnessed much social transformation. The mobility and migration which have become the main characteristics of villages, have created social stratification which is a-historical. To understand contemporary village India it is essential to analyse the stratification. The village studies very vividly show that caste has witnessed new dimensions in rural society. The village which remained isolated from the urban mainstream has now developed a nexus with the urban community. Similar is the emergence of class in rural India. Actually, there is a demonstrable nexus between caste and class in rural India. In the present chapter we analyse the situation of caste and class in rural India. This is what comes under the domain of rural stratification.

Social Stratification

Stratification is ranking of people in a society. Ranking is made on certain criteria. These criteria include power, status and prestige. The mer estate holders in rural society even today hold much power. They are big peasants and occupy positions of power in PRIs and legislatures. At operational level they constitute a considerable rank in both rural and urban stratification.

(4) *Class*

Classes are not established by legal or religious provisions. Nor membership to class is based on inherited position as specified either legally or by custom. Class systems are typically more fluid than the other types of stratification and the boundaries between classes are never clear-cut. There are no formal restrictions on inter-marriage between people from different classes. Some of the characteristics of class include individual's achievement, social mobility, economic status and class consciousness. Thus, class is a large-scale grouping of people who share common economic resources, which strongly influence the types of lifestyle they are able to lead. Ownership of wealth, together with occupation, is the chief basis of class differences. The major classes that exist in India are: (1) upper class, (2) middle class, and (3) working class.

Rural Social Stratification

Indian rural society like any other society has its stratification pattern which is specific to it only. In rural society an individual is normally identified with his village. In the south Indian states the name of a person also includes the name of his village. Irawati Karve, the noted Indian anthropologist, once observed that an Indian is identified by his caste, language and village. Viewed from this perspective the village social stratification is synonymous with village caste. Caste is the chief identification mark of a person in rural society.

Theoretical Approach to the Study of Rural Stratification

Study of rural or agrarian stratification theoretically needs a specific approach. Ramakrishna Mukerjee[1] has attempted to analyse agrarian stratification through following three perspectives:

(1) the property and production relations in agriculture;

(2) status categories in rural society; and

(3) the interactions between the elites and the masses.

Obviously, the perspectives adopted by Ramakrishna Mukerjee are couched in Marxian framework. There are few other sociologists also, particularly P.K. Bose[2], who have also chosen Marxian approach to study rural stratification.

Yet another approach to the study of rural caste is adopted by K.L. Sharma.[3] He emphasises that caste in rural society is so pervasive that it needs to be studied from a particular point of view. He contests Marxian approach to the study of caste and says that "caste is not a mere epiphenomenon of class relations (as it is unquestionably accepted even by orthodox Marxists). Caste is both an actual structure of social relationships and an ideology. As such, caste structure does not rest only upon unequal access to the means of production and the appropriation of surplus by a dominant caste...There are complementary *unequal exchanges* between members of different castes, hence the hierarchy and the exploitation of labour, poor and lower caste men".

Caste in Rural India

Sociologists and anthropologists have defined caste as a major form of stratification. Though this form of inequality is found all over the country, there are a few misconceptions about it. There is a general understanding that caste and class are polar opposites. It is also understood that caste is essentially a rural phenomenon while class is found in urban communities. The misunderstandings are many. The fact is that there are classes in a caste; there are castes in urban communities also. During the last five decades much research has been done in the field of caste. Caste is not regimental; it is always changing. Even the caste structure which prevailed before independence in rural India has changed considerably. But, however, its essential characteristics continue to remain.

It must be admitted that the structure of caste as a form of stratification found in rural society is not different from urban society. The changes are operational only. For instance, in rural society, inter-caste marriages are few and far between; caste occupational mobility is lesser in rural India than urban India. These changes make a difference of degree only. It could be safely said that caste system has greater operational or functional role in the village compared to cities.

Yogendra Singh who holds authority on sociology of social stratification defines caste as a major form of stratification. He writes:

> Sociologists who look across the cultural view of caste have, right from the beginning, associate with an autonomous principle of stratification. The bases of which are institutionalised inequality, closure of social system in respect of social mobility, an elementary level of division of labour, legitimised on ritual bases of reciprocity, and emphasis on quality (ritual purity or racial purity) rather than performance. In other words, caste is associated with an autonomous form of cultural system or worldview.[4]

Thus, according to Yogendra Singh, caste is a cultural phenomenon. Further elaborating the concept of caste he says that besides being a cultural phenomenon, caste is also a structural phenomenon. The structural aspect of caste is stressed by functionalists who very much dwell on structural-functional analysis. Those who consider caste as a structural phenomenon consider it as a system of social organisation, an institutionalised system of interaction among hierarchically-ranked hereditary groups for marriage, occupation, economic division of labour, enforcement of cultural norms and values by caste bodies and performance of rituals based on principles of purity and pollution.

The structural properties of caste, namely, endogamy, caste occupations and hierarchy have a direct bearing on social stratification. The cultural aspects, on the other hand, are value-based. It is in these two aspects, namely, cultural and structural, that the caste system is analysed in our country. When we look at the caste system in rural India we should always keep in mind that there are few specificities in caste system which make caste a particularistic institution in rural society.

Specificities of Caste in Rural Society

We may talk much about the changing caste system in Indian society, but the fact remains that it has a functional role in maintaining the village social system. Some of the special functions performed by the caste in villages are described below:

(1) *Phases of life*

The individual lifecycle passes through birth, betrothal, marriage and death. On all these occasions there is a definite role of caste. Whatever may be the secular status of a Brahmin, his presence is obligatory to officiate at the fulfilment of rituals on major phases of life. A marriage cannot be completed without the Brahmin; a dead body cannot be cremated without his presence. In metropolitan cities some of these rituals might be overlooked or undermined, but in village India caste specialists are essential functionaries.

(2) *Exogamy and endogamy*

One cannot marry with his sister, nor can he marry with any of his agnates. Marriage within the *gotra* or clan is prohibited. This rule of exogamy is observed strictly in village society. However, the urban society can in some situation overlook it. Sometimes there is practice of village exogamy also. The tribals consider it to be their loss of status if a person marries within his village.

(3) *Occupational interdependence*

Caste society is essentially based on an elaborate division of labour. Actually, the village economy a few years back depended on the *jaimani* system. Each caste has had its occupational specialisation. The Darji, Nai, Dhobi, Kumbhar and Chamar are some of the occupational castes. These castes gave their services to their *jajmans* (clients) on exchange basis. The rewards generally consisted of kind payment. On the whole, the caste economy promotes occupational interdependence.

Surely, the *jajmani* system today is on the way to extinction but even then there are few occupational services which are given on cash payment. What is important is that caste system fosters interdependence among different castes in a village.

(4) *Caste associations*

Rural society has got its caste associations much strengthened despite its weakening power. We have enough research material to indicate that caste associations have become stronger in village India today. Ghanshyam Shah informs that in Gujarat the caste has a decisive role in political matters, particularly voting. The kind of caste war that we find in Bihar today is much due to the new strength gained by the caste associations. It is possible that in urban communities caste associations might have become a little weaker, but in rural India many of the political decisions are made by caste associations.

The researches also bring out the fact that the provision of reservation given by the Constitution of India to scheduled castes and scheduled tribes has divided the whole village community into two parts. The caste war has now become multidimensional. M.N. Srinivas has analysed the new form of caste which he calls *avtar*, has much influenced the hierarchical relations between the caste members. It appears that the caste system has weakened in some respects in rural India but has also got strengthened in some of its areas. Such a kind of generalisation about the caste also holds true for urban community.

(5) *Caste is the mirror of rural society*

It is the caste settlement in terms of its power that a particular village is identified in a region. For instance, S.C. Dube[5] in his book *India's Changing Villages* talks about a Rajput village. It means that in a particular village the Rajputs wield power. They maintain the village system. Similarly, we have Jat villages, Brahmin villages and tribal villages. In such villages other castes are also found but they are only subordinate castes. In such a situation the structure of a village is known by the caste groups inhabiting it. It is, therefore, that we call caste as the mirror of a village.

(6) *Dominant caste*

M.N. Srinivas[6] has given the concept of dominant caste. This is a caste which has a numerical strength in the village; it owns major portion of village land and takes major decisions which maintain the village system. It is the dominant caste which rules over the village. The concept of dominant caste very clearly shows that there are few castes which exercise their hold on the village. Besides Srinivas there are a few other sociologists like Andre Beteille, who informed that despite changes in villages the dominant castes occupy a pivotal status in rural society.

In the former princely states and also in the *jamindari* villages, though there has been abolition of intermediaries, there are few castes that wield their influence on the village. They are the big caste peasants who control the behaviour of the subaltern caste members.

(7) *Hierarchical relations*

Social interactions in the village are guided by caste status. Caste, in fact, is a system of hierarchical relations. It is a pyramid of hierarchy, where at the top is Brahmin, followed by Rajput and Bania. A.R. Desai very rightly observes:

> Caste has fixed the psychology of the various social groups and has evolved such minutely graded levels of social distance and superior-inferior relationships that the social structure looks like a gigantic hierarchic pyramid with a mass of untouchable as its base and a small stratum of elite, the Brahmins, almost equally unapproachable, at its apex. The Hindu society is composed of hundreds of distinct self-contained caste worlds piled one over the other.[7]

(8) *Caste and economic life*

A.R. Desai has very strongly argued that the village economy should also be studied from the point of view of caste. It is the caste which mainly determines the economic life of the people. Despite diversification in village economy, even today traditional occupations determined the wealth status of the people. The caste has a role in production relations. For instance, in central Gujarat where the Rajputs are the big landowners, they are being replaced by Patidars as dominant cultivators. It is actually said that in any part of the country habitation pattern of the village is determined by specific caste clusters. Whatever may be the future of caste in India, the fact remains that belongingness to a caste not only determines the pattern of settlement, but also the type of house a person would build.

(9) *Mobility*

Economic mobility of a person or cluster of families is also determined by the caste. Change in a village is relative to the village castes. There are some castes that have given away their traditional occupations while at the same time there are castes that very rigidly follow their traditional occupations. In any study of rural society occupational mobility and social mobility have to be analysed in the context of caste belongingness.

(10) *Caste and joint family*

A.R. Desai emphatically argues that there is a co-relation between caste and joint family system. Actually it is the caste structure which determines the nature of family---joint or nuclear---in the village. It is observed all over village India that a caste in the rural society is essentially a cluster of joint families. Resultantly, the caste moulds the nature of the life of the members of family.

Thus, the caste has a definite role in the structure and functioning of rural society. In contemporary India much changes have come in the caste system. Despite this it is the caste character which determines to a great extent the nature of rural society. Though, most of the facilities of modernity like electricity, tap water, telephone, television, etc., have reached the doors of villagers, but the caste still holds together the village life. It is the task of rural sociology to identify the co-relation between caste and the different aspects of village life.

Changing Rural Caste Stratification

Age-old rural stratification dominated by caste is changing fast. We have argued earlier that we shall discuss the group of Patidars which monopolises the cultivation of commercial crops such as cotton, groundnut, sugarcane and tobacco. A.R. Desai refers to the empirical data of Gujarat generated by S.M. Shah[8] and concludes that the new economic and political forces have undermined the homogeneous functional basis of old castes and also the distribution of property among them. Desai's thrust of argument is that there is a substantial role of caste in the productive system of the village.

Desai also observes that the consumption pattern of the village is also conditioned by the caste. It is the caste which fixes the food, and dress habits or the choice of utensils and other articles of its members. This caste-determined mode of consumption and in fact the total life-style of the villagers influences the production system. "The pure economic theory of consumption would be misleading and result into incorrect conclusions unless its modification due to the intervention of the caste institution is taken into account."

Quite like consumption, the extent of indebtedness is also specific to the caste. S.S. Nehru[9] very categorically argues that "there is a close relationship between caste and indebtedness and credit in the rural India. Certain castes are predominantly composed of members who are almost hereditary debtors; some others of those who are mainly creditors".

Studies on village society have shown clearly that there is a definite pattern of village settlement. This pattern of habitat is determined by the caste. Sociologists have classified the villages on the basis of caste belongingness. There are different patterns of villages based on caste. For instance, the Rajputs and the Brahmins have their settlements closer to the ruling caste. The untouchables and the tribals are always at the fringe of the village. The trading and agricultural castes generally occupy the central part of the village. From all considerations, it must be caste and class as major forms of rural social stratification.

Now, we shall examine the changing rural caste system.

Caste is assuming a new role in rural India. This is the new form or *avtar* of caste. K.L. Sharma provides an interesting social profile of the new caste which is fast emerging in our villages. His descriptions runs as under:

> There are new castes not really in the hereditary/ascriptive sense of the term caste, but in terms of the emergence of new status groups taking precedence over the traditional upper and middle castes. Social mobility in the caste system has been a historical fact, and every new macro-economic and political development has affected the caste system. These changes in the caste system may be seen in the decline of *jajmani* system and emergence of modern occupations, and in the form of new dominant groups and families, decline of untouchability and the pollution-purity principle.'

Significant changes have taken place in the caste system as a form of rural social stratification over the past fifty years. These changes can be conceptualised into two forces: (1) structural changes, and (2) peripheral changes. Structural changes have far reaching impact on the rural caste system. These changes include the abolition of *zamindari* and *jagirdari* systems, introduction of Panchayati Raj, adult franchise, cooperatives, etc. The peripheral changes comprise establishment of modern schools, construction of roads, public health centres, communication links and migration. We shall now enumerate and discuss some of the major structural and peripheral changes influencing the rural caste system.

(1) *Modernisation and Sanskritisation*

Modernisation is a very complex term. It is highly carry out either the traditional occupations or the secular occupations. But the choice of the new occupations or the secular occupations and the rejection of the old ones is much pragmatic and selective. "There are castes which have discarded traditional occupations because they were considered 'impure' or 'unclean' or 'lower', that is, because of the stigma about the polluting nature of their traditional occupations."

K.L. Sharma, while analysing the impact of modernisation on the caste occupations, says that the upper castes have a mere monopoly over the more income, prestige and power providing occupations and avenues.

Modernisation, in fact, is a very comprehensive concept and includes education, politics, power, style of life and a large number of other aspects of life.

The village caste system has received phenomenal change in its structure due to the process of sanskritisation. The change brought by this process is a positional change. In this change there is horizontal mobility in the caste structure. Sanskritisation, as a process of social change or mobility, was introduced by M.N. Srinivas in sixties. It is a social change *within* the caste system. It means imitation of the customs and practices of the higher castes by the lower castes.[13] The castes which sanskritise their pantheon and rituals think that their statuses are lower in social hierarchy, because of the customs, practices and occupations they carry on. These castes try to improve their social status by rejecting some of their traditional styles of life and by imitating the cultural styles of the upper castes.

As stated earlier, some of the lower castes in the villages have given up their traditional occupations which are considered to be 'impure' or 'polluted'. For instance, in some parts of Gujarat, Maharashtra and Uttar Pradesh, the Chamars have given up their traditional occupation of shoe-making, and removal and skinning for carcasses. The Meghwals---a caste of untouchables---have embraced value and ideology oriented life. It includes secularism, democracy, urbanism and industrialism. The sociological thinkers like Durkheim, Weber and Marx have discussed theoretically, some of the major aspects of modernisation. According to Durkheim, the dominant characteristic of modernisation is differentiation. He argues that more a society differentiated more it is cohesive. Thus, with the development of society, there is acceleration of differentiation. Marx, on the other hand, defines modernisation in terms of commodification. He says that in a modernised society everything of society including literature and arts are reduced to the status of a commodity. As the factory products are sold in the market as a commodity, cultural things are also exchanged as a commodity. Modernization for Marx, therefore, is commodification of everything in the society. On the other hand, Weber conceptualises modernisation as rationality.

Taking into consideration the diverse definitions of modernisation it could be said that it includes technology, urbanity, industry, education and many other things which result in the construction of an ideological or value system characterised by differentiation, commodification and rationality. It should also be mentioned here that no society at any point of time is fully modernised. It is a process which goes on continuously. Srinivas[11] argues that modernisation in India began with the coming of British in India. For Yogendra Singh[12] modernisation is basically a value-loaded concept which includes ideology, technology and other aspects of development. The Indian villages received the impact of modernisation through directed change, education, industrial development and agricultural development.

Modernisation has affected the occupational structure of the village caste. It is found that in a large number of villages the majority of castes do not exclusively a sect of Jainism to improve their polluted position. The barbers have now begun to suffix their name with 'Sharma'. The Jatavas of Agra have now become neo-Buddhists. All these occupational changes indicate that sanskritisation has brought about change in the rural caste system.

(2) *De-Sanskritisation*

Yet another change witnessed in the rural caste system is the working of the process of de-sanskritisation. K.L. Sharma, who has intimate experience of working in the villages of Rajasthan, informs that some of the higher castes are giving up their sanskritic values in order to have interaction with the lower castes. For instance, the Rajputs, Jats and Brahmins now do not hesitate to touch the untouchables. Occasionally, the Jats would not mind to share smoking with the lower castes. This kind of change is characterised by Sharma as de-sanskritisation.[14]

(3) *Values of Achievement*

The national idioms of democracy, socialism and secularism have influenced the importance of rituals in the rural life. Actually, the value of achievement orientation is increasingly being accepted by the higher castes. As a result of this value orientation, the traditional rules of food and water taboos are very openly violated. Commensality has become a common thing on occasions of marriage and other celebrations. One can find the lower castes mixing with the higher castes in election and political meetings.

(4) *Education: The Monopoly of Higher Caste*

Education is one of the most significant determinants of status in the present-day village community. Studies conducted on this account show that the higher castes have taken up or rather cornered most of the facilities of higher education. This has opened up new job opportunities for the village higher castes. K.L. Sharma in this respect observes:

> It is college and university education that extends the horizon of occupational possibilities by providing the formal qualifications required for superior occupations and intellectual superiority to those who achieve it.[15]

(5) *Proletarianism*

This kind of structural change is found among the higher castes of rural society. In the process of social change and particularly the opportunities of development given to the lower castes, the higher castes find their status withdrawal. The jamindars of Uttar Pradesh and Bihar, *jagirdars* of Rajasthan and *darbars* of Gujarat are obliged to take to manual labour and lower jobs. Such a kind of process has reduced the status of higher castes to that of proletariat. In the villages one can find the Rajputs doing manual work.

(6) *Hostility and Tension*

A new kind of change is observed among the lower castes of villages. V.S. Naipaul[16] who has taken an account of our country by travelling far wider areas, concludes that there has come an awakening among the subjugated people of the society. The lower castes have emerged with arms in hand as a powerful segment of society to rise against the upper castes. It is a mutiny-like situation. Naipaul observes:

> People everywhere have ideas now of who they are and what they owe themselves. The process quickened with the economic development that came after independence; what was hidden in 1962, or not easy to see what perhaps was only in a state of becoming, has become clearer. The liberation of spirit that has come to India could not come as release alone. In India, with its layer below layer of distress and cruelty, it had to come as disturbance. It had to come as rage and revolt. India was now a country of million little mutinies.

K.L. Sharma, though in different words, also argues that the "fractions of the depressed castes who are benefited by education and employment demand displacement of the traditional oppressive system and in turn they become a target of the hostility and violence of the entrenched upper castes". Sharma, to support his observation, refers to the social mobility found among the scheduled castes in Gujarat.

I.P. Desai[17] also thinks in the same direction. He argues that the safeguard of reservation given to the scheduled tribes has helped them to mobilise themselves against the upper castes.

(7) *Hegemony of the Higher Castes*

Jan Breman[18] has generated some important data on peasants and migrants belonging to Surat (Gujarat) and its *talukas.* He argues that in the whole district the Kanbi Patidars have occupied a higher status in the field of agriculture. They own larger portions of land. The Halpatis, earlier known as Dublas, have been reduced to smaller portions of land. In fact, the Halpatis once an important group of agriculturists, have now become paupers.

In other parts of the country also, the lower castes are fast reducing to the status of marginal agricultural castes. Pauline Kolenda, who has worked in Kanya Kumari district in southern most Tamilnadu, informs that there has definitely come a change in the caste and not in the caste system. Kolenda differentiates in caste and caste system; by caste is meant an individual caste and by caste system is meant a hierarchy of relations. Kolenda's argument is that there is social mobility within a caste but not mobility in the caste system. What she argues is that the upper castes wield much power at the village level. In Rajasthan also, though there is abolition of system of *jagirdari*, the former *jagirdars* even now own large patches of land.

Andre Beteille[19] makes similar observations regarding the landownership in Tanjore district of south India. His thrust of argument is that there is a growing dissociation between caste and landownership. In Tanjore, there are many villages described as *agraharams.* These villages were dominated by communities of landowning Brahmins. These communities lived in a separate part of the village, enjoyed the privileges of both caste and landownership and constituted the traditional village elite. Many of the Brahmins have left the village and sold their land to non-Brahmin tenants. These new owners of land are not necessarily Brahmins but are upper caste Hindus. Thus, despite changes in the rural caste system, so far tenancy is concerned, the upper castes have hegemony over the lower castes.

(8) *Shift in the Sources of Power*

An interesting change is observed in the village caste system. In the past, the status of a person was overwhelmingly determined by the size of land owned by him. Generally, the idiom was: larger the size of land owned by a person, higher was his status. Today new sources of status in the village have emerged. These statuses have their origin in the possession of positions of power. A position in Gram Panchayat, Assembly or Parliament also gives status to a man. Likewise, the status gained by holding a position in the government service also gives some prestige and power. Thus, the power structure associated with different castes has undergone major changes. The members of scheduled caste, scheduled tribes and other backward classes, though have lesser portions of land, occupy higher status.

Andre Beteille has data from Tanjore to substantiate this observation:

> With the introduction of adult franchise and of village councils, landownership and traditional status have ceased to be the only bases of power in the village. The strength of organised members has now become more important than it ever was.[20]

(9) *New Horizons of Caste*

Before the introduction of modernisation the boundaries of caste were limited only to the village or at the most a cluster of villages. Kinship ties were coterminous to the caste. But with the administrative and regional affiliations the caste and kin have got wider networks spread over to the state or a region. Commenting on the extending borders of kinship ties Andre Beteille says that contemporary changes provide the basis for vertical unity in India on the basis of caste. Kinship, on the other hand, provides horizontal links between people living in different villages. Kinship ties in the rural India are numerous and kinship obligations cover a wide range of social activities.

(10) *Extended Patronage*

Status of a caste in the village remained limited to the village itself. But this has experienced change. Now when employment opportunities are available to all the segments of society, naturally the administrative system is highly selective in terms of caste and community at every level, and at lower levels also in terms of kinship and personal dependence. In the beginning the administrative positions were virtually a monopoly of the upper castes, particularly the Brahmins but as Beteille observes, "with the politicisation of the countryside, members of numerically dominant castes are being recruited everywhere. Getting a person a job in an office as clerk, accountant or secretary has developed as an important ingredient of patronage". Beteille has an argument for such an observation. When the selection and promotion of officials is dependent on patronage, it is unreal to expect that their activities will be governed wholly by impersonal rules. Internal relations within the office also represent a variety of compromises between bureaucracy and paternalism.

Scheduled Castes, Scheduled Tribes and Other Backward Classes in the Changing Rural Caste Stratification

A major change that has come in village caste stratification is through the protective and development safeguards given by the Constitution of India to the weaker sections, namely, scheduled castes/tribes and other backward classes. The amended Panchayati Raj Act has further empowered the weaker sections including the women. All these measures have brought substantial changes in the caste structure.

A.R. Kamat[21] informs that education has brought changes within the segments of scheduled castes and scheduled tribes and this has also redefined the relationship between the weaker sections and the caste Hindus. Education, in fact, has brought out an alarming message to the lower castes that the higher castes have no divine power to rule over them or subordinate them. Quite similar to the Kamat's study is the study of Ghanshyam Shah[22] who informs that tribal society has now understood the legends created by the higher castes. There are studies which also bring out the fact that the tribals who have converted to Christianity and have come within the fold of ethnic reform movements are challenging some of the atrocities done by the high castes. Added to it is the political awakening which has mobilized the weaker sections of the society to create a kind of caste war between the backwards and the progressives. The case of Bihar is an interesting example of caste war.

K.L. Sharma[23] on the strength of empirical data has brought out certain structural changes in village caste structure resulting from the mobilisation of weaker sections. He observes:

> The scheduled castes are changing though the process of change is complex, multi-layered and multi-dimensional creating new status distinctions. Initially the lower castes imitated the higher castes in non-economic spheres of social life. Following a considerable degree of socio-political awareness they refused to follow the dictates of their patrons and demanded freedom from the cruel control of the upper caste/class by the scheduled castes symbolise their aspirations for higher status as well as desire to overthrow the existing system.

Yogendra Singh has a strong argument to analyse the change which has come from caste stratification. He suggests that the empowerment of weaker sections in rural society is largely subjective. It means that the weaker sections have got a subjective understanding that they can do anything in the society. A large part of legislation including the constitutional provisions is in its favour. But, Yogendra Singh further examines the changing stratification of caste society and says that in objective terms the benefits of the members of weaker sections are meagre only. K.L. Sharma thinks likewise when he says that "a redistribution of land and power has not taken place (among the weaker sections), but considerable change has occurred in the traditional arrangements of society". To substantiate his position Sharma says that sharecroppers and agricultural labourers of yesteryears have become, after independence, high, middle and low peasants without correspondingly sanskritising their cultural modes of living as a pre-requisite to this basic economic transformations.

It must be admitted that in a limited sense the status of scheduled castes and scheduled tribes has undergone change. Their lifestyle has changed, cultural patterns have gone up and some education has been attained. Leela Gulati reports that "in-migration, out-migration and income from any other source including employment in the Middle East would affect family including marital status, dowry, family networks, living standards, etc."

Despite enough empirical research evidence, it can be said that much remains to be done in the years to come in the field of caste stratification at the village level. It may also be said that at the urban level caste inequalities have much been minimised compared to rural caste inequalities.

Rural Class System: The Changing Patterns

In the preceding pages we have discussed caste and its changing aspects in rural India. Our observations are substantiated by empirical researches done by sociologists and anthropologists. In the following pages we shall discuss the rural class system in Indian society.

There is much controversy at conceptual level on the structures of caste and class. It is argued by some social scientists that caste and class are not polar opposites. There is a continuum between the two. Yet another argument often given is that there is a class in a caste. The Brahmin is a caste, but there are classes of Brahmins—poor and rich—in the Brahmin caste. Recently, a new controversy is raised by Dipankar Gupta, K.L. Sharma and other sociologists.

We do not want to elaborate this controversy but would only say that despite differences in the comprehension of caste and class the fact remains that the Indian society shall have to face for some time to come, social problems relating the caste system. Dipankar Gupta, while raising the controversy between caste and class, puts these two strata of society in the field of culture and Marxism. If we look at caste as an aspect of culture, it is a primordial form of Indian society and is a part of India's rural-urban stratification. From the point of view of

Marxism it is a mode of production. Louis Dumont is the chief architect of the caste as a form of culture. We, however, do not want to enter into this controversy of caste as a form of culture or a mode of production. We only wish to argue that class is not essentially an urban phenomenon, nor the caste is restricted to rural society. Both caste and class as forms of stratification are found in rural society.

Changing Class System in Rural Society

Whenever social scientists and political and social workers including the agricultural workers discuss about rural class system, a question is raised: Is a transition taking place in the rural social structure of India from caste to class? In other words, the basic point of enquiry today is to find out whether caste is changing and taking the form of a class. The question is important. It has taken a form of debate in rural sociology.

On one side of the debate is Andre Beteille who has argued in his article on 'Class Structure in an Agrarian Society' says that the Jotedars of West Bengal, as an agricultural caste, are moving towards the formation of a class. But the change from caste to class is amorphous. By amorphousness Beteille means that the form of class which is emerging among the Jotedars is not of any definite shape or structure of a class. The movement from caste to class is not clear; it is much doubtful. Beteille observes:

> It is frequently argued that in countries like India, the older system of inequalities based on caste is being replaced by a class system not only in the cities but also in the rural areas. If caste stands for a system of inequality in which groups are sharply differentiated and at the same time organically related, then clearly there is evidence of the decline of caste. If, on the other hand, class stands for a system of antagonistic groups based on the polarisation of consciously organised interests, there is no general evidence that this kind of structure is emerging throughout the country: the predominant impression is one of amorphousness rather than structure.[24]

In the above statement Beteille is quite clear when he makes his observation. First, if caste is defined as a form of structural inequality then it has died. Second, if the meaning of class is taken as an antagonistic group then it is not taking a definite shape of a class in village India. Beteille, thus, is very clear that caste is declining in India's villages; he is also certain that class is replacing caste but the form of class which is emerging has not taken a proper shape of class, if we define it correctly.

On the other side of the debate is Pauline Kolenda[25] who has taken a position that village/caste system is changing to village class system. To substantiate her position Kolenda refers to her study of fire hamlets in Kanya Kumari district of Tamilnadu. She deals with four questions: (1) What are the trends of land transfer? (2) What are the factors contributing to these changes? (3) What is the impact of these land transfers on social structure? (4) How to conceptualise these changes?

The data generated by Kolenda reveal that there are a variety of ways through which people lose their land. Some lose it by investing in business that failed. Such castes sold their land to pay the debt. Land is also lost for contesting elections. Some had to dispose of their land to pay for household expenses. Kolenda notes that "Brahmins and Vellalas have been the main losers of land while Thevars, Kallars and Nadars have become the new landowners. Given the stagnant nature of the economy—there has been no green revolution in the area—the rural folk spend their money in the town on education, cinema, medical care and bus travel. The urban folk invest their money in village land. Thus, the earnings of countrymen enrich townsmen who then buy up the land".

Kolenda's findings of Kanya Kumari district very clearly explain that in rural India the caste as a system does not operate. Its place has been taken by class. Kolenda says:

> In neither rural nor urban areas does the old self-sufficient caste system operate, but castes persist as residential locations and as organized communities in the rural area.

Kolenda, in categorical words, observes that in rural India middle class is definitely emerging in place of caste system. The existence of caste is only observable in the habitation pattern of the villages. So far as the agricultural operations are concerned the caste has decayed in rural society.

Kolenda's position in the debate on caste to class is very clear. She says that caste is replaced by class. And the class which is emerging is not a rich class, but a middle class. She further states that the village class system does not enrich a man to become a rich class because there are opportunities outside the village to amass money. She observes:

> Success, in other words, takes place very largely outside of the villages; sons who manage to get jobs at salaries which provide some surplus by land. In the Kanya Kumari area, it is professionals, especially medical doctors and others who have done well in business in town, who are buying land. Whether they will become commercial farmers is yet to be seen...We thus, have the picture of a society which continues to operate in terms of caste communities if not in terms of a caste system in the rural areas, and which operates increasingly in terms of middle-classmen with modern occupations in towns and cities.

In the preceding section we have discussed the caste. Class controversy as is going on in social sciences. The replacement of caste by the form of class in rural India seems to be a certainty. The question now is: What factors are responsible for the transformation of caste into class in rural India?

Factors of Transformation of Caste into Class in Rural Society

(1) *Government policy*

Jan Breman who has experience of working in Bardoli *taluka* of Surat district informs that it has always been the policy of government to pauperise the agricultural labour. The green revolution, white revolution, irrigation and electric supply have gone mostly in favour of the big farmers. In fact, the benefits of development programmes have been largely cornered by the big landowners. It is due to the government policy that agricultural capitalism has come to stay in Gujarat. Not only that Breman goes to the extent of saying that the nationalist movement before independence and the heading political parties have also promoted agricultural capitalism. He observes:

> The advance of a capitalist mode of agricultural production has in essence been pushed through by a class of large and middle farmers, originating from intermediate castes who have gradually gained dominance in recent decades, with the support of the nationalist movement before the coming of independence, and of the coalitions

of leading parties since then. The working classes have derived much less profit from the extension of employment which has accompanied this transformation.

Pauline Kolenda and Jan Breman both agree that in the southern and western parts of India the intermediate castes have become middle classes. And, in this process of social formation, the rural castes are changing into middle class. this kind of social formation is mainly due to the role of state and the policy of rural development. In fact, the government intervention in the rural society has been in favour of principal landowners.

(2) *Correlation between caste and class*

Rural caste and class have been analysed from both Weberian and Marxian perspectives. But if one tries to apply only Marxian perspective to understand the class structure, he cannot do so successfully. Caste and class are a mixed phenomenon in India's rural society. Gail Omvedt[26] argues that there are feudal forces in caste and as a result of it the former landlords, *jamindars* and *jagirdars* have come out as capitalist peasants. It means that the former higher castes have become today higher classes. Where Breman and Kolenda observe that intermediate classes have become classes, Omvedt comes to the conclusion that former higher castes have become higher classes. Despite this difference in findings which is of degree, the fact remains that rural castes are definitely transforming into classes. Another difference is that Omvedt considers caste as a feudal organisation and its change into class is capitalistic.

(3) *Dominant castes replaced*

It was in sixties that M.N. Srinivas gave the concept of dominant caste. But, it has lost much of its relevance today. The big landowners who have migrated to urban and industrial communities, have taken to new sources of income or have been deprived of land due to ceiling legislations. Their dominance in the village has been weakened by several forces. K.L. Sharma presents a new set of data to contest the influence of dominant caste in rural society. He says that the power wielded by the former elites such a *jamindars* and *jagirdars* has decayed because of the abolition of feudal system. On the other hand, members of the weaker sections have got new power from democratic institutions. The new empowerment of weaker sections has brought these sections in close competition with the former power elites. The empirical reality is that the dominant castes have now been deprived by their traditional power of ruling over the village or maintaining the ongoing of the rural system. The dominant castes thus are replaced by new power elites.

K.L. Sharma very emphatically explains the decay of dominant caste in rural society. He writes:

> The idea of 'dominant caste' or group dominance is based on certain assumptions, and since these are not found valid, group dominance tends to be a myth rather than a reality. The new power welders are not the same as they were in the past, however, qualitative difference between the old and the new power elites has been much. The basic difference between the two lies in the fact that rank of a 'group' as a determinant of elite position has withered away. Today, elites are an aggregation and not an active functioning primordial group as the members lack group homogeneity, equality or status and rank, and equal distribution of power and prestige.[27]

(4) *Caste, land and politics make class*

Caste is not only a system of hierarchy; it is also related to land and politics. Viewed from this perspective, the idea of a class is also inherent in a class. Land involves an interaction between the landowner and the actual cultivator. The power is also inherent to the caste. In the changing scene, therefore, when we analyse caste, we must take into consideration the relationship of caste hierarchy, the notion of purity and pollution in relation to land owned by a particular caste and its power structure.

When the land and power undergo change, resultantly the caste structure also witnesses certain changes and these changes relate to class. In the contemporary politics of competing demands of each caste group, naturally the caste assumes the role of a class. Thus, political and economic considerations turn a caste into a class. K.L. Sharma very rightly observes:

> Thus, both caste and class are resources for gaining access to political power. Once political power is gained, it proves to be a further re-

source for the consolidation and improvement of status and class positions. This is how the relationship between land, caste and politics is found in Indian villages today.[28]

When a caste becomes a class, the class conflict which emerges is basically caste war. In Bihar, for instance, the class war that we find between the big landowners and the agricultural labourers is basically and inherently a caste war. Francine Frankel[29] and Zoya Hasan[30] strike criticism of this kind of conflict in Bihar and Uttar Pradesh respectively. In these states "the middle peasants in particular lured the marginal farmers and agricultural labourers on their side preventing them to act on class lines by arousing caste loyalty as most of them belonged to the castes of the middle peasants."

Yet another example of caste becoming a strong class system is that of Karnataka and Tamilnadu. In both these states the caste has been a strong factor of cohesive divisions in society. But the political mobilisations have made the rural society highly class-oriented. There have emerged village factions based on class consideration. This has been referred by D.A. Washbrook[31] in Tamilnadu and James Manor[32] in Karnataka. In the case of Kerala it is found that there has been enough mobilisation in power politics in terms of caste and class. In fact, despite a lack of uniformity in the pattern of caste, class and dominance in the south Indian states, it is different from the north Indian socio-political system obviously due to historical and structural reasons.[33]

In the state of Rajasthan there has been a caste dynamics which has taken the form of a class conflict. The Rajputs have an alliance with the Banias and Jains and have pushed back the Brahmins to a state of oblivion. This has been reported by Iqbal Narain and P.C. Mathur.[34] Ghanshyam Shah[35] also finds similar situation in Gujarat.

(5) *Capitalist mode of production: Turned caste into class*

Admittedly, the agricultural production in rural India has increased tremendously during the last fifty years. Green revolution has come. Green revolution means use of chemical fertilisers and high yielding varieties in farm production. Actually, green revolution coupled with the introduction of new technology have revolutionised the mode of production in agriculture. Advanced technology, new yielding varieties and chemical manure can be fruitfully employed by only big farmers who have capacity to invest in agricultural production. This innovation in agriculture has changed the total mode of production resulting in the emergence of capitalism in agriculture. This form of capitalism has changed the rural caste system into rural class system. Analysing the shift from caste to class in agrarian society, K.L. Sharma very rightly observes:

> The capitalistic mode of production in agriculture has not only polarised the rural class structure further in terms of the rich and the poor, the dominant and the weak, the upper and the lower segments of society, their relationship with the state is also being redefined in favour of the beneficiaries of the state's policies and programme.[36]

(6) *Some new emerging agricultural classes in rural India*

We have argued in the preceding pages about the social formations which have transformed the caste into class. Such a process has been enquired into by a large number of rural sociologists and sociologists. Notwithstanding this, some of the social scientists who have worked exclusively on agricultural classes have brought out a new classification of agricultural castes. These classes do not interview in the caste structure of rural society. The castes work independently in the villages. In the field of agricultural production or in peasantry as a whole there are some classes. These classes are agricultural classes. In other words, landholdings have never been even in rural India. Differences in the size of land have created diverse agricultural classes in rural society. A broad classification of agricultural classes is given below: (1) big farmers, (2) small farmers, (3) marginal farmers, and (4) landless labourers. But such a kind of classification of peasants in terms of class categories does not imply that the institution of caste is transforming into class. Caste-class transformation is different from the classes of peasantry in general. We have mentioned it here because the classes in peasantry in one way or the other also affect the functioning of caste-class formation.

Caste-Class Nexus

In the olden days of school life there used to be debates on country versus town, heredity versus environment, and recently there is controversy on caste versus class. Such debates do not lead us to any understanding of the social phenomena under discussion. There is nothing monolith in social sciences. There are several dimensions of a social theme or a social issue. In this respect it may be said in definite terms that in no period of history caste has been only cultural or structural. It involves power and economy. In hierarchical terms a Brahmin has always enjoyed top rank in the caste hierarchy; but there have been Brahmins who have lived a life of a proletariat. Similarly, there have been Jats who have been in the status of backward caste but there were always some Jats who were rulers and top at the class hierarchy. Thus, historically, it would be true to say that caste includes the attributes of a class also, that is, power and economic status. There has been a historicity of the nexus between class, caste and power in varied forms and contexts. The rural sociologists who try to analyse caste and class as forms of stratification in rural India argue that there is a close nexus in caste-class power. Now caste, class and power are not differentiated in any scheme of stratification. As a matter of fact, caste, class and power are the three inseparable dimensions of stratification. When we talk about nexus we only mean to say that there is a close link between the three—caste, class and power. It would, therefore, be erroneous to analyse the caste in terms of its continuum with class. It would also be wrong that castes are changing to class. It would be better to say that the rural social stratification is changing. It would mean that the caste and the class which is inherent in it, is also changing.

Notes

1. Ramakrishna Mukerjee, *The Dynamics of Rural Society,* Academic Verlag,1957.
2. P.K. Bose, "Dimensions of Agrarian Structure and Change: Issues in Theory", *Sociological Bulletin,* Vol. XIX, No. 40, 1989.
3. K.L. Sharma, *Social Stratification in India: Issues and Themes,* Sage Publications, New Delhi, 1997, p.59.
4. Yogendra Singh, *Social Stratification and Change in India*, Manohar, New Delhi, 1977, p.6.
5. S.C. Dube, *India's Changing Villages,* Routledge and Kegan Paul, London, 1958.

6. M.N. Srinivas, "The Dominant Caste in Rampura", *American Anthropologists*, 1-11, 1950.
7. A.R. Desai, *Rural Sociology in India*, Popular Prakashan, Bombay, 1961, p. 38.
8. S.M. Shah, "Rural Class Structure in Gujarat," in A.R. Desai, *Rural Sociology in India*, ibid., p. 287.
9. S.S. Nehru, *Caste and Credit in Rural India.*
10. K.L. Sharma, *Social Stratification in India: Issues and Themes*, op.cit., p. 160.
11. M.N. Srinivas, *Social Change in Modern India*, California, 1966.
12. Yogendra Singh, *Modernisation of Indian Tradition*, Rawat Publications, Jaipur, 1994.
13. M.N. Srinivas, *Religion and Society among the Coorgs of South India*, Oxford University Press, London, 1952.
14. K.L. Sharma, *Rural Society in India*, Rawat Publications, Jaipur, 1997, p. 183.
15. K.L. Sharma, "Occupational Mobility and Class Structure", *Man in India*, Vol. 48, No. 2, April-June, 1968, pp. 106-144.
16. V.S. Naipaul, *India: A Million Mutinies Now*, Rupa & Company, Calcutta, 1990.
17. I.P. Desai, "Anti-reservation agitation and structure of Gujarat society", *Economic and Political Weekly*, Vol. XVI, No. 18, 1981, pp. 819-23.
18. Jan Breman, op. cit.
19. Andre Beteille, *Studies in Agrarian Social Structure*, Oxford University Press, Delhi, 1983.
20. Ibid., p. 74.
21. A.R. Kamat, 'Politico-economic development in Maharashtra: A review of the post-independence period", *Economic and Political Weekly*, Vol. XV, No. 39, pp. 1627-30 and No. 40, pp. 1669-75.
22. Ghanshyam Shah, "Caste, Class and Reservation", *Economic and Political Weekly*, Vol. XX, No. 3, pp. 132-36.
23. K.L. Sharma, *Social Stratification in India: Issues and Themes*, op.cit.
24. Andre Beteille, *Studies in Agrarian Social Structure*, op. cit., p. 110.
25. Pauline Kolenda,"Foxes, Lions and Bears: The Circulation of Landownership in Southern Most Tamil Nadu", in A.M. Shah et al.(eds.),

Social Structure and Change, Vol. 4, Sage Publications, New Delhi, 1997, pp. 27-49.

26. Gail Omvedt, "Capitalist Agriculture and Rural Classes in India", *Economic and Political Weekly*, Vol. XXIII, No. 27, pp. 1394-96.
27. K.L. Sharma, *Rural Society in India*, Rawat Publications, Jaipur, 1997.
28. K.L. Sharma, *Social Stratification in India*, op. cit., p. 209.
29. Francine Frankel and M.S.A. Rao, *Dominance and State Power in Modern India: Decline of a Social Order*, Vols. I and II, Oxford University Press, New Delhi, 1989.
30. Zoya Hasan,"Power and Mobilisation: Patterns of Resilience and Change in Uttar Pradesh Politics", in F.R. Frankel, and M.S.A. Rao (eds.), ibid., pp. 133-203.
31. D.A. Washbrook, "Caste, Class and Dominance in Modern Tamilnadu", in Frankel and Rao, ibid.
32. James Manor, "Karnataka: Caste, Class, Dominance and Politics in a Cohesive Society", in Frankel and Rao, ibid.
33. K.C. Alexander, "Caste Mobilisation and Class Consciousness: The Emergence of Agrarian Movements in Kerala and Tamilnadu", in Frankel and Rao, ibid.
34. Iqbal Narain and P.C. Mathur, "The Thousand Year *Raj:* Regional Isolation and Rajput Hinduism in Rajasthan Before and After 1947", in Frankel and Rao, ibid.
35. Ghanshyam Shah, "Caste Sentiments, Class Formation and Dominance in Gujarat", in Frankel and Rao, ibid.
36. K.L. Sharma, *Social Stratification in India*, op. cit., p. 203.

9 Rural Social Institutions

Family, Kinship, Marriage and Religion

Institution is a basic concept of sociology. It consists of various aspects of society which do not change immediately. The change is there, but it is very slow. Family, marriage, divorce, kin, religion and economy are some of the major domains of society. J.H. Fitcher has defined an institution as "a relatively permanent structure of social patterns of roles and relations that people enact in certain sanctioned and unified ways for the purpose of satisfying basic social needs."[1] Actually, social structure of a society has certain roles which regularise interactions among the members of the society. These roles and relations continue for longer span of life. These are called institutions. Men have come and gone but the family continuous. And, therefore, family is an institution. There is need of procreation for the society and, therefore, the institution of marriage keeps itself continuous. Whatever may be the type of society, it has the institutions of family and marriage. The basic aspect of institution is the system of social relationships. P.B. Horton defines an institution as given below:

> An institution is an organised system of social relationships which embodies certain common values and procedures and meets certain basic needs of society.[2]

Horton quite like Fitcher makes it clear that the society has certain patterns of relationships which stem from status and role. These patterns of relationships fulfil the needs of the society. The needs of the society, on the other hand, vary from the nature and type of a society. The needs of rural society are different in nature than that of the urban society. And, therefore, the rural social institutions are different from the institutions of the urban society.

There is a controversy on this account. Long back in the irregular journal, *Contributions to Indian Sociology*, Pocock observed that rural and urban communities cannot be differentiated because they belong to the same civilisation, i.e., Indian civilisation. Following Pocock the institutions of marriage and family in rural life are in no way different from the urban community. Such an argument has been contested by anthropologists. It is said that the nature of needs of the rural community are different from the urban community. And, therefore, the rural institutions like family, marriage, kin and religion have to be studied from the perspectives of rural life.

Social Framework of Village Community

It is not recent that rural sociologists dwell on the study of rural institutions. The history of the study of rural institutions goes back to the 18th century when British officials-turned anthropologists studied village communities from the point of view of institutions. The initial interest shown by these writers was inspired by the spirit of official inquiry. Munro, Metcalfe, Maine and Badan-Powell studied the village communities in a systematic way. *They emphasised on the landowning caste.* The British got revenue from the agriculturists and, therefore, it was essential for them to enquire about the agricultural caste. According to the official view, the village was a closed and isolated system. However, the foremost village institution identified by the British officials was the caste system. The common understanding which developed among these writers was that Indian village was static and isolated because of its caste institutions.

Later on, when village studies became very popular in the middle of fifties, a number of other village institutions were studied by sociologists and anthropologists. M.N. Srinivas[3] stressed on the study of caste but he also emphasised the need of the study of religion. Among the Coorgs of south India he found the role of religion quite interesting. A.C. Mayer[4] for the first time studied the institution of kinship in a systematic way and analysed the role of caste and kin in the functioning of rural society. His research work revolved round the towns of central India, that is, Devas of Madhya Pradesh. Marriage, perhaps, is a very important village institution which governs the life of the people. The rules of exogamy and endogamy regulate the relations between the clusters of villages. The village exogamy determines the exchange relations between clusters of villages. The institution of marriage among the village communities has been studied both historically and empirically by K.M. Kapadia.[5]

Perhaps, the most important village institution is that of family. In the fifties, the family life of the village communities has been a part of several village studies. The edited works of Mckim Marriott and M.N. Srinivas[6] include elaborate research articles on village family and marriage. S.C. Dube's *Indian Village*[7] and D.N. Majumdar's *Rural Profiles*[8] carry interesting research documents on several important institutions pertaining to rural life.

All we want to stress is that the social institutions of village communities have been studied systematically right from the 18th century. The flood of village studies which came to India in the middle of fifties took seriously the study of the village institutions. Several of the concepts which have a prime importance in sociology and rural sociology have their origin in the village studies conducted in fifties. The argument is that the Indian village cannot be studied properly without reference to the social frameworks of institutions in rural society.

Rural Institutions and Their Types

It has been a trend in the study of rural institutions to describe family, marriage and kin which are found all over the country notwithstanding rural and urban communities. Admittedly, the institution of family which is found in rural India is different than that of found in urban India. What is necessary is that we describe the rural communities. For instance, the family in a village has a great importance. If a member of the family is defaulter in paying his loan instalments in a cooperative bank, it brings great defamation to the whole family. It is really very difficult for an individual to isolate himself from the family. The place of individualism is marginal in the village. It is this perspective that differentiates the village institutions from the urban institutions.

The bulk of research material that we have very clearly shows that there are few social institutions, such as ecology, family, kinship, marriage and religion, which are found in common in all the villages in our country. Before we discuss some of these rural institutions, we must mention it that besides these institutions, caste, economy and politics are other institutions which need elaborate explanation. We have discussed the structure and role of caste in the previous chapter and also propose to deal with economy and politics elsewhere. What is important here is that we shall keep ourselves restricted to the discussion of rural ecology, marriage, family and religion.

Ecology

Ecology is concerned with the habitat and environment in relation to living organisms. The human settlement thus is determined by its ecology. The rural ecology is substantially different from urban ecology. Agriculture is the major source of income and employment for the rural people. It decides the village pattern, housing design and other such things related to human beings. For instance, the tribals in India construct their houses in a scattered pattern. They keep their fields in the neighbourhood of their houses. On the other hand, in the plains, the villages are compact and the fields are quite away from the habitation. It is in this respect that ecology assumes the status of an institution in village India.

Irawati Karve[9] has discussed at length the institutional aspect of ecology in Maharashtra villages. She finds three types of villages in Maharashtra. The first type of village is highly nucleated with the habitation area clearly defined from the cultivated fields. These villages are situated on high plateau of the Deccan. "In such villages, while the habitation area is well marked, the boundaries of the village together with its fields are never perceived. The fields owned by one village merge into those owned by another except where a hillock or stream or a highway forms the boundary." This type of village settlement is largely determined by the ecology of the plateau.

The second type of village is found in the western coastline of Maharashtra. In this type of village the houses are constructed length-wise on both the sides of a road. These houses stand in their own compounds with their fruit and coconut gardens. These houses are fenced on all sides. In such villages land is cultivated in two ways: (1) horticulture, and (2) agriculture. Horticulture consists of coconut and arecanut palms and plantation, jackfruit and cashewnuts. The agriculture is done a little away from the houses. Though in some areas they come right to the steps of the houses. In such villages, there is no sharp distinction between the habitation area and the cultivated area.

Towards the north-western boundary of the Marathi-speaking region are found the third type of villages. The ecology of this region is constructed by Satpura mountains. There are valleys in between the mountains and the villages are found within the valleys. In this type of villages the fields are found in clusters of two or three huts, all belonging to a single close kinship group. They are either the huts of a father and grown-up sons or brothers and their wives. Sometimes a woman and her husband may have a hut in the same cluster as that of the father and brothers of the woman. The next cluster of huts may be as far as a furlong or two away depending on how big the holding of each cluster is. Generally, in such villages, the boundaries of the village are not clearly defined.

Each ecology of a region has its own village settlement pattern. For instance, houses in the hilly region such as Uttarakhand of Uttar Pradesh, the whole region of Himachal Pradesh and the region of Aravalli ranges determine the pattern of village settlement. It is the ecology of the region which makes the houses compact, scattered or row-wise. The road system and the river system are also shaped by the ecology.

Family

In sociology and anthropology there is no dearth of literature on family. Much has been written on Indian joint family and its changing aspects. The village studies that characterise the decade of fifties carry enough literature on village family. However, no serious attempt has been made to precisely bring out the specificities of rural family. It is not sufficient to say that family is a universal institution. It emphasises relationship between members and guides their behaviour. Writing on Indian family, much emphasis has been put on procreation of children and upbringing them. Rural sociology has certain obligations to bring out the characteristics which are found in the rural family. A.R. Desai has made some attempts to characterise the rural family. In the pages that follow we shall try to bring out some of the major attributes of Indian rural family.

Before we bring out some basic features of rural family we would mention that the portrait of rural family has perhaps been better drawn by writers of Hindi literature in their poems-cum-stories and novels. Prem Chand, the noted Hindi story writer and novelist, has very ably described the character of family found among the Indian peasants. Some of his stories such as 'Panch Parmeshwar', 'Bare Ghar ki Beti' and 'Poosh ki Rat' very characteristically carry the structure of rural family. The Gujarati writer, again a novelist, Panna Lal Joshi has also described the life in rural Gujarat family in his novels.

I.P. Desai who is an authority on family, makes a categorical statement when he says that family in India means joint family. In other words, whatever we may say about rural family, the fact of the matter is that rural family in Desai's paraphrase is a joint family.[10]

We give below some of the major characteristics of rural family in India:

(i) *Clan domination*

Anthropologists who have studied Indian villages argue that Indian family is clan dominated. The nomads such as *Kalbelia* and *Gadulia Lohar* have their families which function around clan ties. The food gatherers and pastorals such as the *Bhotia* and *Rebari* have their families based on clan ties. Irawati Karve wrote authoritatively about the origin of caste and in her conclusion she argues that caste is an extension of kin and clan. The rural family in the present period of history is divided but its essential ties originate from clan relations.

(ii) *Subsistence based family*

Another form of family found in parts of India has subsistence as its base. These families are found among hunters and 'hoe' agriculturists. There are some tribal groups which even today primitive and earn their livelihood by shifting cultivation or 'hoe' agriculture. The Government of India has classified the tribals into (a) primitive tribes, and (b) scheduled tribes. The primitive tribes are at the lowest rung of development, e.g., Saheria in Rajasthan.

(iii) *Agriculture based family*

A.R. Desai considers this family to be the contemporary rural family found more or less all over the country. Such a kind of family links agriculture with the domestication of animals. Generally, the agricultural family is also a pastoral family. It means that rural family has some cattle wealth as secondary source of income, agriculture being the primary. It is the cherished desire of a peasant to have a cow so that bullocks could be used in agriculture.

(iv) *Patriarchal and matriarchal families*

It would be erroneous to think that the rural family is essentially a patriarchal family. Irawati Karve made a penetrating survey of the kinship status found in different zones of India. She informs that in parts of Kerala and Tamilnadu there are castes which practise matriarchal system of family. These families are matrilocal also. The structure of matriarchal or matrilocal family is substantially different from patriarchal rural family. Obviously, the head of the matriarchal family is female and whatever land belongs to the family is in the name of the female head. It is tragic that whenever we think of India, we generalise on north India. The fact of the matter is that Indian social reality is of a composite nature and, therefore, we should take into consideration the diversities of the whole country. In the matriarchal family the status of mother occupies a prime position.

In the patriarchal family which is found generally in north and north-eastern parts of the country has the domination of male. The patriarchal family is also patrilocal. In this kind of family the land is owned by the male head. It is he who decides and officiates at the division of the family. At this stage it should be clearly mentioned that both the matriarchal and patriarchal families could be joint and nuclear.

(v) *Closer degree of relations*

Before the decade of sixties, there was a general understanding that joint family is one which has a (1) common roof, (2) a common kitchen, (3) a common purse (including property), (4) a common religion or object of worship, and (5) a generation depth. These characteristics of a joint family were given by Irawati Karve. At a later stage K.M. Kapadia and others made certain changes in these characteristics of joint family. But, the work of I.P. Desai seems to be a watershed in the field of family studies. Desai argues that the basic character of a family and for that matter rural family, is the degree of relationship which the members of family enjoy.

Desai conducted his research on family in the town of Mahua in Bhavnagar district of Gujarat. He observes that in a town like Mahua the family is knit together by intimate relations. It is this relationship which is the prime characteristic of a rural family. In the urban family, on the contrary, the relationships are not so intimate. Most of the time by both working males and females is spent in offices. It is said that those who work in metropolitan cities leave their house when their children are asleep and come back when they have gone to bed. In the rural family the members work in the field and while working there they never miss any opportunity to have intimate contacts.

Besides closer degree of relations, the members of the rural family share a common ideology. When it is said that there is mass voting in rural areas, it carries the idea that many of the family members share the same ideology and hence mass voting. As a matter of fact, in a rural family, individualism is subordinate to the will of the family head. It is because of this that sometimes a village is defined as a cluster of joint families.

(vi) *Common lifestyle*

All the activities of the members of rural family revolve round agricultural operations. The sowing is followed by weeding. When the crops stand in the field, there is time to keep watch and ward. Finally, there comes time for harvesting. And, what is more, some one has to carry the cattle to the grazing ground. All these activities are related to agriculture. It provides a lifestyle which is common to all the members of the family. Because of the common occupation people have a common way of life. During harvesting time, for instance, no family member can spare time to relax.

(vii) *Health hazards*

There is social medicine also. By social medicine we mean that illness which results from social causes. Because of the similarity of occupation, the rural family members suffer from common diseases. The housing conditions of the village are such that soon after the rains malaria, diarrhoea and other water-borne diseases take an epidemic form. There being meagre availability of medical facilities, many of the rural families suffer from seasonal diseases. Thus, the health hazards with which the rural family suffer are relatively lesser in the urban families.

(viii) *Household division of labour*

There is no specialisation so far the rural family members are concerned in the field of agricultural operations. In practice all the work of the rural household is distributed among members. Writing about the family division of labour A.R. Desai observes:

> Work is distributed among them mainly on the lines of age and sex distinctions. The community house, common land and common economic functions along with the common kinship bond create the peasants household. ... Since the members of the rural family form a single economic unit and constantly cooperate with one another in agricultural operations, since they hold property in common usually managed by the eldest member of the family, since also they spend most of their time together, the psychological traits they develop are very similar.

(ix) *Power of the head of family*

Sometimes it is said that the head of the rural family exercises authoritarian power over the family members. Since the rural family is more integrated and disciplined unit than the urban family, the head of the rural family wields almost absolute power over its members. It is he who distributes the work of the peasant household among the family members on lines of sex and age differences, arranges marriages of sons, daughters, nephews and nieces, administers the joint family property according to his wisdom, and trains the youngsters for future agricultural work and social life. All initiatives and final authority are vested in him. In fact, the head of the family has had the rights and authority to be the ruler, the priest, the teacher, the educator and the manager of the family.

The head of the rural family also subordinates individual members to himself. The members on their part are completely submerged in the family, hence they hardly develop any individuality or personality.

(x) *Family tensions*

It should not be assumed that a rural family does not encounter any stress or strain. There are occasions when the elder son creates problems for the head, particularly at the time of separation. It is common to find violence in a rural family when the land is distributed at the time of separation. All the sons aspire to get the best of the land—irrigated and fertile—in their share. A little lack of wisdom results in bloodshed.

Rural family is thus has its own specificity. But the changes in the rural society have also resulted in the change of rural family. Modernisation, along with urbanisation and industrialisation, has affected the rural family structure. Because of burden on the land, rural economy has been diversified. A large number of villagers migrate to the towns and cities and work as industrial labourer. Those who have got some better education have taken to salaried jobs. The reservation given to the weaker sections has also pushed its members to seek employment elsewhere from the village. Technology has outdated the rural handicrafts. All these factors have influenced the structure of rural family.

Sociologists have argued at length about the future of joint family. Actually, there has been a controversy between joint family and nuclear family. Sometimes advantages and disadvantages of both the types of family are discussed. K.M. Kapadia, M.S. Gore, A.M. Shah, I.P. Desai and others have participated in this debate. It cannot be said conclusively that the joint families are breaking down in rural India. The joint family is linked with occupation. So far the village occupations continue to remain as principal occupations of the village people, it appears the joint family has all the chances of survival in our villages. For any length of time the parcelling of land into sub-holdings and sub-holdings cannot continue any larger. It has to be cultivated with some collective spirit of the members of the family.

Kinship

K.M. Kapadia has written extensively on Hindu kinship organisation. The work published by him in 1947 is the oldest one.[11] Actually, through the analysis of Hindu kinship, Kapadia has built the social history of the people of India. His argument is that the kinship organisation is found in its earliest form in villages and among savage people. Quite like Kapadia, C.H. Cooley[12] referring to the kinship system of Europe makes an important statement and says that kinship and society are twinborn. He says that the solidarity of society is largely maintained by the kinsmen. In a village each person is related to another by kinship ties. Mostly, a village is a collection of persons related by blood. Tracing the origin of kinship system in India and the world as a whole Kapadia observes:

> Primitive society is based on kinship. Every person must have a recognised relationship, nearer or more remote, to every other member of the group or he is an alien—an enemy with no rights whatsoever. The ties of blood are primary and hence natural as opposed to other ties with arise in process of evolution.[13]

If we examine the kinship ties found in villages soon we shall realise that even in cases where blood tie seems to be a mere assumption, or where it is evidently untrue, or where community of blood has to be established artificially, people adhere tenaciously to the doctrine of blood kinship. This implies and emphasises the idea that the thought of the kinship is persistently centred around blood. It is very common to come across brothers and sisters in a village who are not the real brother and sister but become brother and sister on the basis of rituals. "She is my ritual sister." Such statements are common in rural society. Adoption is also a form of contracting ritually blood relationship. All such cases emphasise that kinship relations have deeper roots in rural society. It cannot be denied that such relations, whether ritual or actual, do not exist in urban communities, but their significance and importance is lesser and notional only.

It has been a pervading trend in social anthropology to stress on the need of analysing kinship relationship among the tribals and recently among villagers. A.R. Brown has defined the term 'kinship' as below:

> Kinship is genealogical relationship recognised for social purposes and made the basis of the customary relation of social relations.[14]

The roots of kinship relations arise from genealogical ties, that is, family. These genealogical relations have their origin from the family and depend on the family, but the relations created by the family are not all identical. At times, as among Hindus, they arise from ritual relations and not necessarily physiological relations.

R. Briffault contradicts the family origin of kinship relations. He, on the strength of data generated from the tribals, says that the idea of kinship is earlier to the idea of family. It means that kinship appeared first in human society and later on it was followed by family. His evidence runs below:

> Collective clan relationship appears to be more primitive than the family system of relationship, and the terms by which kinship be-

> tween individuals is denoted in primitive society is not an extension of the meaning they bear in regard to the relations between members of a family.[15]

It appears that the origin of the institution of kinship is difficult to trace. Not among the tribals only but in the village societies also kinship is very old. All the males and females of a village are brothers and sisters. Viewed from this perspective, an Indian village is a cluster of kinship ties. These kinship ties are largely blood ties, for a village in India is by and large exogamous. W.H.R. Rivers, who had experience of working among the Todas of India, maintains that the initial situation of kinship is not individual but communal. In other words, the essential unit of a society consists of a wider group such as the clan, the horde, and the undivided commune.

B. Malinowski, on the other hand, does not agree with the proposition of the origin of kinship from the collectivity or community. According to him, kinship does not have its origin from the communal organisation as held by Rivers. His statement is a little different:

> Kinship, in the first place, is the personal bond based upon procreation, socially interpreted, and in the second place, the wider bonds derived from the primary ones by the process of gradual extensions which occur in all communities during the life history of the individual.[16]

It is really difficult to find out whether the origin of kinship is in the individual or the community. In other words, it is very difficult to say that kinship originated from the tribals and the villages. It appears that the original ties of kinship which are invariably individual, later on develop, multiply and become largely communal, so that, at the end, the individual finds himself at the centre of a complex system of multiple ties—a member of several groups. The family is always the extended household, in many communities, the local group, almost invariably, the clan, very often and the tribe without any exception. And, since kinship results from the family and in the family every child has both a father and a mother and is, therefore, connected with both the father's family and the mother's family, it would seem to be the normal thing in any human society that social recognition should be given to both paternal and maternal kinships, that is, relationship from the side of mother and also father. This is called as bilateral relationship in anthropology.

Importance of Kinship in Rural Society

The study of kinship has far reaching implications in sociological and anthropological theory-building. The latest works of Pierre Bourdieu refer to the importance of kinship study in the building of the theory of structuralism. Besides Bourdieu, Levi-Strauss and Evans-Pritchard have constructed their theories on the basis of kinship relations. It is ironical that Indian sociologists and anthropologists have brought up a large number of studies on village, caste and family, but have neglected the role of kinship in India's villages. This has been stressed by T.N. Madan as below:

> It seems to me that there are two basic reasons for the inadequate attention which Indian and foreign anthropologists have paid to the need for empirical field studies of Hindu kinship. The first has been the preoccupation with caste and its place in Hindu society. ... Second, in the study of caste as well as kinship, modern students have had to reckon with a considerable body of Sanskrit literature, its vernacular translation and commentaries. This has also resulted in the neglect of kinship study.

However, Irawati Karve's *Kinship Organisation in India* (1953) is the only general compendium of kinship terminologies and usages covering most of the linguistic-cum-cultural regions of the country. She has devoted all attention to the status of kinship in rural society. Rivers (1914) has studied the kinship system on the basis of the Dravidian kinship terms. Actually, besides the works of Karve and Rivers, in addition to the work of T.N. Madan's *Family and Kinship* (1965) no substantial book-length work on village kinship has appeared.

Whatever studies that we find on kinship dwell on the nexus in caste, family and kin. And, further, the kinship studies largely relate to the tribals. The importance of kinship both for tribal and rural societies is described below:

(1) *Kinship, family, property and land*

In our villages, the family property mainly consists of land. Land, therefore, is related to the members of the kin. The disputes in the village arise out of land cultivation, encroachment and division. Within a family the land is divided at the time of the separation of sons. And, not only sons but grandsons and other kins related by marriage and blood. Every kinsman has his economic interests related to land.

The women's emancipation movement which has started getting popularity in the villages has now created an awareness among the females that they are also entitled to get an equal share out of the ancestral property. It is demanded that the patriarchal rules inheritance should not deprive the females from share of the common man. In any analysis of village society, kinship and property have to be related.

The ownership of land by the family kins also ascertains the status of the members. Sometimes political status is also determined by the kinship ties. The relations based on blood and marriage go a long way in giving economic and political concessions to the kin members. What is called *Bhai-Bhatijavad*, i.e., nepotism is a glaring example of the strength and weakness of kinship in the village.

Our description about the importance of kinship in rural life does not mean that there is no role of kinship in urban society. But we do want to stress that the urban community is so widespread in its habitation that it hardly provides enough opportunities for the social meets of the people. And, in urban society, secularism and democracy undermine the role of kinship. This is a society which has the value of affective-neutrality.

(2) *Kinship and marriage*

Each group in a society has its rules of marriage, the primary being endogamy, exogamy and incest taboos. There can be difference among groups on the severity or laxity in the application of these rules. The village community, it is found, is more serious in observing the rules of marriage. These rules apply to all the kinsmen.

The villages in our country normally observe rules of exogamy. The members of a village do not prefer to marry in the same village, however, there are exceptions. The village exogamy is reported by Irawati Karve and A.C. Mayer. Mayer, in his study of *Kinship in Central India*, informs that village exogamy is violated in some of the cases but it brings disrepute to the parties involved. It must be observed here that the study conducted by Mayer is an important document on village ethnography. Mayer further informs that inter-caste marriage is in all cases looked down by the village people.

(3) *Rituals related to lifecycle*

The importance of kins lies in the closeness with which they are related to a family. The role of kin can be seen on occasions of birth, betrothal, marriage and death. For instance, it is the *Bhua* or *Bua*, i.e., father's sister who officiates at the naming ceremony of the new born. In urban castes this may take an optional or alternative form. But, in villages, the close relations are always available and the ritualistic payment in cash or kind is given to them. On the occasion of marriage the close relations are expected to offer their gifts which are defined by the customary laws and are also rewarded accordingly. The depth also brings certain obligations on the kinsmen. The close kin are required to observe mourning for all the fourteen days of the death of deceased.

What we intend to argue is that the obligations of kins are very rigidly observed in rural society while in the urban society no such rigidity is witnessed. It is, therefore, the severity or laxity of the observation of rituals connected with the lifecycle which provide specificity to the rural society.

Kinship behaviour in the villages as elsewhere in the country is also changing. There is demand for the ownership of land titles by the women; marriage rules are also challenged and the traditional rules of divorce are getting weakened. But, on the other side, some of the kinship bonds are also strengthening. The kin group is putting a slide stand in the field of politics. The role of kinship is fast increasing in rural elections, more particularly the elections of PRIs. In the distribution of jobs also nepotism is raising its head in the face of democracy and rationality. It appears that in the context of new forces of social formation kinship is likely to assume new structure and function.

Marriage

Admittedly, the institution of marriage is universal. Respond is everywhere in the world, notwithstanding the level of civilisation attained by a society. Despite this uniformity, it should also be accepted that there are various forms of marriage. The pattern of marriage in Europe is fundamentally different from the Indian pattern of marriage. If this logic is further stretched it could be safely said that the forms of marriage and the rules of marriage which are found in rural society are not similar to urban society. Despite this diversity in marriage patterns there are some common features which are shared both by urban and rural marriage patterns. We start with the view that the rural society has its own structure and needs. The rural marriage takes a form which fulfils the agrarian needs. The nature of agrarian society in India is agriculture based. And, the agriculture in most of its form is manually operated. This kind of agriculture prefers a pattern of marriage which suits to the needs of the agrarian economy.

In the discipline of rural sociology we find description about rural marriage. But the institution of marriage which is described in the literature of the rural sociology does not make any departure from the general pattern of marriage. If marriage which is discussed in general sociology is the same in rural sociology, then it challenges the existence of rural sociology as a sub-discipline of sociology. To add it further if rural sociology draws a portrait of marriage which is uniform with the world pattern, we are missing the specificity of marriage in regard to rural society. Our argument is that the institution of marriage is the institution of society but it is relative to the agrarian society, its needs and compulsions. Here, we shall discuss the institution of marriage in the context of the rural society.

The rural society surely is an agrarian society in India. Further, it is a society characterised by the caste system. Caste and class in rural society have a nexus, and can hardly be separated. But the institution of marriage constitutes an inherent part of caste. Quite like caste, marriage is also related to kin and clan. The importance of kin, clan and caste in rural society is different from urban society. When we discuss the marriage system of the rural society, contextually, we also keep in mind the village institutions of kin, caste, class and clan.

At a broader plane the institution of marriage is quite stable compared to other social institutions. Marriage permits a man and a woman to have sexual relations. These relations are legitimised by the surrounding society. If the sex relations are not recognised by the society through a system of marriage, the relations are void, illicit. Second, marriage also permits procreation of children. There is also legitimacy for children.

Edward Westermark is considered to be an authority on the institution of marriage. In his two-volume work, *History of Human Marriage*, he argues that marriage is "the more or less durable connection between male and female, lasting beyond the mere act of propagation till after the birth of offsprings". E.R. Groves, another writer of repute on the institution of marriage defines it as a "public confession and legal registration of an adventure in fellowship". According to Harton and Hunt, marriage is the approved social pattern whereby two or more persons establish a family. All these definitions of marriage stress the single point that when heterosexual relations are recognised by society by some institution, may it be polygamy, polyandry or group marriage, it becomes an institution of marriage. In other words, societal legitimacy is the crux of marriage.

D.N. Majumdar has defined marriage keeping in view the Indian society. He also strikes at the legitimacy of sex relations. According to him, marriage is a socially sanctioned union of male and female, or is a secondary institution devised by society to sanction the union of male and female for purposes of (1) establishing a household, (2) entering into sex relationship, (3) procreating, and (4) providing care for the offsprings. P.N. Prabhu also defines marriage in terms of Hindu society. According to him, the objectives of Hindu marriage include (1) *moksha* or salvation, (2) procreation of children, (3) upbringing of children, and (4) sex. In this hierarchy of objectives of marriage sex occupies the last place.

The characteristics of marriage, as discussed above, are more or less universal. In the universality of characteristics we shall discuss the major forms of marriage with reference to Indian society in general and the rural society in particular.

Forms of marriage

Notwithstanding any society—rural or urban—there are few standard forms of marriage which are found in all the societies. We describe these forms as they are also practised in agrarian society of our country. These are as below:

(1) *Polyandry:* This form of marriage is found in different parts of the world societies. It is also found among the tribals of our country. It is a form of marriage wherein a woman marries more than one man at a given time. It is found among the Khasas—a tribal group residing in the villages of Jaunsar Babar of Dehradun district. The Todas of Tamilnadu also practise polyandry. However, polyandry is not found among the caste Hindus. But surely, it is a rural pattern of marriage found among the restricted segments of tribals.

Among the lower castes, if such marriage takes place, the so-called deviant is penalised by the caste association.

(3) *Sorrorate:* This rule of marriage permits a man to marry his wife's sister, that is *Sali*. This rule is much in vogue among the villagers who practise polygyny. Among many rural castes there is a custom of marrying one's wife's younger sister after the death of the wife. This facilitates the deceased's wife's family. Generally, the lower caste people take to sorrorate marriage. Among higher castes such a marriage is generally not preferred.

(4) *Levirate:* It is the rule of marriage whereby marriage is performed with the deceased brother's widow, that is, *Bhabhi*. A younger brother may marry the widow of his elder brother. This rule of marriage is observed among the agrarian people. Generally, among the lower castes where bride price is paid, while contracting marriage with the widow, efforts are made to save the bride price money for the second wife. The lower castes generally the backward classes, artisans, etc., observe this type of marriage. It must, however, be said that the higher castes, namely, Brahmin, Rajput and Bania look down with this kind of marriage.

(5) *Hypergamy:* It is a custom which allows a man, but forbids a woman, to marry a person of lower status. This practice of marriage is also prevalent among the lower rural castes.

(6) *Hypogamy:* This rule of marriage brings an upper caste woman to marry a man belonging to a lower caste. This system works very well when the ratio of male is lower to the female. Generally, hypogamy is looked down in rural society. But, in cases of love marriage, this rule of marriage is observed in the urban society.

Some specific aspects of marriage in rural society

As have argued earlier that the rural marriage has certain characteristics which differentiate it from the urban marriage. If researches done pertaining to rural marriage system are carefully analysed, we would be able to find out some traits in the rural marriage which are only relative to the rural society. Students of rural sociology should always be able to identify the specificity of marriage which is found in rural society. Some of these specialities are described below:

(i) *Child marriage or age at marriage:* It was for the first time in

1929 that the Child Marriage Restraint Act was passed by the British government. Since then a few amendments in the Act have been made. The prescribed age for marriage today is 21 years for male or 18 years for female. Though the incidence of child marriage is a national problem, its occurrence in rural society is very high. Rajasthan is notorious for solemnising child marriage on the day of *Akha Teej* which falls in the month of June. The day is considered to be auspicious and thousands of child grooms and brides take seven rounds to sacred fire on this day.

The rural society constantly stands in need of additional hands for labour in the field. This need promotes rural people to get their sons and daughters married at an early date. The basic reason for child marriage is the absence of literacy. Female illiteracy in the rural community is colossal. Though there are child marriages in the urban community also, its frequency in the rural side is much large. This happens to be a characteristic feature of rural society.

(2) *Polygyny:* Yet another speciality of rural marriage is the practice of polygyny. Among the tribals more than one wife to a male adds to his status. In the tribal villages one can easily find a *Panch* or a *Pradhan* contracting a second wife the day he assumes his office. Surely, polygyny among the high castes and particularly government servants is a thing of the past, but members of lower caste do not miss any opportunity to go for a second wife. Thus polygyny continuous to remain a characteristic feature of a rural society.

(3) *Marriage by exchange:* Among the lower castes of villages there is prevalence of a form of marriage which is known as *Ata-Sata*. In this marriage, the brother gives his sister in marriage to a man whose sister is in exchange taken by him as his wife. This kind of marriage is found in vogue where there is a striking disproportion of females. This is considered to be a lower form of marriage and is looked down by the village higher castes.

(4) *Bride price:* Marriage by bride price is generally found among the tribals. The amount taken as bride price by the parents of the bride is a compensation money for upbringing the girl. The amount of bride price is customarily fixed by the traditional tribal *panchayat*. However, among the tribals who have attained some education, the practice of bride price is getting weak. But, undoubtedly, marriage by bride price is a characteristic of rural marriage.

(5) *Lower status of women in conjugal relations:* The status of women in rural society is generally lower. As a wife and as a widow she is not given any position of status. As a wife she is considered to be a subordinate partner only meant to do the household jobs. She is not involved in major decisions taken about the family matters. What we want to stress here is that as a conjugal partner she is only required to comply the wishes of her husband. Her lower status is because of her economic dependence and illiteracy. A rural woman is far away from the wave of women's movement.

(6) *Less expensive and less fanfare:* Marriages in urban community, even among the poor masses, are quite expensive. In the countryside the celebration of marriage is highly ritualistic and does not involve much expenditure in respect of fixing of tents, electric decoration, band and other items which exhibit the status of the parties celebrating marriage.

(7) *Marital relations regulated by caste norms:* One striking feature of marriage in villages is the gap between the ritual of marriage and consumption of marriage. If the bride has not attained maturity the consumption of marriage is postponed for a future date. In all cases, in rural India, there is a gap in the solemnisation of marriage and consumption of marriage. The system of *gauna*, that is, bringing the wife from her parents heralds the date of consumption of marriage. This practice of marriage consumption is almost absent in urban community.

(8) *Arranged marriage:* Yet another speciality of marriage in rural society is the preponderance of arranged marriages. In the interior villages there is no practice of allowing the prospective groom and bride to meet before marriage. Love marriage or inter-caste marriage is a news in rural side. It is the responsibility of the parents to arrange the marriage of their wards.

(9) *Lesser frequency of divorce:* Hindu marriage is a sacrament. Higher castes do not practise divorce. The frequency of divorce among the higher castes in both rural and urban areas is similar. But, permitting divorce to a wife is not looked down among the lower castes.

(10) *Procreation of children*: One very conspicuous feature of marriage in countryside is the procreation of children within a reasonable period after marriage. Family planning or no family planning—it is

expected of a couple to give birth to a child. If no child is born to a woman after marriage there are many rumours afloat in the village. All sorts of remarks are made against the husband and wife. Even the potentiality of man is challenged and the female is charged for being sterile. Thus, in rural society, procreation is an essential part of marriage.

Thus, surely, rural marriage is not similar to urban marriage. The local traditions and practices give a specific shape to marriage in rural society.

Religion

It is interesting to know that a large number of social thinkers have written extensively on the role of religion in society; for example, Emile Durkheim, Max Weber and Karl Marx have discussed the impact of religion on European society. Besides, among these thinkers may be included Tylor (1871), Spencer (1896) and Frazer (1890) who have argued that it is the religion which creates solidarity in human society. In fact, religion is the need of a society.

India's villages are highly disposed to religion. Religion and its associated aspects such as ritual and magic also influence the society. It may be said at the outset that Indian rural society is much characterised by the observation of rituals and magic than religion itself. The rural society is basically a caste society. And, caste has religion as its inherent part. In practice caste and religion can hardly be separated. Even the origin of caste system stressed from religion when mythologically it is said that the Brahmins have originated from the mouth of Brahma, the Rajputs from the arms and the Vaishyas from the thigh. The *Purush Sukta* further informs that the Shudras have been created from the legs of Brahma.

It is the search for the ultimate reality of world which has given emergence to religion. There is great diversity in world's religions. Not all religions worship one god or even several gods. Hinduism believes that there are lakhs of gods. If we look at the pattern of worship all over the world we will find that there are people who even worship animals or other geographical features. This frame will show that in spite of vast differences among religions, the various forms share four basic elements, viz., recognition of the sacred, ritual, a system of beliefs and organization.

The social institution of religion is defined as the system of norms, guiding behaviour, related to man's search for ultimate truth. A concern for the ultimate truth—a search for explanation of the meaning of life, death and other difficult events to explain—is the basic theme in religious behaviour.

According to Durkheim, "religion is a unified system of beliefs and practices relative to sacred things, that is to say, things set apart and forbidden beliefs and practices which unite into one single moral community called a church by all those who adhere to them". Like other social institutions, religion exhibits certain cultural universals and variations and performs functions related to personalities and societies.

Most of the work recently done in the field of rural and tribal societies goes to the credit of anthropologists. Clifford Geertz, for instance, considers religion as a cultural system. According to him:

> A religion is a system of symbol which acts to (1) establish powerful, pervasive, and long-lasting moods and motivations in men by (2) formulating conceptions of a general order of existence, and (3) clothing these conceptions with such an aura of factuality that (4) the models and motivations seem uniquely realistic.[17]

Perhaps, the oldest definition of religion is given by Tylor. He defines religion simply as beliefs in supernatural beings. The question of supernatural beings puzzles anthropologists. After all one may ask what is supernatural? Is it a form of knowledge? Is it ritual and magic? These questions have not been satisfactorily answered. But, the fact remains that religion is essentially a cultural phenomenon which works for the solidarity of society. Each society has its own perception of religion and, therefore, the rural religion is different from urban religion. If we analyse the rural society we will immediately find that it depends very much on the factor of fate. Agriculture is rainfed; a single crop standing in the field can be destroyed in no time by flood waters or lack of rains. Any mischief-maker can set the whole crop to fire. The peasant's total earnings of a crop either stand in the field or harvest. Such a situation makes the economy and security of a peasant vulnerable to all the hazards and unfriendly acts of nature. This creates a strong belief in religion among the peasants.

The close association between rural society and religion makes the study of latter quite important in rural society. However, religion is not monolith. It also contains rituals and magic. The Indian peasant is mostly described as superstitious and fatalist. Such an understanding of rural society requires to establish a nexus between religion and economy of the rural people.

Significance of religion in rural society

Throughout the present work it has been our effort to discuss different aspects of society with the reference of the historicity and societal needs of rural society. The same argument is raised here and in the following pages an attempt has been made to discuss the importance and significance of religion for the rural people. Following are some of the reasons which explain the status of religion in rural society:

(1) *Economy is dependent on nature*: Though agricultural scientists have developed enough scientific knowledge to increase the farm produce, land fertility by applying chemical manure and introducing an appropriate technology for saving manual labour, much of our agriculture still depends on nature. The villagers do not have much of scientific knowledge for the protection of crops. Nor can they afford to spend on technology. All these factors make a farmer to depend on nature.

(2) *Religious outlook dominates other aspects of rural life*: The history of rural society makes it obvious that the people living in the countryside not only depend on nature for their agricultural operations, but their whole life is dominated by religion. In other words, not only the village economy but the total mindset of the people is determined by religion and rituals. This distinguishes it from the urban life. A.R. Desai scores a point when he stresses the importance of religion in rural India:

> The religious outlook of the rural people overwhelmingly dominates their intellectual, emotional and practical life. It is difficult to locate any aspect of their life which is not permeated with and coloured by religion. Their family life, caste life, general social life, economic and even recreational life are more or less governed by a religious approach and religious norms. Religious concessions also largely dominate their ethical standards; the form and content of their acts like painting, sculpture, architecture, folk songs, and others, as also

their social and economic festivals."[18]

Religion occupies a core place in all the activities of rural life. In fact, the history of village settlements begins with the provision for the worship of a deity. There is a saying among Telugu people that for the habitation of a village settlement it is essential to have economic safeguards, some kind of medical facility, some provision for potable water and some Brahmin to officiate at the religious ceremonies.

(3) *Priestly leadership in rural society*: Whoever may have been the ruler of the village—a Rajput, a jamindar or a *jagirdar*, the intellectual and economic life of the people was controlled by priestly class. Here priestly class means the Brahmins. The traditions and conventions of the rural life were historically laid down by the Brahmin leaders. And, hence the life of the village aggregate in all spheres was moulded in the spirit of religious ideas and dogmas and was controlled by religious institutions and leaders. Contrarily, in the urban community, the priestly class does not succeed much in influencing the educated and scientifically awakened people.

(4) *Religion at the crossroads*: Admittedly, the role of religion in rural society even today continues to occupy an important place. In fact, its importance is at the crossroads. There has come a new economic and political environment which strikes at the importance of religion. More and more people are becoming secular, democratic and oriented to scientific ethics. It indicates that the battle line between religiosity and secularism has been drawn. It appears that soon rural religion would take a course of change which is evident in urban society. A.R. Desai writes:

> The contemporary rural society in India has become a battle ground of struggle between the forces of religious orthodoxy and authoritarian social conceptions on the one hand, and those of secular democratic advance on the other. It is essential for the student of Indian rural society to follow this conflict.[19]

Thus, the causes discussed above explain the importance of religion in rural life. Though this importance is increasingly declining, it appears certain that till the rural masses are educated, and scientifically oriented in their outlook, religion will occupy a prime status among them. It should not mean that there is no religiosity among urban people. The reality is that the practice of religiosity is deeply rooted in rural society. The urban people have developed refinedness in their observation of religious rites. The rural sociologists should make an effort to distinguish between the crude, almost static rural religion and the refined and highly abstract urbanised religion which soars in the stratosphere of speculative thought and grapples with ontological, epistemological and other basic problems of philosophy. The rural sociologists should also note that rationlist and materialist philosophical thought currents found in the urban society are almost absent in the rural people.

As a matter of fact rural religion has its roots in the rural natural environment. Explaining the specificity of rural religion vis-a-vis urban religion, A.R. Desai writes:

> The roots of rural religion lie principally in the great, almost abysmal, ignorance and resultant fear of the forces of environment prevailing among the rural people. Refined urban religion, even if based on the erroneous idealistic interpretation of the world, is not born of mere fear. This distinction regarding the psychological roots of rural and urban religion is important.[20]

Rural Religion

The religion has certain aspects which make it relative to the rural society. Some of the major characteristics of rural religion are discussed below:

(1) *Sense of the world*

Religion has its theory and philosophy. It has its rituals and festivals. But the rural religion creates an understanding among the people as to the meaning of the world as the people reside. It explains the meaning and direction to human existence. Rural religion gives an idea, however, vague it may be, to the people about their ultimate survival in the world.

For instance, Hinduism is based on the broader theory that the life is a cycle of births. This theory guides the day-to-day life of the rural people. Everyone knows it very well that if he does not behave well in the present life, his next birth would be full of sorrows and misfortunes. Such a translation of the Hindu theory of transmigration of soul regulates the life-cycle of the people. In the urban society this theory has become weak and got dominated by scientific ethics. The non-Hindu groups in the village also interpret their life according to the theory and philosophy of the religion which they follow.

It may further be said that the world outlook of the village people is also characterised by the forces of nature and also the temperament of the man. The village people accept the theory of transmigration of soul also because they are ignorant about the reality of world and accept whatever is given by the religion.

(2) *Body of rituals*

Anthropologists have defined ritual as the practice of religion. As a matter of fact, if religion is the theory and philosophy of life, ritual is its social aspect. Defining the status of ritual within the concept of religion T.H. Eriksen observes:

> Ritual has been defined as the social aspect of religion. If we may define religion as systems of notions about the supernatural and the sacred, about life after death and so on (with the obvious political implication), then rituals are the social processes which give a concrete expression to these notions. Very generally speaking, we may suggest that rituals are rule-bound public events which in some way or other thematise the relationship between the earthly and the spiritual realms.[21]

The Indian rural religion is basically the observation of rituals. The rural masses are generally illiterate. They cannot make out the meanings inherent in the classical and sacred texts. In such a situation almost all of them observe the rituals. The theories behind the rituals are never taken care of. The village festivals of Raksha Bandhan, Dassehara, Diwali and Holi are all characterised by the observation of rituals. Even the theory behind the seven rounds taken in presence of sacred fire is hardly interpreted in theoretical context. Because the Brahmin officiating the ritual requires them to do a particular ritual, people do it without knowing the theoretical interpretations.

Quite like the observation of Hindu religion in the form of rituals, the other religious groups such as Jains, Muslims and Christians in the countryside perform the rituals only in the name of rituals. It is called the *lokik*, that is, society's approach to religion. In rural India there is so much predominance of rituals that the finer values of religion continue to remain hidden within the theory of religion.

The religious practices which constitute the body of religion include prayer, sacrifice to gods and goddesses and rituals. Prayer is offered to various deities at home as well as outside the home. Actually, prayers offered at the home are addressed to the family gods and deities. Sometimes, on occasions of festivals, all the members of the family offer prayer to the family deity. Prayer outside the home is offered at the village temple. It is not necessary that all the members of the village assemble at the temple regularly. Those who are devotees, particularly the aged persons, visit the temple regularly.

People at the rural side offer a variety of sacrifices to gods and goddesses. Describing the sacrifices made by the people at the shrine A.R. Desai writes:

> The rural religion prescribes a variety of sacrificial acts to its adherents, which range from the sparkling of some drops of water and scattering of leaves or grains in front of the various deities to the offering of animal and though rarely even of human sacrifices to them. The rural religion is composed of various sub-religions and each sub-religion prescribes to its followers a particular set of sacrificial acts.

The villagers observe a variety of rituals. The conception of purity had been elaborated in the past Indian society to such an extent that it became a veritable principle. Rituals are the religious means by which the purity of the individual and the social life becomes guaranteed. The inherited rural religion prescribes a complex pattern of behaviour for the individual as well as for social groups in all spheres of life, complex because rituals are associated with their numerous significant and even insignificant activities.

It must be mentioned here that there are a large number of ethnic groups in the country. Each group has its own body of rituals. It is really very difficult for any ethnography to prepare a catalogue of village rituals. However, it must be observed that whatever may be the ritual, and its structure and function, people without any hesitation observe it. It is because if the observation of rituals is violated, there is always a fear that some misfortune might fall on the family.

The village people have a mindset which is very superstitious and, therefore, they dare not overlook any ritual observation. The rituals which are related to death are taken quite seriously.

(3) *Religion as an institution*

There is pan-religion which covers the whole country. The census reports divide the population of country into various religions. Accordingly, the followers of Hinduism constitute the majority. Other groups of followers include Jain, Sikh, Christian, Buddhist, Muslim, Parsi and others such as tribals who have their specific religions. The census enumeration thus very clearly indicates that notwithstanding the various religious cults, religion constitutes an important rural institution.

Max Weber who made an attempt to study six great world religions showed that each religion has some property, some organisation and above all a rationality to keep the followers held together. There are some religions based at the village level that own their own temples, gurudwaras, maths, and churches. The Jains have their own temples at the village level. In states like Bihar the *maths* have hundreds of acres of land attached to them. The priest clergy, the *Jathedar*, or *Pujari* take care of all the activities which are held at the shrine.

All the characteristics of a social institution such as economy, politics and education are found in the religious institution. If a single village is taken up for elaborate study one can find different aspects of educational and ritual institutions. The institution of religion is no exception to change. With the spread of scientific knowledge and awakening of the people the institution of religion is also changing. What is interesting to note is that with the spread of urbanisation, agricultural capitalism and general awakening, a few of the rituals at the village level are observed with greater enthusiasm, exorbitant expenditure and higher pomp and show. Again, with the increasing pace of modernisation, the old shrines are renovated, new cults are emerging and frequency of visit to shrines is fast increasing. Modernisation and vigorous observation of rituals, obviously, is contradictory. It does not suit to the rationality. It is an interesting subject for the students of rural sociology.

Functions of rural religion

Rural sociologists have stressed on some of the social functions of rural religion. Sociological thinkers have also stressed on the positive functions of religion in maintaining the unity of village. Historians throughout the different periods have brought out the fact that our villages have maintained unity. Village unity has been a silver line in our annals of village. Recently religion has also fractured the traditional village unity. The caste politics has affected the cohesion of society. The following are some of the functions of religion—good or bad—for the maintenance of rural society.

(1) *Preservation of rural social order*: Admittedly, religion is a belief of a person towards the supernatural. But it is also a moral code for its followers. The moral code gives social order to the society. The fear of the wrath of the god compels a man to live a moral life, follow the sacred and avoid the profane. Thus, the fundamental function of the religion is to maintain social order in the socicty. Once a promise is made to the deity it is fulfilled at any cost by the village people. There are instances in our struggle for independence that whenever a crisis came, the national leaders sought the involvement of the village people in the name of religion. When the division of Bengal was made in 1905, the Bengali leaders of Calcutta addressed a crowd of 10 to 12 thousand people to take a dip in water of the Ganga making a promise that they would participate in the movement against the division till the day. The division was withdrawn. Similarly, Bal Gangadhar Tilak in 1893 started the practice of using the traditional religious Ganpati festival to propagate nationalist ideas through patriotic songs and speeches. In 1896, he started the Shivaji festival to stimulate nationalism among young Maharashtrians. The history is replete to bring home the fact that whenever a crisis gripped a village, religion is sought after to keep the people united.

The prescriptions, moral order, *katha, kirtan,* lectures of saints are all used to maintain the social order of society. The villagers very well know that any erosion in the fabric of religious life leads to the breakdown of social order.

(2) *Means of social control*: Whatever may be the kind of religion, it is held by all the religions that whatever you do in this life, you will reap the same in the next life. Charged by the general ethos of religion, the villagers try to lead a sacred life. Almost all of them are scared of the tortures of hail. This fear motivates them to choose a life which is approved by the religious norms. We have a rich literature to show that the deviants in the village have been asked to host a dinner to the community or a dip in the holy waters of Ganga. Religion in the rural side is used for maintaining social control over the people. The social control is exercised through the rigid observation of village traditions, customs and conventions.

We want to mention it here that there is always prevalence of some religion in the urban community. But the strength of religion, its power is diluted here. Scientific ethics and rationality replace the urban orthodoxy. Rural conservatism, however, survives unabated.

(3) *Opportunity of recreation and leisure*: The rituals provide opportunities to the rural people to relax and enjoy the life. All over rural India there are always some rituals which are related to sowing and harvesting. Some of the rituals served after the harvesting have gained regional prominence. The *Baishakhi* of Punjab, *Navratri* of Gujarat and *Ganpati Mahotsava* of Maharashtra are ritual observances related to the agricultural cycle. There are fairs also organised in the name of religion. It must be observed that round the year, the villagers get opportunities of leisure and recreation due to religious celebrations.

(4) *Hierarchical order*: The stratification of society is also maintained through the customs and traditions advocated by religion. The caste system, despite the efforts made by secular forces, continued to survive because of the values inherent in caste system. Louis Dumont has stressed this value aspect of caste system. MacKim Marriott has also identified the ritual and religious aspects of hierarchical relations in the village life. The commensal relations in the village are, even today, regulated by the concept of purity and pollution. In the cities there are no taboos so far commensality is concerned.

(5) *Impurity rules over human behaviour*: During the past fifty years

the village life has been characterised by a new wave of change. These changes are largely in the realm of economic, educational, political and secular life. Many of the notions charged by pollution, even today, stigmatise the human life. The village women, even among the high caste Hindus do not enter kitchen and water places during the period of menstruation. Widows are discouraged to participate in auspicious occasions. They are considered to be persons of glooms. Nor they are allowed to visit the cremation ground even when their own kins die.

(6) *Cult war*: There is enough evidence in our history to demonstrate that there has been war between the followers of diverse religions. Jainism and Buddhism emerged as the revolt against fundamental cult of *karmakanda*. Even Jainism and Hinduism also witnessed schisms in their cult. Rural India today is also faction ridden owing to the prevalence of different religious cults. However, the severity of religious cult war is in a low key compared to urban community. The regional and national politics all over the country has taken to religion as a force for creating divisions in the society. It appears that if chances are made available to politicians, the day is not far away when religion would prove to be a highly divisive force in the villages. On the other hand, the capitalist economy which has made its penetration in the village life would also reduce the importance of religion.

Notes

1. J.H.Fitcher, *Sociology*, University of Chicago Press, Chicago, 1964.
2. P.B. Horton and C.L. Hunt, *Sociology*, McGraw Hill, New York, 1964.
3. M.N. Srinivas, *Religion and Society Among the Coorgs of South India*, Asia, London, 1952.
4. A.C. Mayer, *Caste and Kin in Central India*, University of California Press, Berkeley, 1960.
5. K.M. Kapadia, *Marriage and Family in India*, Oxford University Press, London.

6. M.N. Srinivas, op.cit.
7. S.C. Dube, *Indian Village*, Routledge and Kegan Paul, London, 1955.
8. D.N.Majumdar, *Caste and Communication in an Indian Village*, Asia, Bombay, 1958.
9. Irawati Karve,"The Indian Village", *Deccan Bulletin*, Vol. XVIII.
10. I.P. Desai, *Some Aspects of Family in Mahua*, Asia Publishing House.
11. K.M. Kapadia, *Hindu Kinship*, The Popular Book Depot, Bombay, 1947.
12. Cooley, C.H., *Social Organization.*
13. K.M. Kapadia, op. cit., p. 311.
14. A.R. Brown, *Man*, Vol. XXIX, p. 50.
15. R. Briffault, *The Mothers*, Vol. I.
16. B. Malinowski, 'Kinship', *Britannica*, XIV edition, Vol. XXX, 17, pp. 23-26.
17. Clifford Geertz, *Agriculture Involution: The Process of the Ecological Changes in Indonesia*, University of California Press, Berkeley, 1963.
18. A.R. Desai, op. cit., p. 54.
19. Ibid., p. 55.
20. Ibid., p. 56.
21. T.H. Eriksen, *Small Places, Large Issues*, Pluto Press, London, 1995, p. 203.

10 Rural Aesthetics

Aesthetics is the perception of people about possessing sense of beauty, an idea about artistic things. If a casual round of a village settlement is taken it would be immediately found that the villagers have a strong sense of beauty coupled with utility. This kind of aesthetics is visible in the adornment of village dwellings and in the embellishment of their household goods. There are always some artists in the village, such as the *khati*----carpenter who makes wooden carts, bedposts, doors and awnings; the *kumbhar*----the potter who turns out a variety of earthen crocks; the *basera*----basketeer who interweaves bamboo strips and twigs to produce wicker baskets; and even the ordinary housewife who makes her own mudbowls and sundry containers, all have tectonics as their basic idea and perception.

Villages in north and western India draw paintings of peacock on their walls. Peacock is associated with Lord Krishna. It is symbolic of love and is a popular theme for village people. It is a carpenter who turns an ordinary wooden wheel of a rustic cart into an exciting article of attention by decorating it with beautiful designs in indigenous colours while giving it a protective covering. One can find that the village art and painting are closely related to the religious beliefs of the people. Recently rural aesthetics has become a part of debate among the artists. For instance, Rustom Bharucha[1] has come out with a thesis that the contemporary cultural activism in the country should take a secular form. His argument is that modern aesthetics should part with the burden of religion and religious beliefs. The politicisation of Ram by political forces is a truism and needs to be warded of.

Rustom Bharucha very emphatically argues that contemporary aesthetic culture in rural India is characterised by the global trend of capitalism. The village artisans, folk singers and village theatres are all of creative villains of the erosion of indigenous culture. In the words of Bharucha:

> Differences in India are perhaps most marked through the economic inequalities that pervade the country. With the rise of global capitalism in India the effects of these inequalities have become more marked.[2]

The debate about the place of secularism in rural aesthetics need to be explored: However, at present, we only want to say that rural life is not without aesthetics. There is a definite place for beauty in different aspects of people's life. It is tragic that despite our having voluminous research material on village communities, we have almost no details about village aesthetics. On the contrary, there is an understanding among the general masses of people that the villagers are rustic and have no perception about beauty. As a matter of fact, the villagers exhibit a strong sense of aesthetics in all their performances. For instance, and historically it is true, that in each state of the country the rural society has more than one cultural performances known far and wide. The *bhand-pratha* of Kashmir is famous for the performance of rural artists. Punjab villages give a beautiful display of *nakal* and *bhangra.* No folk dance at the television screen is complete without *bhangra.* The *swang* of *Bahurupia* of Haryana and Rajasthan is well known in the neighbouring states. Uttar Pradesh has the famous artistic display of *notanki.* The *jatra* of West Bengal provides an excellent artistic performance. The Chhatisgarh performance of *pandri* is held all over central India. Teejan Bai is a popular artist for the masses of rural people. The region of Dholpur in Rajasthan is known for its cultural performance of *Alha-Udal*---the two rural heroes who fought bravely. Instances after instances may be given to demonstrate the point that the rural people have an excellent sense of beauty.

What Does Aesthetics Mean?

Aesthetics is the sense of beauty; it is a thing of art, both in material and abstract form. A.R. Desai[3] has analysed the dimensions of rural aesthetic culture and argues that the whole of rural India is, in fact, a museum of folk culture, folk ways, folk dances and folk musical instruments. He has explained the term 'aesthetic' with reference to rural culture. He writes:

> Aesthetic culture is an integral part of the total culture of a society. It expresses, in art terms, the ideals, the aspirations, the dreams, the values and attitudes of its people, just as its intellectual culture reveals its

knowledge of the natural and social worlds which surround them.

Aesthetic culture, thus, has a wider body of values, ideals and beliefs of the people. These ideals and beliefs relate to history, mythology, religion and above all a sense of traditional beauty.

Art Forms

The artists who have developed a theoretical framework of aesthetics have given the following types of art:

(1) *Graphic Arts*

It includes drawing, painting engraving and other such art forms. These forms have ordinarily two dimensions.

(2) *Plastic Arts*

These arts involve the manipulations of materials to yield three dimensional forms, that is to say, carving and modelling in high and low relief and in the round.

(3) *Folklore*

It includes myths, tales, proverbs, riddles, verse and music.

(4) *Dance and Drama*

Actually, dance and drama also include song. In fact, it is a synthetic form of art.

All the above forms of aesthetic arts are not static. There is a constant change in the themes of art. In the rural aesthetic art the change sometimes is very conspicuous. The villagers are very strong in robust commonsense and they display the contradiction of our life in a fairly good way.

Status of Art in Rural Society

The status of art in rural society is all-pervasive. One can see the people's sensitivity to art and beauty in their manner of embellishing their dwellings with *mandhna*, the artistic drawings on the facade, walls and floors which they do themselves or through the services of the village artists known by different names as *Chatera*, *Kalakar* and *Chitrakar*. Some of the other expressions of their aesthetic sentiment are the adornment of their bodies by henna or tattooing in a large variety of designs. They also have a large number of interesting patterns of hair-dressing, beard and moustache styles and an impressive array of curious ornaments and apparels.

The women-folk all over the countryside are much fond of decorating the walls and floors of their dwellings. Their art of designing broadly revolves round a few simple motifs—some floral, some frenzy and others used as fillers or fringers. Looking at the aesthetic culture of villagers in all the aspects of their life, one can bring out certain characteristics of these village artistic forms. Some major characteristics of these aesthetics of rural culture are given below:

(1) *Roots in rural life*

Rural aesthetic is rooted in the reality of people. The people pass their time around the natural environment. The nature is characterised by an orderliness. There is a real beauty in the name. This gets manifestation in the performance of rural art. The countryside is marked by earth of different kinds. In the villages, in the plains, a combination of *khadia*---the white earth, and *geru*---the red earth is made and ornamental designs on the floors and walls are made. This kind of drawing immediately emerges from the grassroot---the earth itself. Nature's beauty gets representation in several other forms of art in the villages.

(2) *Involvement of the masses*

One of the specialities of village art and cultural performance is that it involves the people in the total process of the display of culture. When there is a *Ram Leela* or a *notanki*, the village artists themselves are selected to take part in the art activity. Bengal's *jatra* is a classical example of the participation of the folk masses in the cultural display. A.R. Desai has analysed the mass participation of village people in the collective artistic rural activities:

> A social group, a family or the village people as a whole did not break itself into actors and spectators when they engaged themselves in artistic activity. Men, women and children of the group, all participated in it; they were both the actors and the audience. There

were very few professional artists in that society. In the social division of labour artistic work was not still separated from the total social work. So as to create a special body of social workers like artists.

An interesting example of the participation of people in the cultural performance is that of *Navratri*—nine days preceding *Dasshera.* In the Gujarat region, the masses of rural people including the urban observe dance festivity throughout nine nights. Dances in *Navratri* are quite fanciful and exhibit an aesthetic performance which is unusual. Similarly, during the *Ganpati Mahotsava* in Maharashtra, the common masses have all opportunities to exhibit their artistic talent. In Punjab, *bhangra* is everybody's cup of tea. In the rural aesthetic performances it is the people who themselves participate. In urban community, however, there is a marked distance between a professional artists and the ticket- paying audience.

(3) *Art related to phases of life*

Broadly, the rural art and aesthetics has two dimensions: (i) familial, and (ii) collective. The familial art is related to the major phases of life, namely, birth, marriage and death. For instance, on the birth of a child in the family, the courtyard is decorated with *mandhna.* Drawings of elephant and horse with rider putting on a head dress are made on the walls. On the death of a person a bamboo ladder is constructed which, it is assumed, would be used by the deceased to climb to heaven.

From all considerations it appears that the rural art is predominantly influenced by the ties of family and the major phases of life. P.A. Sorokin and C.G. Zimmerman who have examined the art forms at rural global level observe:

> The significance, the manifestations, the content and the symbolism of rural aesthetic activities, permeated with familism, births, marriages, deaths and sickness of members of the family were the main subjects of rural art.[4]

(4) *Rude artistic forms*

The sophistication that we find in traditional art is almost absent in the rural art forms. The folk artists give expression to their feelings in a very simple form which could be described rustic or rude. The artists draw their paintings out of the things of nature. For instance, the musical instruments used by the folk musicians or singers are prepared by the local artisans. A drum, *dhol, nagara, dholak, duff, khanjari* and *navati* are all manufactured at the local and regional levels by the local artisans. The folk artists traditionally divide various types of musical instruments into two categories: (i) enhancers or embellishers, and (ii) rhythmers or time keepers. The embellishers include different kinds of string instruments and wind instruments. The rhythmers comprise percussive instruments, tintinnabulary instruments and rattling instruments. These forms of instruments include *khartal, drum, nagfani, murali* and *thali.*

(5) *Agrarian life as the theme of aesthetic art*

Agrarian life is conditioned by the agricultural operations. It is the cropping pattern which determines the ritual celebrations and performances of folk songs and folk dances. The agrarian people become busy soon after the sowing. The crop season ends with the harvesting. And, then, the *rabi* crop comes. These days, where irrigation facilities are available, there is also a third crop taken during summer days. India, throughout its period of civilisation, has been predominantly an agricultural country. Rural dances and songs, therefore, have grown out of the continuity of civilisation. However, some new cultural forms have taken their entry in the rural culture. It has also happened that the cultural practices of a particular region have crossed the administrative boundaries of other states. In such a situation, the co-relation between the cultural celebrations and the agricultural cycle has been disturbed. For instance, the *Navratri* of Gujarat or the *Baishakhi* of Punjab has entered into the cultural domain of Madhya Pradesh, Rajasthan and Haryana. As we find today the rural folk song celebrations involve the whole community in collective performances.

The theme of the rural folk songs and dances generally relates to agriculture. The deities, which are related to rains, protection of crops, are worshipped through the folk dance performances. However, some new things also take place in the cultural performances. Sorokin and Zimmerman talk about the folk arts generally found all over India pertaining to agrarian life. For instance, they observe:

> Some of their religious and magical songs were concerned with love, death, mourning, health and fertility, others deal with agricultural activities and were sung as a part of the religious and magical rites connected with spring, summer, fall and winter festivals, still others honoured the grove, wood, field and corn deities. ... both, work song and religious song were inseparately connected with daily life and with the religion and magic that centred in agriculture.[5]

The tribals of the country have also become agriculturists. They have also taken to a settled agricultural life. Their art forms and performances are different from the non-tribal populations. Their dances and songs are performed according to their history and mythology. Tribes like Gond, Muriya, Bhil and Chaudhra have definite occasions when they perform their art. It must be observed here that the tribal cultural performances are invariably collective performances. It is not heard that they have taken to modern forms of dance and song. It all goes to suggest that the perception of art and items of culture is relative to the tribal and agrarian way of life.

The village art, painting, tattooing and other such things are related to the environment which surrounds the people. A.R. Desai makes his observation in this respect as under:

> Ornamental and decorative rural arts also bore the impress of the rural environmental and social milieu. The specific flora and fauna found in the rural area provided material for design. Rural artistic creations in these in other spheres are based on rural environment and occupation; trees, flowers and plants, horses, cattle and other animals, birds and fish and peasant houses. Further, geometrical designs characterising those arts had a magical meaning bearing as various agrarian life processes.[6]

It should also be mentioned that the contents of folk cultural performances manifest songs, music, dances, stories, proverbs, riddles, literature, pantomimes, festivals, dramatic performances and similar forms of arts.

(6) *Rural aesthetics takes collective forms*

The basic difference in a rural and urban society is between individual and collectivity. There is a definite place of individual artist in an urban society. Normally, he earns his livelihood by performing his professional art. This is not the situation in rural society. Generally, art performances at the rural side take a collective form. This is the striking difference between the urban and rural sense of aesthetics. As a result of such a collective approach to rural cultural practices, art has been overwhelmingly collective in spirit. This art has expressed the fears, joys, aspirations and dreams of the collectivity even more than most of the social art of the urban society. Further, it has been marked with profound naturalness, sincerity and spontaneity. This is in contrast to the urban art which is either commercialised and, therefore, caters largely to the emotions of its potential buyers or is super individualistic, and embodies the individualistic caprices and momentary emotions of the artist. Further, rural art has expressed the sentiments and life experiences of countless generations. It has been, therefore, also more organic and durable than most of the urban art.

(7) *Rural art is necessarily a lesser commodity*

One very striking feature of cultural performances at the rural side is its non-commodification. If there is *tamasha*, *dandia*, *dance* or *alha-udal* recitation there is no ticket for it. These songs and dances which are participated by the rural community as a whole do not carry any price-tag. These are only expressions in the diverse forms of culture. The rural artist, in fact, is not motivated by the urge to make profit through his art creations, his artistic activity is prompted by the growth of art only.

(8) *Artistic skills are traditionally transmitted*

There are no training schools in the village where one can learn the art of folk song and folk dance. It is only by regular participation that the art is learnt. Actually, the cultural forms at the village level are transmitted from generation to generation. In other words, as traditional occupations travel from one generation to another, the cultural practices dance, drama and song also pass from one generation to another. This, however, does not mean that the cultural practices remain sterile. As it happens, each generation takes away something from the old tradition and always adds something new. This makes the rural cultural practices lively.

(9) *Changing rural aesthetic forms*

The content of the rural art and its cultural practices relates to the forms of the rural society. The form are actually determined by its organic relationship with the content. The rural style of painting, engraving, sculpture and architecture; the designs of costumes and ornaments; the tunes of folk songs and the rhythms of poetry; the structures of folk tales, dances and drama is determined by the rural aesthetic culture. The rural culture is marked with symbolism and it is the task of the rural sociologists to penetrate through the symbols and uncover the hidden significant ideas conveyed in an art work.

The rural aesthetic culture, as a whole, consists of a large number of regional ethnicities. For instance, we have varied forms as *sorathas, dohas, chaupais, chhappas, kirtans, bhajans, abhangas, pavadas, destis, hories, kajaris, kawalis* and others in the domain of poetry and song, and *rasas, garbas* and others in the field of drama. Similarly, the words of other rural arts also reveal a rich diversity of forms.

As a matter of fact, if we survey the regional rural ethnicities, we would find that there are a variety of cultural forms. All these forms are basically related to the forms of culture. For instance, the desert culture of Rajasthan gives a specific form of musical instruments, songs and dances. In their culture, sand dunes, camel and desert bushes occupy an important part. These cultural forms are manifest in the songs and music of the Longa and Maganiyar who happen to reside in the desert area.

The diverse regional culture leads us to inform that there is a great deal of specialisation in rural arts. It is because of the fact that the art is fused with concrete activities like sowing, reaping, harvesting and keeping a watch on the crops. Since the art creates a thematic continuity, the arts dealing with them are enriched and keep continuity from generation to generation. Resultantly, there is a constant improvement and enrichment in village arts, their forms, styles and patterns. In no case the rural art or the rural aesthetic is static.

Conclusion

Rustam Bharucha has very rightly raised the question that the new forms of culture should have a large degree of secular ideology. We find today that a larger portion of rural aesthetic culture is characterised by religion and diverse types of rituals. This can be explained by the fact that the total rural life is regulated and maintained by the natural order. The peasant's prosperity or his pauperness is determined by the environment and the gifts of nature. But this kind of historical fatalism is being changed by the efforts of government. It must be accepted that to certain extent the nature is tamed by constructing dams, providing chemical manure and controlling plant diseases. Such an entry of secularism in the form of new technology and varieties of agriculture does infuse the role of secularism. It is hoped that the new rural cultural forms must manifest some proportion of the secular ideology.

The new analysts of rural aesthetic culture express the fear of the disintegration of traditional rural aesthetics. In contemporary India the communication net is far expanding. There is also a spread of education. A large number of non-governmental organisations are mobilising the people to avail the new transport and communication facilities. Cinema, television and computer are coming to the village in a larger way. This has influenced the rural aesthetic forms of art and culture. The traditional rural melodies are now sung in the tune of film songs. The village streets echo with the TV dialogues and performances. The factory manufactured musical instruments are replacing the traditional rural instruments. Can this wave of revolution in communication check the erosion of the basic forms of rural culture? Perhaps, the future would decide.

Notes

1. Rustom Bharucha, *In the Name of Secularism,* Oxford University Press, Delhi, 1998.
2. Ibid., p. 28.
3. A.R.Desai, op. cit., p. 77.
4. P.A .Sorokin and C.G. Zimmerman, *Systematic Sourcebook in Rural Sociology,* Vol. II, p. 445.
5. Ibid., p. 458.
6. A.R. Desai, op. cit., p. 79.

11 Agrarian Unrest

Unrest among the Indian peasants is not new; it is historical. Bipan Chandra observes that peasant movements had been a part of national movement since 1920. With the emergence of agricultural capitalism, the growth of green revolution and the spread of education alongwith the development of agriculture, unrest among peasants has increased. The tribals of the country who are late comers to agriculture have also raised their head high to agitate against the government for the fulfilment of their demands. Land and agriculture are the state subject. And, therefore, the peasant unrest is the concern of the state governments. There are some vital questions related to the peasantry of our country. The route of peasant unrest, therefore, lies in the social structure of peasantry, its history and processes of agricultural modernisation.

Importance of Peasantry in India

Gandhiji was the architect of rural India. His dream was to give autonomy to our villages. Long back, in 1909, he wrote a letter to the British government in which he advocated his pet theory of *Hind Swaraj.* He suggested that India must do away with hospitals, railways, etc., and stick to plough. He argued that plough has given a peaceful life. If our villages prosper, the country would also prosper. It is also said that when the first draft of India's Constitution was referred to him, he tore it off that it did not contain anything about *Gramraj* or Panchayati Raj. It was on his insistence that an elaborate provision for Panchayati Raj was made in the Directive Principles of State Policy.

Why in India, as elsewhere also, land is something which is the property of the community. It should be used by all. During the 18th century, the US President asked American tribal chiefs to sale their land to the government. One of the tribal chiefs immediately reported: "How anyone could purchase or sale land. Sky and earth cannot be transacted. They are the warmth of the people." Land, therefore, and for that matter agriculture which feeds people, occupies a prime place in all our priorities. We give below some aspects of our agriculture which show its importance:

(1) *Agriculture determines mode of life:* Surely, agriculture is the source of generating income; it also feeds people. But, above all, it is the agriculture which decides the mode of our life. The lifestyle of a community is the result of our agricultural produce and agricultural calendar. In fact, our cultural life in terms of celebration of festivals and rituals is determined by agriculture. What we wear, what we eat and in fact how do we pass our life is decided by agriculture.

(2) *Source of national income:* It is roughly estimated that a little less than our national income is derived from agriculture. During periods of history the kingship has survived out of the revenue drawn from agriculture. Several battles were fought, lost and won, but no ruler ever tried to disturb agriculture. It was known that if agriculture is disturbed, the royal treasure would receive nothing . It, therefore, goes very well with the state governments that revenue of agriculture is the major source of income.

(3) *Strength of power:* Agriculture is also a source of power. Those who hold larger portions of land, yield greater power. One of the characteristics of dominant caste is the size of landholding. The group of peasants, which has larger portions of land, rules the village. In any consideration land gives power to the peasant. Agricultural labourers are looked down in the village hierarchy.

(4) *Status drawn from agriculture:* Yet another importance of agriculture, which is both social and cultural, is that it gives status to the tiller. Marriages, betrothals, loaning are all determined on the possession or non-possession of land. One who does not own any portion of land is the poor, the wretched of the earth. Admittedly, land not only gives income but also bestows status to a person.

(5) *Rural stratification and landholding:* The importance of agriculture also lies in the fact that it ascertains the stratification of society. Land is not divided equally. There are big farmers, small farmers and agricultural labourers in a village. These inequalities arise out of unequal distribution of land. Land is owned on heredity basis. And,

therefore, the social stratification, which results from unequal possession of land, creates problems of inequality.

The contemporary Indian society is now characterised by industrialisation also. Industrial development all over the world seems to have become a dependable alternative for raising the quality of life of people. Surely, there is a talk about *swadeshi* movement. But, in the current situation of globalisation and liberalisation, it is difficult to go back. And, when the country attains some goals in this respect, agriculture is destined to be an important aspect of economy. Even in advanced countries such as US, agriculture has not been marginalised. Looking to this trend of transformation, agriculture for all time to come would occupy a prime place in our efforts of nation building.

Some Basic Statistics about Indian Villages

We are a country of more than five lakhs villages. These villages are not homogeneous. They are diverse in ethnicity, quality of land, hills and plains and even diversified by geography. We give below some of the basic factual data about our villages:

(1) *Heterogeneity:* As stated above, India's villages are not homogeneous. There is enough heterogeneity among the peasants. It means that if there is an agrarian movement it has to mobilise peasants of various strata. The ethnicity, caste and class come in the way of homogenisation.

(2) *Land parcelling:* Roughly it is said that about 15 per cent of peasants hold 60 per cent of total land. And, 85 per cent of peasants possess only 40 per cent of land. Besides this, a larger portion of peasants own land which is not viable economically.

(3) *Green revolution and its impact:* It must be accepted that the green revolution (1967) has contributed substantially in the farm produce. But it was not without its impact. It is a reality that this revolution had created a class structure in rural society. Inequalities in rural society have increased.

Some Erroneous Assumptions about Peasantry

The urban dwellers suffer from some biases against village people. There is a feeling that the rural people are quite backward and weak in their wisdom. They are rustic and do not have a wide worldview.

Some of the biases are given below:

(1) *A lot of docile people:* Generally, the historians and the official ethnographers have described the villagers as passive docile and fatalistic. This is not true. As a matter of fact, the peasants have a robust common sense. They are expert in their occupation. The skills they are having have come to them through the experience.

(2) *Peasant problem is non-issue:* Yet another erroneous view about the peasantry is that they have no real issues with the government. They do not pay any income tax. They are given a number of subsidies. Their consumption of electricity is subsidised. The facilities of irrigation are given to them liberally. There has not been any substantial rise in the land tax. Looking from all these, it is believed that the agrarian unrest is a non-issue. The real problem is that of law and order. And, therefore, what has to be done with the peasants is to tackle them sternly.

(3) *Ethnic diversity:* Somehow an understanding has gone with the leaders, bureaucrats and government that in the long run no peasant movement can succeed in India. Failure seems to be in-built in any peasant movement. It is because of the fact that the peasantry as a whole is highly heterogeneous. It is a divided house of a variety of peasants---big and small. Add to this heterogeneity are the class and political party orientations. All these economic and cultural diversities come in the way of peasant movement. The general understanding of a peasant movement is that it should be curbed.

Such a prejudicial view about peasant movement is belied by the success of some of the movements. The reality is that some of the peasant movements have become movements of class war. And, a few of the movements have been initiated and monitored by left parties.

Who is a Peasant?

Jan Breman[1] has discussed the problems of peasants and agricultural labourers. He says that there is a close relationship between the owner of the land and the worker in the field. This is agrarian relationship as he defines. Talking in terms of peasant castes he observes:

> The peasant castes tilled the soil and exchanged part of their crops for the goods and services of the non-agrarian specialist.

Literally, a peasant is one who tills the land. But such a definition is not so simple as it appears to be. It was true in the past but today there are gentleman peasants who are absentee landlords. There are also peasants who practise sharecropping. Breman considers agricultural labourers also a part of peasantry. For our purpose a peasant is one who generates income out of the land owned by him.

Categories of Peasants

Indian peasantry as elsewhere is not a homogeneous category. There are different types of peasants and the criteria taken for the heterogeneity of peasantry are also varied. Some rural sociologists have taken the ownership of land for peasant categorisation. For instance, Daniel Thorner takes the landownership as a basis for peasant typology. The peasants who have the landownership document---*patta*---in their name are *malik;* those who do not own the *patta,* but cultivate the land are typed as *kisan*---the tiller of the land; and the *mazdoor*, that is, the agricultural labourers. There are some rural sociologists who consider other assets besides agricultural landownership as the criteria for peasant categorisation. Then, the peasant categorisation is made only on the total earnings of a peasant. As a matter of fact, no strait-jacket typology of peasants can be made. The categorisation varies from one empirical situation to another. However, we shall try to present a modest categorisation of peasants in India as under:

(1) *Landownership*

On the basis of landownership as referred above Daniel Thorner has given three categories of peasants as under:

(i) Malik: Who owns the ownership of land or *patta* in his name.

(ii) Kisan: He is the actual tiller of land. This category includes the sharecroppers also.

(iii) Mazdoor: This includes agricultural labourers who earn their livelihood by working in the field.

(2) *Typology by size of landholdings*

Some state governments have defined the types of peasants on the basis of the ownership of size of land. Accordingly, the types of peasants according to the size of landholdings are given below:

(i) Rich peasants: This category includes peasants who possess more than 15 acres of land.

(ii) Small peasants: In this category are included peasants having land between the size of 2.5 to 5 acres.

(iii) Marginal farmers: Those who own land below 2.5 acres.

(iv) Landless peasants: The peasants who earn their livelihood as sharecropper and sub-tenant and have no land in their possession. Actually, they earn their livelihood by manual labour without having ownership of land.

(3) *Class basis of peasant typology*

There are some Marxist sociologists who have taken class approach to the typology of peasants. For instance, Utsa Patnaik[2] observes that class differentiation within peasantry is relevant. There has been growth of capitalism in rural peasantry. In the wake of labour exploitation the Indian peasantry has really taken a class character. Use of outside labour in relation to the use of 'family labour' is the most reliable single index of categorising peasantry. According to her, there are two categories of peasants: (i) big landlords, and (ii) agricultural labourers including the sharecroppers.

Patnaik's categorisation is not acceptable to some Marxist sociologists. For instance, Rudra argues that the essential basis of class categorisation in the peasantry is the contradiction between classes. The non-Marxists criticise class approach to peasant categorisation. They argue that the essence of the process of differentiation lies in the historical conversion of the peasantry, which is not a class as such, into two differentiable classes which are ranged at the opposite ends of a capitalist social relation. A. Saith and A. Tankha[3] on the one hand find that there are rich, middle and poor peasants, and on the other the rich peasants are transforming into capitalist farming households as they use hired labour produce for market and also use modern technology.

(4) *Resource ownership*

There are some sociologists who categorise the peasants on the basis of several other resources like (i) utilisation of loans, (ii) repayment capacity, (iii) tenancy, (iv) ownership of assets, and (v) credit from bank.

K.L. Sharma[4] thus finds five types of peasant groups. They are as under:

(1) owner-cultivator,
(2) largely owner-cultivator,
(3) largely tenant-cultivator,
(4) tenant-cultivator, and
(5) total poor peasant.

It must be admitted that due to the variety of criteria used for categorisation of peasants it is difficult to present a uniform typology of peasants. There would always be as many types of peasants as the criteria we employ. It addition to the criteria used by sociologists, there are economists also who have also used certain criteria for peasant types. For instance, they classify the peasants into (1) landlords, (2) rich peasants, (3) middle peasants, (4) poor peasants, and (5) agricultural peasants. Despite the diversity of criteria for peasant categorisation, it must be said that in any classification of peasants, tenancy, that is, the right of holding land tenancy and and the land size owned, play an important role. Thus, tenancy and land size combined together function as determining criteria for peasant classification.

Agrarian Unrest

Indian peasantry has witnessed certain ups and downs in its long history. There was a time in ancient and medieval history when the country experienced long battles and constant bloodshed. But these long-term disturbances did not affect our peasantry. The wars were fought by the warriors and the peasants with plough on their shoulders to the field for cultivation. Even during the feudal rule the cases of land eviction were few and far between. But, this peaceful and quiet peasantry has now been transformed into an agitating peasantry. A.R. Desai[5] very rightly observes that our peasants today are up in arms. The history of peasant unrest goes back to the first quarter of 1920s. The rural sociologists have analysed the peasant unrest in different terms. For instance, A.R. Desai[6] calls the unrest as the peasant struggle, Kathleen Gough[7] terms it as peasant uprising, for N.G. Ranga[8] again it is a struggle of the peasantry, and it is peasant revolution according to Hamza Alavi.[9] It appears that the sociologists who are oriented to Marxism have analysed the peasant agitation as struggle on the pattern of class struggle and class war. These sociologists look at the peasant agitations from the perspective of class antagonism.

There are few other sociologists who analyse the peasant unrest from the liberal point of view and call it simply a movement. For them, the agitation among the peasants is nothing but only a movement which started as a peasant movement during the struggle for independence in 1920s. D.N. Dhanagare[10] reviews the peasant agitation also as a peasant movement. Whatever term we may give to the peasant agitation, the fact remains that in the post-independent India there has come a revolution in agriculture. It has increased the farm produce. The subsistence farm produce has now become a surplus produce for the market. The agriculture has become capitalistic. With the transformation in agriculture the situation of peasants has also undergone change. And, this change has given rise to many problems. The peasants have demands. The relations between peasants and agricultural labourers have also undergone change and all this requires a through analysis for students of rural sociology. Anyone who decides to understand peasantry must take into consideration all these factors.

Peasant Movements in Pre-Independent India

Peasant discontent as recorded by historians has been a familiar feature of the 19th and 20th centuries. During the first quarter of the 20th century, the peasant movements became much more violent. These movements were deeply influenced by the struggle for national freedom. Though, in different parts of the country, there were several peasant struggles, but here we will discuss the following important struggles only:

(1) Santhal Insurrection (1855-56)
(2) Peasant Revolt in Punjab (1930)
(3) Champaran (Bihar) Movement (1917-18)
(4) Kheda Peasant Struggle (1918)
(5) The Bardoli Satyagraha (1920)
(6) Moplah Rebellion in Malabar (1921)

Writers of India's struggle for independence described that the peasants of the country began to develop political consciousness only after 1918. They started taking part in national struggles and rose in revolt with their own problems. In course of time they constituted their own organisation, framed their own flag and programme. It is enumerated that a few peasant movements also took place before 1918. And, then, the period between 1870 and 1897 was interspersed with severe famines in India. Famines in India, particularly those of 1870, 1896 and 1897 were most devastating. This led to great misery among the *kisans* in affected areas. Periodically occurring economic depressions also led to great hardships among them. As a result of this, occasional peasant struggles brought out against the *jamindars*, moneylenders and the government.

In the pages that follow, we shall describe the above mentioned peasant movements which took place before the attainment of independence.

Santhal Insurrection (1855-56)

The Santhals are a group of tribals largely concentrated in Bihar. They are mainly agriculturists. The first peasant movement which took place in India dates back to Santhal insurrection of 1855-56. This insurrection has reference to the establishment of the Permanent Land Settlement of 1793. The settlement pattern initiated by the British took away lands from the Santhals which they had cultivated for centuries. The *jamindars* took land on auction from the British government and gave it to the peasants who took it for cultivation. The *jamindars* and moneylenders and also groups of Europeans and government officers increased the land tax and oppressed the common peasantry. The Santhals were subdued to an extent that they decided to rise against the *jamindars*, moneylenders and traders.

In the beginning, following Permanent Land Settlement, the Santhals in Bihar did not resist much. They even took to limits of retreat and moved towards the borders of the plains of the Ganga at the very place where the competition for land was the keenest and the rents were the highest. This was unbearable for the Santhals. They took to insurrection. Following were the main causes for the agitation:

(1) The *jamindars*, the police, the revenue and court exercised a combined action of extortions. The Santhals were obliged to pay all kinds of taxes and levies. They were dispossessed of their property. They were abused.

(2) *Violence*: The representatives of *jamindars*, that is, Karendais inflicted personal violence on the Santhals. A variety of *petty* tyrannies were exercised on the timed and yielding Santhals.

(3) *Trespass on Santhal Land:* The rich peasants trespassed on the land of the tenants. They took away their cattle.

(4) *Exorbitant Rate of Interest:* The moneylenders charged interest which was incredibly high. These moneylenders came to be known as *diku*, that is, exploiters by the Santhal. For this matter all the Bengalis who ran their trade in the Santhal areas were known as *dikus.*

(5) *Oppression by Europeans:* The Europeans were employed in Bihar for railroad construction. These Europeans more than often forced abduction of Santhal women and even murder and some unjust acts of oppression. For all this no payment was made by the Europeans employed on the line of the railway.

The *jamindars*, moneylenders, traders and European employees thus oppressed the Santhal peasants to such an extent that there was no alternative left for them rather than to take to insurrection.

Enough is enough; the Santhals could not bear the operation any further. The leading Santhals began to rob the *mahajans* (moneylenders) and the *jamindars* of their ill-earned wealth. But the officials took the Santhals in a very non-serious way. This was far away from reality the Santhals assembled in early part of 1855 in thousands of number. The assembly of Santhal complained that their comrades had been punished while nothing had been done to the *mahajans* whose exactions had compelled them to take the law into their own hands. In course of time the insurrection spread all over the Santhal areas. The Santhals took to guerrilla fighting. This was a new experience for the whole of Bihar. It was surprising to see the Santhals making their own armies, composed of rebellious peasants marching against their oppressors. It was a supreme tribute to their organisation and voluntary discipline that without any pervious military training, such a large number of persons, exceeding 10,000 assembled and disassembled at a very short warning. The Santhal army broke down the postal and railway communications. The government realised that the Santhal rebellion had all the characteristics of defying the government.

Surely, the Santhal insurrection was very strong but it could not succeed against the power of the government. It was suppressed. However, despite failure, the insurrection was successful.

The following measures which taken by the British government an account of the Santhal insurrection:

(1) Before the insurrection, the settlement area of the Santhals was broken into several parts for the purpose of administration. Then, a change was made. The government declared the Santhal concentration area as the *Santhal Pargana.* It was due to the Santhal insurrection that the British government recognised the tribal status of the Santhals. Now they came under uniform administration.
(2) The *diku* population realised that now the Santhals were not an unorganised mass of people. They are organised and have a vibrating enthusiasm. Not only the Santhals of Pargana but the tribals as whole who were agriculturists got united. This was by no means an ordinary achievement. Actually, the Santhals gave a message to the peasants of country as a whole to resist the operation of *jamindars* and moneylenders. The Santhal blood etched the slogan that they were bold and large group of people.

Peasant Revolt in Punjab (1930)

In the first quarter of 1930 the region of Punjab also got the wave of peasant unrest. This movement owned its activities due to the working of the All India Congress Committee. Actually, the peasant movements which took place during the decades of 1920s and 1930s were a part of the struggle for independence. The peasants normally were against the British government. Second, their targets were the *jamindars* and moneylenders. The peasant movement in Punjab was mainly located in the central districts, the most active being the districts of Jullundur, Amritsar, Hoshiarpur, Lyallpur and Sheikhpura. In these districts, most of the peasants were self-cultivating Sikhs. They were already in the national mainstream of freedom struggle. In the beginning, the Muslim and Hindu peasants kept away from the movement but at a later stage they also sought their incorporation in the movement.

There were several causes for the Punjab peasant movement. However, two basic causes as under occupy a pivotal position:

(1) There was the problem of the resettlement of land revenue. Actually, the government wanted to increase the land tax. The increase was phenomenal. The peasantry resisted it.

(2) Yet another increase in the tax was in the form of canal tax. The water rates given by the government were very high and the people opposed it.

During the course of movement which culminated in 1939 the peasants were organised in a forum. The small peasants and sharecroppers got an opportunity to demonstrate their resistance to *jamindars.*

Though the movement was mainly located in the central districts of Punjab, the princely states also witnessed a major outbreak of peasant unrest. In Patiala, which was a princely state the demand of the peasants was to get back the land which was seized by the combine of landlords and officials. Here, the tenants refused to pay the *batai* or share rent to their *biswedar*, that is, landlord. The rebel peasants were suppressed and their leaders were put behind the jail. There was not much loss of men but there were several occasions when there were encounters between the police and the peasants.

Following were the outcomes of peasant revolt in Punjab:

(1) The movement was successful to the extent that by 1953 a legislation was made which enabled the tenants to become owners of their land. This was the height of the success of the Punjab peasant movement.

(2) Beyond Punjab, the impact of peasant movement was widespread. In other parts of the country, the peasants were given some relief in the reduction of taxes and also debt relief. Some security of tenure was also given to the tenants.

Champaran (Bihar) Movement (1917-18)

The Champaran peasant movement was also a part of the wider struggle for independence. When Gandhiji returned from South Africa, he made the experiment of non-cooperation in a smaller way by giving leadership to the peasant struggles in Champaran (Bihar) and later on in Kheda (Gujarat). These struggles were taken up as a reformist movement but the idea was to mobilise the peasants for their demands. The Champaran peasant movement was launched in 1917-18. Its objective was to create awakening among the peasants against the European planters. These planters resorted to illegal and inhuman methods of indigo cultivation at a cost which by no canons of justice could be called an adequate remuneration for the labour done by the peasants.

Gandhiji studied the grievances of the Champaran peasantry. The peasants opposed not only the European planters but also the *jamindars*. Some of the important causes of Champaran peasant struggles were as under:

(1) In Champaran and as a matter of fact in the whole of Bihar, there was an enormous personal increase in the land rent.

(2) The peasants were obliged to grow indigo and this curtailed their freedom of cultivation.

(3) The peasants were compelled to devote the best part of their land for growing particular crops as desired by the landlord. They were also required to give their best time and energy to the crops decided by the landlord.

(4) The peasants were paid very poor wages. These were so meagre that it was very difficult for them to earn their livelihood.

Briefing the situation of peasants in Champaran D.G. Tendulkar writes: The tale of woes of Indian ryots, forced to plant indigo by the British planters, forms one of the blackest chapters in the annals of colonial exploitation. Not a chest of Indigo reached England without being stained with human blood.

(5) One very important reason for the Champaran unrest was the sub-human life led by the people. Gandhiji when visited Champaran was very much displeased by the abject poverty of the peasants. He expressed his feelings in the following words: "The peasants in Champaran are leading their lives like animals, suffering from all kinds of miseries."

The Champaran peasantry suffered terribly at the hands of European planters. The landlords and the government officials combined together also oppressed the peasantry. Gandhiji, who had returned from South Africa, wanted to experience his non-cooperation movement and *satyagraha* in India. Champaran seemed to be a suitable place for making such an experiment. The people were also ready to accept the leadership of Gandhiji, though in the end the incidence of Chauri-Chaura turned the movement to violence. Gandhiji was not happy with all this. However, we would reiterate that the Champaran peasant movement was a part of the national movement of independence.

The course of events that led to the Champaran peasant struggle can be described as under:

(1) One very important feature of Champaran movement was that it was led by intelligentsia. Some of the prominent leaders of the country, namely, Gandhiji, Rajendra Prasad, Brijkishore Prasad and Muzharul Haq participated in the movement. This provided strength and direction to the movement.

(2) On 10th April, 1914 the sufferings of the Champaran peasants were discussed thoroughly at the annual conference of the Bihar Provincial Congress Committee, which found that the Champaran peasants were in a serious situation.

(3) Next year, in 1915, the Provincial Congress Committee recommended for the constitution of an inquiry committee to take stock of the Champaran peasantry.

(4) It was in 1916 that the Indian National Congress, in its Lucknow session, discussed the peasant situation of Champaran. It was decided that something had to be done to give immediate relief to the Champaran peasants.

(5) On 14th May, 1917 Gandhiji wrote a letter to the District Magistrate of Champaran, W.B. Heycock, wherein he showed his concern to give the peasants freedom from landlords and government. Gandhiji wanted to improve the relations between the *jamindars* and tenants.

(6) Rajendra Prasad[11] was very much unhappy with the inhuman life led by the Champaran peasants. He himself was an eye-witness to the poor and miserable condition of the peasants.

(7) It was in 1908 that the peasants at the Sathi factory and other neighbouring factories stopped the cultivation of indigo and organised an agitation. To quell it, 19 persons were convicted in

December 1908. Nearly 200 prisoners awaited trial at Motihari under different charges including assaulting planters and arson.

(8) The struggle of the Champaran peasants took place in April 1917. The British government adopted very serious methods to oppress the peasants. They were tortured for not paying the excessive revenues. "Among the methods adopted were setting Dhangars and Doms, the low caste people, on the high caste tenants decides the policemen tying them down and beating them, and putting logs of wood on their chest. In another method of torture the hands were put underneath the leg and tied to the neck, the leg being raised. If the peasants did not pay even then, they were brought to the factories. They were forced to embrace a neem tree with both their hands tied together, and set upon by policemen. On such occasions, the indigo planter used to be present on the scene. On the other hand, the red ants on the tree would bite the man tied to the tree, but he could do nothing as his hands were tied."[12]

The Champaran peasant movement had to undergo severe sufferings. But the participation of the general peasantry and the ideology of non-violence gave strength to the peasants. It is interesting to look at the outcomes of this movement.

The Champaran movement is described to be a success story in the history of peasant movements in India. Some of the important outcomes of the movement are given below:

(1) One very important outcome of the movement was the enactment of Champaran Agrarian Act assented by Governor General of India on 1st May, 1918.

(2) E.M.S. Namboodripad, the leader of the left movement in India, considered Champaran movement as a contribution to the development of nationalism. He observes:

> ...despite stiff opposition by the European planters and their protectors in the bureaucracy, Gandhiji and his comrades were able to bring the struggle to a successful conclusion.[13]

(3) There were few scholars who did not consider the Champaran movement as a success story. The movement did not succeed to strike against the exploitation and discrimination with which the peasants suffered. Ramesh Chandra Dutt, for instance, argued that the settle-

ments made between the government and the peasants did not embrace the exploitation of our peasants by *jamindars*, so also this agitation led by the Mahatma in Champaran did not lead up to any fight against the main causes for the terrible poverty and sufferings of Champaran peasants, namely, the excessive rents and exorbitant incidence of debts... it does strike us rather significant that both he (Gandhiji) and Rajendra Prasad should have remained scrupulously silent upon the ravages of the *jamindari* system.

Kheda Peasant Struggle (1918)

The Kheda peasant struggle is also known as no-tax peasant struggle. It was a *satyagraha* launched in March 1919 under the leadership of Gandhiji, Sardar Vallabhbhai Patel, Indulal Yajnik, N.M. Joshi, Shankerlal Pareekh and several others. It was again an experiment, quite like that of Champaran, made on non-violence. It was also participated by intelligentsia. Incidentally, the movement provided an opportunity to the educated public workers to establish contact with the actual life of the peasantry. The educated workers learnt to identify themselves with the peasantry and made themselves available for sacrifices.

The Kheda peasantry mainly consisted of the Patidar peasants. The Patidars have always been known for their skills in agriculture. The land of Kheda---a part of central Gujarat---is quite fertile for the cultivation of tobacco and cotton crops. Educationally also, the Patel cultivators are well-off.

The struggle of the peasants was organised for several causes. However, a few important causes are given below:

(1) The government reassessed the Kheda land and the cultivated crops. On the basis of land data, collected in this way, the revenue was increased. This was unacceptable to the peasants.

(2) The peasants had suffered a famine and this had resulted in a large-scale failure of crops. The government, however, did not accept the failure of crops and insisted on the full realisation of land tax. The peasantry, on the other hand, made its own inquires and emphasised persistently that the government was not justified in demanding the full land tax.

The Gujarat Sabha consisting of the peasants, submitted petitions and telegrams to the highest governing authorities of the province requesting for the suspension of the revenue assessment for the year 1919. But the officials maintained and rejected the popular demand for non-payment of tax. When the government refused to consider the demands of the Kheda peasants for non-payment of land tax, Gandhiji exhorted the peasants to resort to *satyagraha.*

In some cases, the government removed the opium crop by alleging that it was without permission. This was considered to be a mischievous technique adopted by the government.

The Patidar peasants and the intelligentsia developed its faith in *satyagraha*. Gandhiji observed:

> The beginning of an awakening among the peasants of Gujarat has come.

The non-payment of land tax led the government officials to auction the peasants' cattle, confiscate their houses, and take away their movable property. The peasants were given notices of fines and penalties.

The Kheda movement was terminated owing to the acceptance of some of the prime demands of the peasants. Some of the achievements of the struggles were as under:

(1) It was settled that the well-to-do Patidar peasants would pay up the land rent and the poorer ones would be granted remissions. The bulk of the peasant mass who constituted the small farmers were by and large satisfied.

(2) What is important about the movement is that it created an awakening among peasants about their demands. On the other hand, they sought their involvement in the struggle for independence. The impact of the success was also realized among the peasants of Gujarat and the neighbouring states.

(3) Writing about the wider success of Kheda movement Sukhbir Choudhary observes:

> The acceptance of the peasants' demand brought a new awakening among the peasantry. The struggle brought home to them that their complete emancipation from injustice and exploitation would not take place so long as their country did not achieve complete independence. The bureaucracy appeared to these people no longer their

well-wisher but only an agent of the alien regime.[14]

Bardoli Satyagraha (1928)

Quite like Kheda peasant struggle, the Bardoli (Surat, Gujarat) movement was also a no-tax movement. It would not be wrong to say that the Bardoli *satyagraha* of the peasants was the child of the non-cooperation movement started by Gandhiji. Gandhiji selected Bardoli as a suitable place for launching civil disobedience campaign because the place had witnessed and participated in the constructive work. D.N. Dhanagare has sketched a portrait of the socio-economic background of Bardoli. He says that Patidars were the dominant cultivators in Surat *taluka.* They were divided into two classes: (1) Kali Paraj, and (2) Ujta Paraj. The 'Kali Paraj' class of peasants literally means black skinned. It included the lower castes, tribals, backward classes and untouchables. The 'Ujla Paraj' literally means fair-complexioned people comprising all upper and well-to-do castes such as Patidar, Vania, Brahmin and so on. Gandhiji observed that the Kali Paraj were living in dire poverty. Actually, they survived a near-slave life in Bardoli.

The Patidars were a well-to-do class of peasants. Their relations with the lower caste, that is, small, marginal and agricultural labourers were quite unsatisfactory. The land with the poorer peasants was very meagre and largely unproductive. The wages of the agricultural labourers were so small that they could hardly keep their body and soul together.

The Patidars could afford to invest their surplus money in the improvement of land. Some of the Patidars also worked in London and Africa. Whatever surplus money they got from foreign countries was also invested in the purchase of new land and provision of irrigation facilities. It may also be pertinent to mention here that the land of Surat *taluka* was quite fertile. The black soil was quite suitable for taking cotton crop.

The Bardoli *satyagraha* was launched in mid-February 1928. By July all noon-agriculturists' holdings were forfeited by the government. Out of the land taken over about one tenth was sold. As regards the cultivating landowners, 50,000 acres of land were forfeited though not sold. The movement thus became serious during the months of April and May. Some of the causes of the Bardoli movement are given below:

(1) Jan Breman[15] has very elaborately discussed the causes by providing historical review. His main argument is that the relations between the Kali Paraj and the landlords were characterised by exploitation. The stock of Kali Paraj people mainly consisted of Dubla, also called Halpati. The Ujli Paraj peasants cornered most of the benefits in terms of ownership of land and other facilities. All this created an antagonism between the rich and big Patidar peasants and the poor and slave-like small, marginal peasants and agricultural labourers.

(2) At the initiation of Gandhiji some constructive work was started in the entire Bardoli *taluka*. On the one hand schools, *ashrams* and hostels were started whereas on the other hand reform movements were begun. This created an awakening among the peasant masses to get mobilised for fulfilling their demands. The constructive programmes also trained the youths to prepare for non-violence and *satyagraha* movement.

(3) Interestingly enough, the *Patidar Yuvak Mandals* were constituted for the social reforms of the members of Patidar community. These youth associations had not only created unity among the Patidars but also developed among them a sense of antagonism against the peasants of lower castes. There is an interesting anecdote given by Gandhiji in *Harijan*. He happened to visit Bardoli and was accompanied by Mahadev Desai. Desai reported the anecdote in *Harijan* in the following words:

> In 1921 when Gandhiji asked some one about the population of Bardoli *taluka*, he said it was 60,000, the poor Dubla (Halpati) and the Chaudhra (tribal) not counting at all, whereas, they were not less than one-third of these.[16]

Dhanagare argues that the status of the Kali Paraj peasants was that of a serf of medieval Europe. What is worse, the slave in America before the abolition was the legal property of his master. The Dubla or the Hali has never been that kind of poverty. He borrowed money and in repayment of it worked as his master's permanent agricultural labourer for a lifetime, simply because he could never repay the loan.

(4) As a result of the constructive work done by Gandhiji the spinning wheel—*Charkha*—had become popular among the backward castes and tribes. A *Swarajya Asharam* was established in Surat and six similar centres were set up in Bardoli *taluka* to carry out con-

structive activities and to diffuse new political culture.[17] Though the Patidars appeared to be benevolent to the lower castes, the harmonisation of the latter prepared a suitable ground for peasant *satyagraha*.

(5) The *Hali* system, though was prevalent in south Gujarat, was a speciality of Bardoli. This system is based on the tribal agricultural labourers and the high caste landlords, that is, Patidars. Explaining the *Hali* system which is largely responsible for Bardoli *satyagraha*, Dhanagare observes:

> Relations between a *Hali* labourer and the landowner who hired him were the same as those between a serf and his master in medieval feudal society. This system of recruiting agricultural labour had grown out of moneylending practices. When a poor *Dubla* borrowed money for the marriage of his son, he in return, agreed to work on his creditor's farm. Wages, just enough for subsistence, were paid in kind and were so low that the amount borrowed could never be repaid. Consequently, for a *Hali* the chain of bondage continued from one generation to another.[18]

The fact of the matter is that the *Hali* cultivated the lands owned by upper caste people like Patidars, Anavil Brahmins and also Rajputs. What is worse, the higher castes only helped to reinforce the economic ties between the serfs, that is, tenants and their owners. And, the fact that until 1938 no movement was launched for freeing the *Dubla* agricultural serfs. And, the abolition of the *Hali* system in Surat district, suggests how deeply serfdom was rooted in the agrarian system there.

The Bardoli *satyagraha* thus was much against the *Hali* system.

(6) It was in January 1926 that Jayakar who was incharge of reassessment of land revenue had recommended a 30 per cent increase over existing assessment. This increase in land tax was immediately opposed by the Congressmen. They set up an inquiry committee to go into the issue. Its report, published in July 1926, came to the conclusion that the increase was unjustified. At a later stage, in July 1927, some reduction in land tax was made. The Congress Party found the concessions too meagre. These were not acceptable to them.

The course of events that led to the Bardoli *satyagraha* can be described as under:

(1) The Bardoli peasant agitation had the sympathy of educated

persons and also nationalist leaders. Vallabh Bhai Patel was contacted by the local leaders to take up the leadership of movement. A meeting of representatives of 60 villages at Bamni in Kadod division invited Sardar Patel to lead the campaign. The local leaders also contacted Gandhiji and after having assured him to observe non-violence, seriously launched the movement.

(2) Sardar Patel assumed the leadership and went to Bardoli. He wrote to the government to fulfil the demands of the peasants. Meanwhile, a meeting of a peasants of Bardoli *taluka* passed a resolution advising all occupants of land to refuse payment of the revised assessment until the government appointed an independent tribunal or accepted the current amount as full payment. Describing the decision of the peasants committee, Bipan Chandra observes:

> Peasants were asked to take oaths in the name of *Prabhu* (the Hindu name for god) and *Khuda* (the Muslim name for god) that they would not pay the land revenue. The resolution was followed by the recitation of sacred texts from the *Gita* and the *Koran* and songs from Kabir, who symbolised Hindu-Muslim unity. The *satyagraha* had begun.[19]

In this connection it may be said that Patel was incharge of the whole agitation. His capacity as an organiser, speaker, indefatigable campaigner and inspirer of ordinary men and women was already known. But these were the women of Bardoli who gave him the title of 'Sardar'.

(3) The Bardoli *taluka* was organised in such a way that the agitation could be started effectively. The whole *taluka* was divided into three camps, *chhavanis*, each under the charge of an experienced leader. One hundred political workers, drawn from all over the province, assisted by 1,500 volunteers, many of whom were students, formed the army of the movement. It was for the first time that an army of non-violent workers was developed.

(4) An extensive network of mobilising the peasants was made. Regular meetings, speeches, distribution of pamphlets, door-to-door persuasion and other things of propaganda were taken up by the volunteers. The important point is that the organisation of movement was so very well executed that the peasants of the whole *taluka* demonstrated their strength through rallies and strikes to the government.

(5) The government of Bombay became stern and took all repressive measures such as attachment of land, and crops, and confiscation of cattle and other movable property. The government forfeited a large chunk of land, say 50,000 acres. At their level, the agitating peasants boycotted all government officials and purchasers of auctioned property. And, thus, drove them to desperation. In short, the government's handling of Bardoli agitation was both impolite and crude.

(6) The national leadership was much influenced by the *satyagraha* displayed by the Bardoli peasants. The members of the Bombay Legislative Council from Gujarat resigned *en masse* as a mark of protest against the government's policy; this was followed by Vitthalbhai Patel's threat to resign. Vallabhbhai was a big leader who was president of the Bombay Legislative Council. As a matter of fact, the pressure of the legislative assembly was so strong that the government was obliged to take a soft stand against the movement.

(7) The Bardoli peasant movement, in course of time, took an altogether new dimension. Workers in Bombay textile mills went on strike and there was a threat to bring about a railway strike that would make movement of troops and supplies to Bardoli impossible. Even the flames of Bardoli had reached to Punjab and many *jathas* of peasants were despatched to Bardoli. Yet another strength of the movement came from Gandhiji who shifted to Bardoli on 2nd August, 1928.

(8) An enquiry committee was constituted by the government under the presidentship of a judicial officer, Broomfield in association with Maxwell, to find out the details about Bardoli agitation. The findings of the committee came to the conclusion that the increase had been unjustified. The committee also suggested to reduce the enhancement of land tax.

Soon, the Bardoli peasant movement became a national issue. Gandhiji, alongwith Patel, conducted the movement in such a way that it carried, throughout the period, its non-violent character. The national leaders linked the movement with the movement for freedom. The British government thus had high stakes in the Bardoli agitation. The Simon Commission was about to come in India and the Congress declared that it would have nation-wide boycott of the Simon Commission. Looking to the national importance of Bardoli the British government took a softline. Sardar Patel was contacted and some kind of agreement was struck. Referring to the outcome of Bardoli agitation D.N. Dhanagare writes:

> Accordingly, on 18 July, 1928 Wilson offered terms to Patel whereby the peasants of Bardoli paid the full assessment or the differences between the old and new revenue demands, and abandoned the *satyagraha* first so that a special inquiry into only the disputed facts regarding revenue settlement in Bardoli *taluka* could be conducted. Patel once again rejected them and insisted on the release of all prisoners---satyagrahis, restoration of forfeited lands (whether sold or not) to original landowners and appointment of an impartial committee as his pre-conditions for withdrawing the agitation.[20]

The withdrawal of the movement was not a happy affair. Verbally the government agreed that the pre-conditions of Patel would be fulfilled but informally it was decided that the full enhancement of rent would not be paid. Nobody took the governors declaration seriously when he declared that he had secured an unconditional surrender. In fact, it were the peasants who laughed the last.

The Bardoli *satyagraha* influenced not only other peasant movements in the country, but it also provided a new strength to the national freedom movement. Gandhiji very rightly observed on the success of Bardoli agitation:

> Whatever the Bardoli struggle may be, it clearly is not a struggle for the direct attainment of *swaraj.* That every such awakening, every such effort as that of Bardoli will bring *swaraj* nearer and may bring it nearer even then any direct effort is undoubtedly true.[21]

The Bardoli movement has been criticised from varying perspectives. D.N. Dhanagare has raised the issue as to what extent the *satyagraha* was a reality or a myth created by the Gandhians. At a broader plane it could be safely said that the Bardoli agitation was more a national issue for experimenting *satyagraha* as a method for freedom struggle. Definitely, not much attention was paid to the basic problems of the peasants. The problem of *Hali Pratha*, which was highly exploitative was not raised at all by the movement. Dhanagare argues that the movement pleaded the cause of the rich and middle class peasants. The poorer masses of peasantry who had very little land in their possession were altogether neglected. But, surely, the movement provided a strength to the national freedom struggle.

Moplah Rebellion in Malabar (1921)

The Moplah peasant movement was engineered in August 1921 among the peasants of Malabar district in Kerala. The Moplah tenants were Muslims and they agitated against the Hindu landlords and the British government. Their grievances related to lack of any security of tenure, renewal fees, high rents and other oppressive landlord exactions. In the 19th century as well, there had been cases of Moplah resistance to landlord oppression but what erupted in 1921 was on a different scale altogether.

Actually, the freedom movement covered a span of long decades, beginning from 1835 to 1947. The social and economic background of the Moplah has been quite heterogeneous. The elites among the Moplah earned their livelihood by working as petty traders and merchants. However, the masses of Moplah earned their livelihood by working as small agriculturists. They were the tenants of the big landlords who happened to be high-caste Hindus. Though the Moplahs were poor they imitated the traditional ways of Nayars and acquired the reputation of warriors. There was British rule in Malabar. The officials in collaboration with Hindu landlords exploited the Moplahs and oppressed them a great length.

The Moplah agitation of 1921 was preceded by several movements between 1835 to 1921. D.N. Dhanagare elaborates the series of Moplah movement which took place before the major Moplah movement of 1921. He traces the history of Moplah movement as under:

> Significantly, as soon as the *Jenmi* landlords, backed by the police, the law courts and the revenue officials, tightened their grip on the subordinate classes, the Moplah peasantry in its turn started to revolt against its oppressors. The first such outbreak occurred in 1836 and thereafter between 1836 and 1854, 22 similar uprisings occurred, of which two, one in 1841 and the other in 1849, were quite serious. In general, outbreaks followed a similar pattern, almost invariably it would involve a group of Moplah youths attacking a Brahmin Jenmi, a Nayar official or a Jenmi's servant; sometimes it also involved the burning or defilement of temples, and occasionally the burning or looting of landlords' houses. Such a rebels often took refuge in a mosque or seized a Hindu temple for their final stand against the police or troops, who in the end would shoot them down.[21]

The Moplah movement of 1921 was altogether different. First, it erupted among the Muslim peasants against the Hindu landlords. Second, it was characterised by violence. Third, the movement as the history goes, fell in the trap of Hindu-Muslim riot. During this period there was Khilafat movement—a movement raised for the attainment of freedom for Muslims.

Some of the causes of Moplah peasant movement are given below:

(1) Any analysis of the peasant movement of Moplahs should take into account that the Moplahs were Muslim peasants. Their landlords who were called *Jenmis* were mostly Hindus. The relations between the *Jenmis* and the Moplahs were historically quite unfriendly. In other words, the relations were both economically and religiously antagonistic. Since 1835 the Hindu landlords suppressed the Moplah tenants. Thus, the basic cause of the Moplah agitation was the operation against the *Jenmis.*

(2) The land tenure system in Malabar was quite unfavourable to the Moplah tenants. There was total insecurity of tenure to the Moplahs and they could be ejected from their land without any appropriate notice.

(3) The immediate cause of Moplah agitation was the renewal of fee at an exorbitant rate fixed by the *Jenmis.* This was unbearable for the Moplahs.

(4) The exactions practised by the *Jenmis* were of very high order. More than often the Moplahs were discriminated against the Hindu tenants.

The course of events that led to the Moplah movement can be described as under:

(1) The first impetus for Moplah resistance against the landlords came from the Malabar District Congress Committee held at Majeri in April 1921. This conference supported the tenants' cause and demanded legislation to regulate landlord-tenant relations.

(2) Following the Minjeri conference of 1920, the Moplah tenants formed an association which had its branches in the whole of Kerala. This brought the Moplah tenants under one organisation.

(3) Yet another motivating factor for 1921 Moplah agitation was the Khilafat movement which constituted a wider part of national struggle for independence. This movement developed its roots in

Malabar also. The Moplahs took active part in Khilafat movement also. Actually, in practice, the meetings of the Moplahs and the Khilafat could hardly be separated. The bonds between the Khilafat movement and Moplah tenants became so much mixed that the government issued prohibitory notices on all Khilafat meetings on 5th February, 1921. This displeased the Moplahs and ended up with the agitation of the Moplah peasantry.

(4) The British government was weakened as a result of the First World War. It was not in a position to take strong military action against the Moplahs. As a result of this, the Moplahs began to exhibit increasing science of turbulence and defiance of authority. The final break came only when the district magistrate of Eranad *taluka*, on 20th August, 1921, raided the mosque at Tirurangadi to arrest Ali Musaliar—a Khilafat leader and a highly respected priest. The people were quiet and peaceful, but the police opened fire on the unarmed crowd and many were killed. A clash ensued and government offices were destroyed, records burnt and the treasury looted. The rebellion soon spread into the Eranad, Valluvanad and Ponnani *talukas*—all Moplahs strongholds.

(5) In the agitation the targets of Moplah attack were the unpopular *Jenmis*, mostly Hindus, police stations, treasuries and offices, and British planters. The Hindu landlords who were lenient in their relations with the Moplahs were spared by the latter. Interestingly, the Moplah rebels travelled several miles through territory populated by Hindus and attacked only the landlords. This gave a communal flavour to the peasant agitation. As a matter of fact, the Malabar people in general lost all their sympathy with the Moplahs. Communalisation of peasant agitation was suicidal for the Moplahs. Commenting on this new aspect of the Moplah agitation Bipan Chandra observes:

> The communalisation of the rebellion completed the isolation of Moplahs. British repression did the rest and by December 1921 all resistance had come to a stop. The toll was heavy indeed: 2,337 Moplahs had lost their lives. Unofficial estimates placed the number at above 10,000; 45,404 rebels were captured or had surrendered. But the toll was in fact even heavier, though in a very different way from then onwards, the militant Moplahs were so completely crushed and demoralised that till independence their participation in any form of politics was almost nil.[23]

The movement of Moplah is a failure story. Much of its defeat lies in the fact that it took to communal swing. Secondly, when the Khilafat movement stood for non-violence and also the struggle for independence the Moplah took to violence as a method of agitation. Thirdly, the movement did not motivate the peasantry of the neighbourhood to stand in arms against the landlords. It was perhaps a lone tragedy of Moplahs that their landlords happened to be Hindus. This was never a case in any of the agitations which took place during 1920s and earlier.

To conclude, it can be said that the peasant movements which took place in 19th and early 20th centuries were a part of wider national struggle. On the one hand, these movements were influenced by the freedom struggle and on the other hand they had their impact on the struggle also. Most of these movements were the experiments in *satyagraha* and non-cooperation of Gandhiji. Then, there was participation of intelligentsia and educated people in these movements. There were several causes of these movements; the major the being increase in land tax, security of tenure and exploitation of the poor peasantry by the landlords. The big and middle peasants also participated in the movements. Most of the movements, leaving aside Moplah, were characterised by non- violence.

In the next part of the chapter we propose to discuss the peasant movements which took place either at the transitional period, that is, the end of freedom struggle and the attainment of freedom or soon after independence. This will be followed by an analysis of a few of the ongoing peasant movements in contemporary India.

Peasant Movements at the Eve of Independence and Afterwards

Telangana Peasant Struggle (1947-51)

This movement was launched in the state of Andhra Pradesh against the former Nizam of Hyderabad. The agrarian social structure in the Nizam's Hyderabad was of a feudal order. It had two kinds of land tenure systems, namely, *raiyatwari* and *jagirdari.* Under the *raiyatwari* system, the peasants owned *patta* and were proprietors of the land; they were registered occupants. The actual cultivators of the land were known as *shikmidars*. *Khalsa* lands were chieftain's lands, and out of revenue collected from these lands, personal expenses of the royalty were met out. The *Deshmukhs* and *Deshpandes* were the hereditary collectors of revenue for *khalsa* villages. In *jagir* villages, the tax was collected through *jagirdars* and their agents. Both the *jagirdars* and the *Deshmukhs* wielded immense power at the local level.

The region of Telangana was characterised by a feudal economy. The main commercial crops, viz., groundnut, tobacco and castor seed, were the monopoly of the landowning brahmins. The rise of Reddis and peasant proprietors further strengthened the high castes and propertied class. The non-cultivating urban groups, mostly Brahmins, Marwaris, Komtis and Muslims, began to take interest in acquiring land. Consequently, the peasant proprietors slided down to the status of tenants-at-will, share-croppers and landless labourers.

Following were the main causes of the movement:

(1) The Nizam's former Hyderabad state had a feudal structure of administration. In the *jagir* area, the agents of the *jagirdar* who were the middlemen, collected the land taxes. There was much of oppression by the *jagirdar* and his agents. They were free to extort from the actual cultivators a variety of taxes. This condition of exploitation remained in practice till the *jagirdari* system was abolished in 1949.

On the other hand the *khalsa* land or the *raiyatwari* system was also exploitative though the severity of exploitation in the *khalsa* system was a little lesser. In the *khalsa* villages, the *Deshmukhs* and *Deshpandes* worked as intermediaries. They were not in the payroll of the *jagir* administration; they were only given a percentage or the total land collection made by them. The *Deshmukhs* and *Deshpandes* then developed a habit to cheat the peasants by creating fraud in the land records. This, in countless instances they reduced the actual cultivator to the status of tenant-at-will or a landless labourer.

In both the systems of administration, i.e., *jagir* and *khalsa*, the peasants were exploited by the intermediaries appointed by Nizam. High taxes, fraud with the record and exploitation resulted in creating discontent among the poor peasants.

(2) Yet another cause of peasant movement in Telangana was the exploitation of the big peasants. D.N. Dhanagare informs that the

jagirdars and the *Deshmukhs* had thousands of acres of land in their possession. The families of these big peasants and their heads were called *Durra* or *Dora*. It means, the master or lord of the village. Dhanagare says that the *Dora* exploited the small peasants and agricultural labourers. This exploitation, in course of time, became legitimised with the big farmers. It was considered to be the privilege of the *Dora* to exploit the masses of peasants. Dhanagare observes:

> Such exaction had become somewhat legitimised by what was known as the *vetti* system under which a landlord or a *Deshmukh* could force a family from among his customary retainers to cultivate his land and to do one job or the other—whether domestic, agricultural or official, as an obligation to the master.[24]

(3) In the whole former state of Nizam a system of slavery, quite like that of *Hali* of south Gujarat, was prevalent. This system was known as *Bhagela*. The *Bhagela* were drawn mostly from aboriginal tribes who were tied to the master by debt. According to *Bhagela* system, the tenant who had taken loan from the landlord was obliged to serve him till the debt is repaid. In most of the cases, the *Bhagela* was required to serve the landlord for generations.

(4) The Reddis and Kammars were notable castes who traditionally worked as traders and moneylenders. They exercised a great deal of influence in the countryside. They wanted to pull down the dominance of Brahmins as agriculturists in the state.

(5) The Telangana region was economically backward. The development of agriculture depended on the facilities of irrigation. The commercial crops could hardly be taken without irrigation facilities. Though, the lack of irrigation was realised by Nizam and he provided irrigation facilities to the peasants both in *khalsa* and *jagir* villages. *But, these facilities were largely cornered by the big farmers.*

(6) Land alienation was not new to the former Hyderabad state. Between 1910 to 1940, the frequency of land dispossession increased. On the one hand, the land possessed by the non cultivating urban people, mostly Brahmins, Marwaris, and Muslims increased and on the other hand the tribal peasants got reduced to the status of marginal farmers and landless labourers. Describing the impact of

land alienation on the poorer peasants D.N. Dhanagare writes:

> As a result of growing land alienation many actual occupants or cultivators were being reduced to tenants-at-will, sharecroppers or landless labourers ... in fact, where rich *Pattadars* held holdings too large to manage, they tended to keep a certain amount of irrigated land to be cultivated with the help of hired labour and turned over most of their dry lands either to *Bhagela* serfs or to tenant cultivators on very high produce rents.[25]

The Telangana peasant unrest did not erupt over night. It took about three to four decades. Actually, till 1930, the poor condition of the peasants had reached its culmination. Meanwhile, there had been much transformation in agricultural economy. The Telangana economy, which was only subsistence economy, had grown into market economy by the 1940s. With the change in capitalistic agricultural economy, there was no change in the status of the tenants and sharecroppers. Actually, the modes of production and exchange remained pre-capitalist or semi-feudal and emerged as the major source of discontent among the poor peasantry in Telangana. On the other hand, with the termination of Second World War, there was a terrible fall in wholesale prices. The price trends strengthened the position of moneylenders and traders who tightened their grip on indebted small *Pattadars* and tenants. One of the bitter consequences of the forces of change has been an increase in the number of agricultural labourers. It appears that there was enough discontent among the lower segments of peasantry. Peasants were only waiting for some opportunity to engineer some insurrection.

The course of events that led to the Telangana peasant struggle can be described as under:

(1) The Telangana peasant movement was engineered by Communist Party of India (CPI). It is said to be a revolution committed by Communists. The Communist Party started working in Telangana in 1936. Professor N.G. Ranga had laid down the regional level peasant organisation in Telangana. This regional organisation was affiliated to the All India Kisan Sabha---an organ of CPI. Within a period of three or four years, say by 1940, the CPI had established its roots in the former Hyderabad state. During the period from 1944 to 1946, the Communist activities increased in several of the districts of Hyderabad. A proper framework was, therefore, prepared for launching a

peasant movement in Telangana.

(2) The next event which took place in Hyderabad and more actually in Telangana was the famine of 1946. All the crops failed and there was a crisis of the availability of fodder. The prices of food, fodder and other necessities of life increased. This was a crisis for the tenants and the sharecroppers. Actually, the year 1946 provided all opportunities for engineering the peasant struggle. In the early July 1946, the peasants resisted the government orders. Militant action was taken by the CPI-led peasants.

(3) The CPI made an objective to mobilise the peasants. It took up a campaign to propagate the demands of the lower peasants. By the middle of 1946, the Communist propaganda was fully intensified and covered about 300 to 400 villages under its influence. The movement during this period was slow but the peasants showed enough resistance to the government dictates. However, it must be mentioned that in the mobilisation of peasantry, only Telangana local peasants participated.

(4) The second conference of CPI was held in March 1948. It resolved to give a revolutionary turn to the peasant movement in Telangana. The peasants later on were organised into an army and intermittently fought guerrilla wars. Writing about this part of the course of events of Telangana peasant struggle Hamza Alavi observes:

> ...Telangana movement had a Guerrilla army of about 5,000. The peasants killed or drove out the landlords and the local bureaucrats and seized and distributed the land. They established governments of peasant 'soviets' which were integrated regionally into a control organisation. Peasant rule was established in an area of 15,000 sq. miles. with a population of four million. The government of the armed peasantry continued until 1950; it was not finally crushed until the following year. Today, the area remains one of the political strongholds of the Communist Party.[26]

(5) Besides the peasant agitation, a parallel discontent was also taking place in Hyderabad. A para-military voluntary force, organised by Kasim Rizvi, was taking its roots. The members of this voluntary organisation were known as *Razakars*. This organisation was against the peasants. The peasants consolidated their movement in the face of the oppression of Nizam, activities of *Razakars* and the authority crisis in Hyderabad.

(6) On September 13, 1948, the Indian army marched into Hyderabad and within less than a week the Nizam's army, police and the *Razakars* surrendered without resistance. The police action, taken by the newly framed Central Government of independent India, was very quick to suppress the peasant movement. D.N. Dhanagare elaborates the police action as under:

> On India's part the 'police action' was taken to stop the *Razkar* frenzies as they not only created anarchic conditions within the state but also posed a serious threat to the internal security of neighbouring Indian territory. The police action was, therefore, unsavoury but essential ... once the *Razakars* were overpowered, and a military administration set up... the offensive was immediately directed at the peasant rebels in the troubled districts of Telangana. The superior Indian army spared no measure to suppress the communist squads.[27]

The peasant movement in Telangana had to be withdrawn. Actually the police action gave a death blow to the Communist-led Telangana peasant movement. In this struggle, the movement had to suffer a lot. Fighting with the Indian army over 2,000 peasants and party workers were killed. By August 1949, nearly 25,000 Communists and active participants were arrested; by July 1950 the total number of detainees had reached 10,000. This should suffice as an index of the intensity of Telangana peasants struggle.

The Telangana peasant movement continued for about five years. Its outcomes can be enumerated as below:

(1) The struggle had the participation of a mixed class of peasantry. Though the rich peasants, mainly the Brahmins, had their involvement in the struggle, the major achievement was that the struggle for the first time brought together the tenants, sharecroppers and the landless labourers. This was by all means a very big achievement of the struggle. The Kammar and the Reddy castes who belonged to the rich class of peasants though gained enough but the movement consolidated the strength of poor peasants, particularly the tribals, who were the victims of *vetti*---the bonded labour.

(2) Yet another benefit of this struggle was in the favour of the Communist Party. The Communist, for a long time to come, exercised their hegemony over the entire state of Hyderabad.

(3) Though the Communist Party, as a whole, benefited from the Telangana peasant struggle, it had its own losses also. Ideologically,

the party got split from top to bottom. One group of Communists supported the struggle while other decried. The second group argued that the struggle was in no case less than terrorism. Writing about the division of Communist Party during the struggle, P. Sundarayya writes:

> It is relevant to mention here that during the course of the struggle, particularly during the phase of its last two years, the Communist Party from top to bottom was sharply divided into two hostile camps, one defending the struggle and its achievements and the other denouncing and decrying it as terrorism, etc. Those who opposed this struggle had even openly come out with the press, providing grist to the mill of the enemies in maligning the struggle and the Communist Party that was leading it. This sharp political ideological split, though enveloping the entire party in the country, was particularly sharp and acute in Telangana.[28]

(4) So far the demands of the poor agricultural classes were concerned the movement was a failure. Surely, there were some gains to Kammar and Reddy---the rich peasant, but the gains of the poor peasants such as sharecroppers were quite meagre.

The Telangana peasant struggle, it must be boldly said, was from above and not from the peasants themselves. No single agrarian stratum initiated the movement. It was all the handy work of the Communist Party. Despite the failure story of Telangana struggle it must be admitted that it was a source of inspiration for the Communists as a whole in the country. D.N. Dhanagare very rightly makes his conclusive statement about the outcome of the movement when he says:

> ... Telangana insurrection was no more successful than other peasant resistance movements in India. Like all other movements, though, the Telangana struggle has become the source of legends and inspiration for the radical left in India. Recently, there has been renewed interests, academic as well as political, in the study of the Telangana struggle, its silver jubilee celebrated by all shades of Communist Party in India, became, however, an occasion for mutual mud-slinging; but that must be left out of this study.

Naxalbari Peasant Struggle

The Naxalbari peasant struggle was launched in March-April 1967.

This movement had Tebhaga (1946) peasant movement as its torch bearer. The light provided by Tebhaga inspired the Naxalbari movement. The prime objective of this movement was to change the whole society, not the conditions of peasants only. Then, the Naxalbari movement was highly charged by the ideology of violence. The idiom of the movement was that power comes from the barrel of the gun and not by slogans and non-violence. The movement was aimed at the total annihilation of the big farmers, landlords and jagirdars. Nothing short of it could change the structure of society. Naxalbari is a police sub-station in the Darjeeling district of West Bengal. It is in the name of the police sub-station that the movement is known all over. At a later stage it took an ideological flavour.

One principal feature of the region of Darjeeling is the high percentage of sharecroppers. It is because of this that the Naxalbari movement was essentially a movement launched by sharecroppers. In the beginning the movement remained restricted to three police stations only, namely, Phanisidewa, Naxalbari and Khoribari, having a population of about one lakh. The percentage of sharecroppers in and around these three police stations came to be 65 and 50 respectively. The commonly grown crops by the people predominantly include paddy and jute.

The *Rajbansis* are the most preponderant community of the region. They constitute more than 50 per cent. It is said that earlier this community was a tribal group known as *Koch*. With the growing influence of Brahminism in the region, some affluent sections of *Koch* adopted the nomenclature of *Rajbansis.* This created social differentiation among the *Kochs*—one section became *Rajbansi*, another converted to Islam, and the third one adhered to the original *Koch* stock.[29] In the process of political development which took place in the Tarai region, the *Rajbansis* acquired larger portion of land and came to be known as *Jotedar.* A *Jotedar* is a person who holds in severality, joint or in common, a piece of land for which he pays revenue directly to government through his agents.[30] At a later stage, the *Jotedar* legally became the owner and controller of *jotes. Jotes* could also be purchased or acquired as gift.

The *Jotedar* was the peasant proprietor. He leased-out lands to tenants—*raiyats*, who paid annual rents to him. He also granted land to tenants-at-will, *praja*. The *praja* paid rent in kind. The tenants-at will, as elsewhere in the country, were fully dependent on *Jotedar* for their seed, plough, cattle and agricultural implements. The seed advanced was deducted at harvest time from the produce and the balance was shared equally.[31] Below the *Jotedar* were small farmers, *adhiars* who cultivated small patches of land on equal share basis.

The production relations in the Darjeeling district, where the uprising was concentrated, consisted of the nexus of *Jotedar-rayat-praja-adhiar.* Under this system, the cultivator was merely reduced to the status of a sharecropper. The sharecropper was completely in a state of dependency, and suffered exploitation and succumbed to bondage.

While writing anything on the Naxalbari peasant movement it must be observed categorically that the movement was started by sharecroppers. Second, it was inspired by Tebhaga, the region now being in Bangladesh. Following are some of the important causes of the movement:

(1) The landlord used to take a larger share out of the produce made by the sharecropper. The general share taken by the landlords varied from one-half to one-third. It was quite excessive. The sharecroppers, which included *rayat*, *praja* and *adhiar*, demanded reduction of the share of produce.

(2) Another cause of the movement was the demand for the regulation and distribution of *benami* lands in an appropriate way by the peasants.

(3) The sharecroppers had no power with them. They were helpless under the bondage of the big landholders. It was the major cause for the uprising.

(4) The Naxalbari movement was admittedly a movement of the peasants but above all the major cause of the movement was the class war, between the big farmers and the ordinary peasants.

(5) The sharecroppers alleged that they were against their dependency on the big farmers. The big farmers were guided by the motto: "I will feed you; you produce for me." Such a kind of dependency was not acceptable to the tenants-at-will, the *praja* and the landless labourers.

(6) The *praja* had to submit to *begar*, that is, to work as *Hali* or *Vetti.*

(7) The judiciary of the district was in all cases in favour of the big farmers. The *praja* were always victimised by the judiciary.

The production relations between the *Jotedar*, that is, former *Rajbansis* with the *praja, adhiar*, that is, sharecroppers were strained. The exploited masses of peasants were groaning to engineer a revolutionary struggle.

The course of events that led to the Naxalbari movement can be described as under:

(1) Charu Majumdar was the leader of Naxalbari movement. There was a group of revolutionary leaders known as Siliguri group. This group gave out six documents known as the guidelines for the peasants. The document advocated the ideology which worked behind the Naxalbari movement. The sum and substance of the six documents include that militancy was the guiding ideology for capturing power. Majumdar and his group preached violence to the peasants saying that land was to be given to the tiller and Congress was to be defeated. The mobilisation of the peasantry was made on the lines of class consciousness. It was planned to establish a people's government after annihilating the jotedar-jamindar through armed revolution. The participants to the struggle were the peasants who were sharecroppers and who identified big farmers—*jotedars* as their class enemy. Thus, the movement was mobilised against the landed propertied class. For this movement it can safely be said that the broad-based peasantry, inclusive of all its strata, was involved in the struggle.

(2) During the month of March 1967, the violent leaders of the movement killed a moneylender within the jurisdiction of Naxalbari police station. This murder was followed by a series of other murders and one after another the *jotedars, sahukars* were killed by the participants of the movement.

(3) The messages of the movement were given through several slogans. Some of the slogans were borrowed from Tebhaga peasant movement. Throughout the area the leadership to movement was given by Panchnam Sarkar, Kanu Sanyal and others.

(4) In course of time the movement got ablaze in different parts of West Bengal. College students including females participated in the movement. The movement, thus, was not only a movement of the peasants but the society at large.

The Naxalbari movement was essentially against the big farmers, that is, *jotedar.* Though there was no immediate gain of the struggle, it definitely influenced the course of peasant movements in the country. The Naxalbari movement was a specific struggle ideologically oriented to Marxian socialism. In the *jotedar-adhiar* relation there was a visible contradiction in capital and labour. The deprivation of *adhiar* and for that matter for *rayat* and *praja* was due to the process of differentiation resulting from the force of history and modernisation. The rank and file of the Communist Party had made the adhiars conscious of the contradiction which turned them to pauper. Yet another outcome of the Naxalbari movement was that like other movements of the country, it did not stand for or put the demand for structural changes in the old feudal system. Instead, the movement, ideologically and operationally too, stood for a systemic change which could end exploitation and operation inherent in the semi-feudal system.

Some Other Contemporary Peasant Struggles

There have been some effective peasant uprisings in the recent past. Kathleen Gough, who has Marxist orientation to peasant uprisings, takes a review of all the peasant struggles which have taken place in India during its period of long history. Gough is credited to have pioneered to write about the poor peasantry in India. Her empirical study was concentrated in the state of Tamilnadu. She says that peasant revolts have been common in India both during and after the British period. Every state of present-day India has experienced several struggles over the past 200 years. She observes:

> Thus, in a recent brief survey I discovered 77 revolts, the smallest of which probably engage several thousand peasants in active engage several thousand peasants in active support or in combat. About 30 revolts must have affected several tens of thousands, and about 12, several hundred of thousands. Surely, the Kheda and Bardoli peasant struggles were important; certainly, Telangana and Naxalbari uprisings were significant but in contemporary India there have emerged a few new peasant struggles. It is really very difficult to keep track to all the contemporary movements. However, we shall mention a few important movements.[32]

Earlier, the CPI (M) and other left-wing political parties had their separate peasant organisations. The All India Kisan Sabha (AIKS), led by Mahendra Singh Tikait and its sister organisation, the All India Agricultural Workers Union (AIAWU) are some of the peasant unions based on political ideology. Recently, Sharad Joshi of Poona, Sharad Pawar of Bombay and Narayan Swami of Tamilnadu have formed separate peasant organisations which claim to dissociate themselves from all political parties. In fact, Sharad Joshi more than often has put his pet theory: "no political party can be seriously interested in helping the farmer." This Shetkari Sanghatan, he claims, has carried forward the peasants' cause as a non-political issue.

If we look at some of the peasant uprisings in contemporary India, we would notice that peasants are mobilised as a group to effect change in the face of resistance. The peasant movements, though have been widespread, are stronger in some areas than others. In Maharashtra, which abounds in the production of onion and sugarcane, Sharad Joshi has been leading an independent agitation in the Nasik-Pune region. His movement of peasants took off in 1977-78. He says:

> When there was crisis in the onion market following the Janata government's ban on exports, prices of onion collapsed to just Rs. 15-18, entirely divorce from politics. But then government started buying onion to raise prices and there was no need for an agitation. In mid-1980, however, there was an onion glut and prices again fell sharply, so we started an agitation.

The Shetkari Sanghatan adopted a new strategy to launch the movement. It included blocking of roads and non-payment of land revenue. It took to *gherao* of elected representatives, occupation of government offices and other such ways. The demands put up by the peasants were unhistorical. These included higher prices for peasants' produce and lower costs for inputs like water, electricity, fertilisers and pesticides. In the earlier peasant movements such methods were never employed. Then either the movements followed the ideology of freedom struggle or in some cases violence.

Sharad Pawar of Maharashtra, the Congress leader, with the alliance of other six parties, took out a long march from Jalgaon to Nagpur with a peasant strength of 8,000. In Tamilnadu Narayan Swami organised the peasants under the forum of Tamilnadu Agriculturists' Association in December 1983. His demands included a hike in paddy prices, writing off loans and remunerative prices for produce. The Krishi Rakshak Sangh-the peasant organisation of the Patels of Mehsana district of Gujarat, blocked roads and railways and fought pitched battles with the police. They also demanded better prices for groundnut and milk. The movement started by the peasants of Karnataka, who took to high-risk modern farming in places of traditional cultivation, demanded a hike in a support price of jowar and maize. The peasants of Uttar Pradesh and Bihar have also expressed their grievances against the increase in the price of input. Movements on the pattern of Nasik were launched by cane- growers in both these states. Their demands included a fair share in the crops grown on the land owned by *Mahants.*

Concluding Observations

An analysis of the peasant struggles in India makes us to make the following observations:

(1) The struggles of the peasants, it should be amply clear, are not the struggles of the deprived and relentlessly exploited landless labourers or untouchables which simmer ominously beneath the apparent stillness of the countryside. Not, again, it is the localised caste-based rural resurgence.

(2) The peasant struggles as we find in the contemporary India in different states are rooted in the process of modernisation. Their leadership is provided by the kulak peasants, rich farmers and the boggy of ex-jagirdars and *jamindars*. The struggles are mobilised to fulfil the vested interest of the better off segments of the country.

Soon after 1965, the peasants contributed to increase productivity as a result of green revolution. The objective of the revolution was to increase food production to achieve to self-sufficiency in foodgrains.[33] Undoubtedly, since the onset of green revolution, there has been a substantial rise in foodgrains production from 47 million tonnes in 1947 to 135 million tonnes in 1981. The increase in production has not improved the level of living of average peasant. The living has rather worsened. Modernisation has polarised the agricultural income, for it enriched the larger owners while tenants and labourers gained little.

(3) The study of contemporary struggles reveals that the demands of the peasant struggles revolve round the interest of the rich farmers who have marketable surplus. It is this segment of the vast peasantry which has become cost conscious. These farmers demand remunerative prices for their produce. All their strategies move round questions

of income, prices and inputs which in some parts of the country are beginning to loosen agriculture from its traditional feudal moorings. It is the surplus producing cultivators, who constitute a tiny minority of 15 per cent of the 72.5 million rural landowning households in the country, who are asking for higher produce prices and thereby holding the urban-oriented economy to ransom.

(4) The study of a large number of peasant struggles further shows that the leadership of these movements rests with the left-oriented political parties. The objective of these parties is to gain political power by mobilising the peasant masses as their support base. It is argued that at a broader plane the peasant struggles are mechanisms to combat the rural leadership at the pan-regional level. For long the urban leadership has dominated the national politics. The new peasant leadership today wants to push back the urban leadership. In fact, the struggles suggest the beginning of socialism in traditional rural-urban relationship. There appears an end of the urban phase of national politics and the birth of a new rural chapter.

(5) There is yet another observation which pins heavy hope on the contemporary peasant struggles. It argues that the present-day ills of the country manifesting themselves in poverty, famine, unemployment and economic inflation can be solved only by a peasant-backed revolution. The peasantry is not passive today and for more than 200 years, "it has repeatedly risen against landlords, revenue agents and other bureaucrats, moneylenders, police and military forces. The uprisings were responses to relative deprivation of unusually severe character, always economic, and often also involving physical brutality or ethnic persecution."[34]

Notes

1. Jan Breman, *Patronage and Exploitation*, Manohar, 1979.
2. Utsa Patnaik, "Class differentiation within the peasantry", *Economic and Political Weekly*, Vol. IX, No. 39, 1976.
3. A. Saith and A. Tankha, "Agrarian transition and the differentiation of the peasantry: A study of west U.P. village", *Economic and Political Weekly*, Vol. VII, No. 14, 1972.

4. K.L. Sharma, *Rural Society in India*, Rawat Publications, Jaipur, 1997, p. 161.
5. A.R. Desai(ed.), *Peasant Struggles in India*, Oxford University Press, Delhi, 1979.
6. Ibid.
7. Kathleen Gough, "Indian Peasant Uprising", *Economic and Political Weekly*, Vol. IX, 32-4, Special Number, August 1974.
8. N.B. Ranga, "Indian Peasants' Struggles and Achievements" in A.R. Desai(ed.) op. cit.
9. Hamza Alavi, "Peasants and Revolution", in A.R. Desa(ed.), op. cit., p. 671.
10. D.N. Dhanagare, *Peasant Movements in India 1920-1950*, Oxford University Press, 1991.
11. Rajendra Prasad, *Champaran and Mahatma Gandhi*, Delhi, 1955, pp. 63-65.
12. Ibid., pp. 29-31.
13. *Gandhi Smarak Nidhi Papers.*
14. Sukhbir Choudhary,"Early Struggles 1905-18", in A.R. Desai (ed.), p. 233.
15. Breman, Jan, op. cit.
16. Mahadev Desai, *Harijan*, Poona, Vol. VI., No. 523, 1939, p. 455.
17. A. Bhatt, "Caste and Political Mobilization in a Gujarat District", in Rajni Kothari (ed.), *Caste in Indian Politics*, New Delhi, 1970, p. 327.
18. D.N. Dhanagare, op. cit., p. 91.
19. Bipan Chandra et al., *India's Struggle for Independence*, Viking, 1988, p. 206.
20. D.N. Dhanagare, op. cit., p. 100.
21. Mahadev Desai, *The Story of Bardoli*, Ahmedabad, 1957.
22. D.N. Dhanagare, op. cit., p. 61.
23. Bipan Chandra et al., op. cit., p. 203.
24. D.N. Dhanagare, op. cit., p. 185.
25. Ibid., p. 187.
26. Hamza Alavi, *Socialist Register*, 1965. Also reproduced by A.R. Desai, *Rural Sociology in India*, Popular Prakashan, Bombay, 1978, p. 416.
27. D.N. Dhanagare, op. cit., p. 199.

28. P. Sundarayya, *Telangana People's Struggle and its Lessons*, Communist Party of India (Marxist), Calcutta, December, 1972, pp. 1-5
29. W.W. Hunter, *A Statistical Account of Bengal*, Vol. X, D.K. Publishing House, New Delhi, 1974.
30. Partha N. Mukerji, *Naxalbari Movement and the Peasant Revolt in North Bengal*, Centre for the Study of Social Systems, Jawaharlal Nehru University, New Delhi, 1978 (Mimeographed).
31. W.W. Hunter, op. cit., p. 260.
32. Kathleen Gough, op. cit., p. 86.
33. Frankle Francine, *India's Green Revolution: Economic Gains and Political Costs*, Princeton University Press, 1971. Also, see in this connection, Mohan Ram, *Marxism in India*, Vikas, Delhi, 1971, pp. 185-186.
34. Kathleen Gough, op. cit., pp. 1391-1412.

12 Rural Development

During the struggle for India's independence Gandhiji reiterated that the development of country and its prosperity depend on its villages. He emphasised that if the villages are ruined, who can save the country? When we discuss the programmes of rural development we must always keep in mind that our rural society has never been and is not even now a homogeneous society. Our peasantry is highly stratified. Despite land ceiling, land reforms and tenure legislation there are *kulak* or big farmers, small farmers, original farmers and at the bottom there are masses of agricultural labourers who live on subsistence economy. They are below the poverty line.

The development programmes which the country is implementing are aspects of directed change. Plans and programmes which are especially meant for rural development have objective to make a change in the quality of lifestyle of the rural people. The development efforts are not new today. The British government was very clear that more than half of their revenue came from the land tax. They also knew that the import of raw material to Britain was also in their interest. They tried to improve the farm produce to attain agricultural growth. The independent India also has the objective to increase the produce of the peasants. It is very much desired that the peasant crosses the subsistence economy and brings his surplus to the market. So far as the agricultural development is concerned, there is no argument, no debate. But the crucial thing is that the poor peasants should also get a substantial benefit out of such development. Or the rich peasants should not corner the major benefits of development at the cost of smaller peasants and the agricultural labourers.

If we critically review the record of the benefits of peasant struggles throughout the periods of history, we would soon realise that the rich farmers have got the lion's share. If the history of peasant struggles is repeated in the history of rural development, the whole purpose of our efforts would be lost. Our idiom should be that in any effort of rural development the peasants should be the first in the queue for benefits. Let the rich Farmers be at the end of the queue.

Yet another important point we should have in our mind is that the development of rural India mainly depends on agriculture, irrigation and village industries. For agricultural development we should apply improved inputs of manure, technical implements and high yielding varieties of seed. The farm produce needs to be carried to the market and for that the farms should be linked with the nearest market. Nehruji, while launching the First Five Year Plan, observed rather it was his favourable observation that for a village to develop there are three prerequisites: (1) school, (2) cooperative society, and (3) village industry. Surely, there are several prerequisites for the development of village which are termed as infrastructural needs. These needs include public health centre, transport, housing, electricity, potable drinking water, village roads, and a large number of other such facilities.

In this chapter, we propose to discuss the history of village development in India from the British period to the present day. The introduction that we have provided above serves as a canvas for proper evaluation of development. In any such evaluation the basic criterion is the consumer. If, for instance, the consumer and in this case the peasant is satisfied, the programme would be evaluated as a successful one. Gandhiji put a very simple question to our development administrators: What does the poor man get out of your development programmes? If the poor farmer benefits more than the rich farmer, the development has made a mark. It is this perspective which dominates our history of development efforts since the coming of British.

Rural Development Before Independence

It would be prejudicial to say that the British government totally neglected the problems of India's villages. Even we would go a step further and say that during the feudal period the Muslim rulers and their counterparts in princely states did not neglect the village people. In the medieval period several battles were fought, lakhs of people were killed, and tonnes of money was looted. All this was ghastly but the history tells us honestly that these feudal rulers did not disturb the village life. Close to the fields, the battle was fought and the cultivator ploughed his fields while singing the verses of the *Ramayana*. All this happened peacefully because it was the prime interest of the feudal ruler to get regular revenue from the peasants. The revenue was the only source of maintaining the kingdom.

What we want to stress is that the British did not totally neglect our villages. In fact, several of our village agricultural problems were for the first time identified during the British period. Beginning from the 17th century to the attainment of independence, a large number of development programmes were implemented for the development of India's villages only. Here, first we take up the efforts made for development during the British period. These efforts could be put into two heads:

(1) development efforts made by British government, and
(2) efforts made by voluntary organisations or NGOs.

Development Efforts Made by British Government

During the British period India's villages and their economy encountered a crisis. The industrial revolution which took place in 18th century influenced our villages also. The British government brought steam engine and steam power in India. This revolutionised our traditional production system along with transport. The factories and the railways disturbed our indigenous village production. The factory production which was on mass scale and also cheaper made our village industry irrelevant. The village artisans became unemployed for their market was replaced by factory produce. Railways and road transport linked the village industry with the world. This resultantly gave a new market economy to our villages. On the one hand the British policy was to encourage agricultural output in the fields and on the other hand part of it was used in the factories and a part of it also exported. It was a strange situation. The production increased but the peasantry did not gain much. And if there was some gain to the peasantry it was mostly cornered by the big farmers. The artisans in all cases were losers. The interest of the British government was to help the peasants so that the farm surplus could be used by it for its own economic consolidation. It should be very clear that the British policy was oriented to the increase of agriculture produce not for the welfare of the peasants but for satisfying their own vested interests. However, whatever the British government did for the development of agriculture is mentioned as under:

(1) *Cash Economy*: The traditional barter system was getting increasingly weaker during the British period. The colonial rulers introduced cash economy. This introduction encouraged the peasants to take commercial crops. The peasantry produced whatever it wanted for its consumption. The commercial crops were taken for market only. Thus, it was for the first time that agricultural subsistence economy gave place to commercial crops.

(2) *Famines and Irrigation Facilities*: The British government wanted to consolidate its regime in India. Any unrest launched by the people strengthened the freedom struggle and weakened the government. This was not acceptable to the British government. In such a situation the occurrence of famine was a threat to the colonial rule. During the British period, the famines took place more than often. Every second or third year was a famine year. The greatest famine in India took place in 1899. In the year 1901, the British government appointed a Famine Commission which suggested that the government should constitute a committee of experts to comprehend the agricultural problems. It also suggested the strengthening of the staff of agricultural departments in all the provinces. The commission further recommended that legislation should be made on the lines of the Punjab Alienation of Land Act, 1901 to restrict the transfer of land. It also suggested to establish a Cooperative Societies Act. This particular suggestion obliged the government to have co-operative societies in 1904 and 1905. According to the advice of the commission there was expansion of irrigation in the next few years.

All these measures show that the problem of Indian agriculture was assuming a new aspect in that the emphasis was changing from palliatives like famine relief, *tacavi* grants and revenue remissions to more positive measures. But, on the whole, the total impression made by these steps on rural economy was quite insignificant at least up to the end of the First World War.

(3) *The Royal Commission on Agriculture*: It became clear to the government that to combat the scarcity created by famines, some permanent efforts should be made to provide irrigation facilities. It is only through irrigation that the challenge of famine could be partly

met. The idea of providing irrigation facilities prompted the government to appoint the Royal Commission on Agriculture in India in 1926. It was to examine and report on the prevailing conditions of agriculture and rural economy in British India. And to make recommendations for the improvement of agriculture and the promotion of the welfare and prosperity of the rural population. However, the problems of land revenue and land tenure were excluded from the terms of the commission. The commission submitted its report in 1928. The crux of the suggestions made by the commission dwelt on the theme that the real problem in India was to improve the indian village life. It also suggested that land fragmentation should be immediately stopped. It further suggested that the government should establish the Imperial Council of Agricultural Research which would provide guidance to the provinces. The suggestion for the constitution of Imperial Council was a step further to improve the agricultural production.

Besides the above mentioned efforts made by the British government a few minor actions were also taken by the British provinces. It must be observed that undoubtedly the colonial rule was keenly interested to improve the situation of agriculture in India. The challenge was from the frequent occurrence of famines and the resultant unrest. The government also wanted to increase the farm production. To face the agricultural crisis which emerged during the British period, the government precisely took three steps: (1) provision of irrigation facilities, (2) establishment of cooperative societies, and (3) creation of a research committee for the comprehension of problems in agriculture.

The efforts of improvement made by the British government were hardly taken seriously by the peasantry. Actually, by the first quarter of 20th century, the freedom movement had reached to the villages. There was non-cooperation movement, there was no-tax payment movement. The awakening which came to the peasants brought home the fact that the British government was doing all this for its own interest and the welfare of peasants was alien to them.

Efforts Made by Voluntary Organisations or NGOs

When the British government had its policy oriented towards the improvement of agriculture, our national leaders were engaged in the task of mobilising the villages for their involvement in the freedom movement. Though the first major challenge that was thrown to the British government was the revolt of 1857, after the foundation of the All India Congress Committee, the village masses were organised. It was in the beginning of 20th century and particularly during the non-cooperation movement (1920-22) that our national leaders took up constructive work for the awakening of people. A large number of voluntary organisations emerged in the countries. These organisations were mainly based in villages. The constructive works, such as included opening of schools, adult classes and hostels, led the villagers to implement the plans which could give self-reliance to them. The national leaders were convinced that freedom could only be gained with the participation of the masses of people. No history of village development could be complete without some description of the voluntary organisations which worked among the villagers. Besides Gandhian workers there were some moral organisations and missions such as Ram Krishna Mission which also worked for the upliftment of villagers. Even the Christian missionaries, though they had their interest in religious conversion, also worked in the field of education, health and sanitation. Thousands of social workers worked among the villagers for the cause of development. Admittedly, these voluntary organisations could not provide any physical infrastructure to the villagers, but they definitely provided social education to the villagers to fight against social evils of illiteracy, intoxication, *purdah* and backwardness of women. These reforms, by any standard, were not ordinary.

We shall now discuss some of the voluntary efforts made by non-governmental organisations during the British period. These are enumerated as below:

(1) *Seva Gram Ashram*: Gandhiji had his definite ideas about India's villages. He, throughout his life, fought for the autonomy of village people. *Gram Swaraj* or village autonomy was his often repeated theme. He argued that the villages should be given power to rule over themselves. He stood for the decentralisation of power to the villages. Inspired by this ideology he established the Sabarmati Ashram at Ahmedabad. This ashram in the beginning was in a village outside the walled city.

Later on Gandhiji established *Seva Gram Ashram* in 1935. It was based in Wardha, and imparted education to the weaker sections of villages surrounding Wardha. The development programmes for the villages at Wardha included sanitation, adult education, promotion of village industries (such as *tel-ghani*) and potable water. The villagers were encouraged to fulfil their own needs and not to seek any help from the government.

One very notable feature of Wardha Ashram was the promotion of *buniyadi shiksha* or basic education for the development of villagers. Gandhiji was against the formal school education which depended largely on lectures. Education in the right sense should be the vocational education. At the school level, the children should be educated to do their own work from cooking to cleaning and spinning. He argued that a village should fulfil all its needs by itself. Dependence of any kind should be warded off.

Then, the constructive work on the pattern of Wardha Ashram was started in different parts of the country. Gandhi's economy revolved round the *charkha*, village industries and manual work. We only want to emphasise that a network of voluntary agencies based in villages gave the message to the people that the village to attain self-sufficiency, that is, autonomy in all aspects of life.

(2) *Shantiniketan*: Quite like Gandhiji, Rabindranath Tagore was also influenced by the idea that the village should stand in its own legs. Tagore did not like the crowded life of Calcutta. He, therefore, started his *ashram* a little away from Calcutta. Though Shantiniketan, today, has the status of a university, Tagore started it with the objective of bringing the villagers closer to the youths. The educational part of Shantiniketan was very closely linked with the village life—its sanitation, health, cottage industry and welfare. Though Shantiniketan did not provide any infrastructural facilities to the surrounding villages, it created an awakening among the villagers to develop self-reliance. Shantiniketan became an ideal of imitation in the whole of West Bengal.

(3) *Flood of Literary Works*: Besides the constructive work based on manual labour through the Gandhian workers, there is evidence to show that the persons belonging to Hindi and regional literatures also highlighted the village problems and suggested reasons for the amelioration of backwardness. For instance, Hindi fiction writers such as Prem Chand, Jaya Shankar Prasad, Fanishwarnath Renu and Sharat Chandra created works which presented the abject poor condition of the village people. The village indebtedness, *jamindar's* exploitation

and government's apathy are well documented in the works of these writers. By all standards the fictions given by these authors have contributed substantially towards the awakening of the village people.

A review of the rural development works done during the struggle for independence brings out the fact that both the British government and the national leaders were convinced that nothing fruitful can be done without involving the village people. The objective of the government was surely more production in agriculture but it was not a gesture of welfare for the village people. The voluntary agencies, however, did the development work a little differently. Efforts to uplift the village people were made to make the village people or the village community autonomous. The idiom of village development which worked with the voluntary agencies and also the fiction writers was to help the people to stand on their own. However, despite differences in objectives, the village life touched by these agencies included public health, education, reform and promotion of village industries.

Rural Development After Independence

In this section, first, we will discuss the programmes of village development taken up during the transitional period between the end of feudal rule and the implementation of Five Year Plans.

(1) *Firka Development Scheme* (1947): On the eve of the attainment of independence, the former Madras state launched a new scheme of village development known as Firka development scheme. It was inspired by the ideology of Gandhiji. The scheme emphasised a perfect coordination of different state departments that were engaged in rural development. Such departments included agriculture, industries, irrigation and veterinary. "Under the Firka development plan the five main centres of activity were agriculture, village industries, sanitation, health and housing, education and village social and cultural activities." Rural water supply and health facilities were given priority over other aspects of village development.

The scheme was evaluated in 1952. It was found that with some drawbacks it was a successful story. However, when the community development projects were started in 1952 the Firka scheme was merged in it. The experience of Firka was much useful for running the community development projects.

(2) *Nilokheri Project* (1947): Nilokheri is located in Karnal district of Punjab (now in Haryana). The Nilokheri project was launched for the settlement of refugees who migrated to Punjab during the riots which took place soon after independence. The project was initiated by S.K. Dey who was then, the Minister of Community Development. The original plan of Nilokheri was to have a township of 5,000 people and to link it with villages having a population of about 25,000. It was contemplated that the Nilokheri town would have centre of medical relief, Public health and sanitation. There was also a provision for high school education, technical and vocational training, horticulture, poultry, piggery, fishery, sheep breeding and other farms of animal husbandry. It was within the scope of the project to change the villages according to the scheme of development. It was planned to accommodate the refugees who were then living in the camps. However, the complete scheme for urban and rural area could not materialise as the Ministry of Rehabilitation was concentrated only with the displaced persons who could be settled in the new town, and in the villages around there were already old inhabitants. Alongside technical and vocational training, work centres were started in all the crafts which were taught in the former institutions. Weaving calico printing, soap making, laundry, bakery, tinsmithy, blacksmithy, general mechanics, leather and a multitude of other crafts and trades came in as production nucleus.

The Nilokheri project was unlike any other village development project. Its objective was to rehabilitate the refugees in a planned settlement where they could get everything which is required for a town or a village. The clusters of neighbouring villages were also planned to be attached with the Nilokheri town. But, this could not be done as the villages were already settled and had their felt needs fulfilled. The project did not have a formal role of non-officials. S.K. Dey who was basically an engineer did not pay much heed to social and cultural aspects of village. Despite this weakness Nilokheri was an excellent exercise in the planning of a town. It would be worthwhile to say here that Indian villages are never found in planned settlements.

(3) *Etawah Project* (1948): The project was conceived by Albert Mayer who was an American town planner and remained in India during the Second World War. The project started at Mahewa in the district of Etawah of Uttar Pradesh in 1948 with the aim to develop villages in the fields of agriculture, cooperation and public health. The

Etawah district was divided into a number of blocks, each block having 64 villages with a population of 70,000. The village development programmes included improvement of land, agricultural practices, educational facilities and sanitation in villages; local cooperatives and panchayats were to propagate the message of development.

The Etawah project was the forerunner to the Community Development Project (CDP) which later on started in 1952. It should also be observed that the project was supervised by experts in different walks of village life. The project personnel was expected to provide expert guidance but the people were required to make the project self-running. No financial assistance, however, was given to the people. The project belonged to them and, therefore, they had to run it. Another speciality of the project was that it emphasised on agriculture, cooperatives, health and sanitation, and education. Such an approach to village development makes two things clear: the development of villages occupies a top most priority and agriculture, cooperatives and education are the prime areas that no development effort could afford to neglect.

Community Development Project (1952)

The Directive Principles of State Policy put down that the state would make all efforts to improve the life of the scheduled castes, scheduled tribes and weaker sections of society. It is in accordance with the provisions of Constitution of India that the states launch special development programmes for the weaker sections. Add to it is the objective of developing our villages that live under conditions of poverty. It was a historical obligation to prepare plans for village development. The All India Congress Committee, in several of its conferences, reiterated the need for village development. Gandhiji had his support for such a plan.

It was in 1951 that the Planning Commission submitted its draft report to the government. It was unhistorical for India to have adopted a uniform approach for the development of villages. When the draft plan was still under consideration of the public, the Colombo Plan for India, Pakistan, Sri Lanka, Borneo and Sarawak, that is, all Commonwealth countries was drawn up. This plan was also incorporated in our plan and in December 1952 the First Five Year Plan in its final shape was presented to the parliament. The Second Five Year Plan came out in 1956 and the Third Plan in 1961 and so on after every five years. Now, we are at the stage of Ninth Five Year Plan.

It was on 2nd October, 1952—the day of Gandhi Jayanti—that the Community Development Project (CDP) was launched in the country. In the beginning 55 areas comprising 27,338 villages and a population of 16.7 million were selected for intensive development. By the end of the First Plan, the CDP and National Extension Service (NES) had been taken up in about 1,40,000 villages situated in 998 development blocks and serving a population of 77.5 million persons. By 1959 the CDP was finally withdrawn and redesigned in the form of Panchayati Raj. The new incarnation of community development involved the participation of the people, that is, non-officials in the statuses of *Zila Pramukh, Pradhan, Sarpanch* and *Panch.*

The CDP was mainly aimed at the development of villages. It meant development of (1) agriculture and related matters, (2) irrigation, (3) communication, (4) education, (5) health, (6) supplementary employment, (7) housing, (8) social welfare, and (9) training. Agriculture and related matters included the intensive development of agriculture alongwith reclamation of wasteland, provision of improved seeds, and supply of chemical manure through village cooperative society, improvement of livestock and intensive cultivation through the production of fruits and vegetables.

Irrigation included provision of water by minor irrigation works, namely, tubewells, tanks, canal etc. It was planned that out of the total cultivable village land half of it should be irrigated.

Communication meant road system in the countryside to be developed. Wherever necessary, approach and linked roads should be constructed. It was estimated that no village under the CDP should be more than half a mile away from the main road.

The educational programme included social education for adults, expansion and improvement of primary and secondary education and programmes for removal of social evils.

Serious concern was shown to health and sanitation. It was planned that each development block should have one primary health unit. The block headquarters should possess a secondary health unit with a hospital and a mobile dispensary. Public health programmes included provisions for water supply, control of epidemics like malaria, cholera etc., and training to villagers in public hygiene.

Within the supplementary employment, the villagers were given opportunities for gainful employment by the development of cottage and small-scale industries, construction of brick kilns, saw mills etc. The CDP also planned to give opportunities in the tertiary sectors which could be created.

In the field of housing the plan provided demonstration and training in improved techniques and designs for rural housing. In congested villages action in the direction of development of new sites, opening of village parks and playgrounds had been planned.

The social welfare activities included provisions for audio-visual aids for instruction and recreation.

The CDP also considered training for the village level workers and other personnel who were to be employed in these programmes.

One very important part of the CDP was the establishment of Programmes Evaluation Organisation under the Planning Commission. Its main functions were as under:

(1) current appraisal of the ongoing projects;
(2) identification of the projects which made successful stories;
(3) plugging the programmes which are accepted or rejected by the people; and
(4) providing explanation for the response given by the people to the projects which are implemented.

Some Salient Features

When the CDP was launched in 1952, there were some strategic assumptions about the development of India's villages. The government assured the villagers that they should accept the various projects given to them, as expert advice would always be made available to them. The CDP has also the services of experts in various fields, such as agriculture, irrigation, education and veterinary science. Their services can be given without any payment to the people. The CDP also, in a larger way, promised the villagers to make them available the required amount of money by way of loan on easy terms. It was also contemplated that the project personnel would provide some infrastructural facilities to the village people. A school, a dispensary, an approach or link road, a cooperative society and other such minimum needs for the people would be given out of project funds. The broad objective of the CDP was to make the villagers self-reliant. The people will have to stand on their own legs, the government would provide the required expertise and financial assistance.

The CDP was designed and implemented initially for three years. It was guessed that during this period the villagers would be self-supporting; they will have their own irrigation facilities, their own school and cooperative. In 1959, the project was withdrawn with the hope that the villages would march ahead on the road to progress without any financial assistance. This, however, did not happen. At the end, the CDP proved to be a project of failure. Out of it there emerged a new form of community development following the recommendations made by Balwanth Rai Mehta Committee in 1959. Before we discuss the new transformation of CDP, let us analyse the drawbacks of the project.

A Critique

The Programme Evaluation Organisation (PEO) and a large number of social scientists including sociologists, anthropologists and economists have criticised the CDP. Some of their major criticisms are as under:

(1) The project became highly bureaucratised. It was a development of the village people from the above; the people of the below were only passive receivers. There was least involvement of the masses of people.

(2) The needs of the people were perceived by the project personnel or in other words by those who were at the planning level. The felt needs of the people throughout the period of implementation of project, remained unidentified by the government.

(3) The PEO reiterated in its reports that a few of the schemes were implemented only on paper. In reality, on verification, it was found that no wells were created, no community halls were made, no parks were erected though all these appeared very much in the official records. For the people the programmes of the CDP were farce and full of scandals.

(4) Corruption plagued the implementation of various programmes

under CDP. The point which came home with the people was that the total bureaucracy was corrupt. Only a meagre part of the budgetary allocation was actually spent for the people.

(5) Despite huge expenditure on agricultural development the food production did not increase.

(6) The benefits of the CDP went to the rich and big farmers at the cost of small and marginal farmers.

(7) There was a dismal lack of coordination among different development departments. As a result, there was much overlap in the programmes.

(8) The programmes were implemented uniformly as they were tailored at the central level. The diverse situations at the local level denied the acceptance of these programmes.

When, during the year 1959, the CDP was finally withdrawn from the villages, it gave a relief to the people. During the period, when the project was in operation, the villagers more than often acted as host to various development officials. It appeared that the visits were unending. And, indeed at the winding up of the project, one old man observed, as the survey report observes: "We took a sigh of relief; now the visits are finally over."

The Emergence of Panchayati Raj

There came as drastic change when the Balwanth Rai Mehta Committee suggested for the creation of Panchayati Raj for implementing the CDP. The basic argument given for the establishment of Panchayati Raj was that people should be given power to rule over the villages. The *Panchas* elected by the village people would implement the programmes. This will ensure the involvement of the people in the development of villages. The development, thus, under this scheme, was contemplated from the below, from the masses of people.

Keeping in view the role of Panchayati Raj, the Third Five Year Plan was also revised. The Planning Commission in the Third Plan suggested several new strategies for the development of villages. Stress was also given to increase agricultural production. The Third Plan also suggested a new approach to some of the already ongoing schemes. The new form of development programmes included:

(1) increase in agricultural production,
(2) area development programme, and
(3) programme for special target groups.

The three major programmes introduced for increasing agricultural production were the Intensive Agricultural Area Programme (IAAP), Projects for Intensive and Integrated Agricultural Development, and the High Yielding Variety Programme (HYVP) which concentrated on improving agricultural productivity. Some of the programmes were designed to help special areas; for instance, Drought Prone Area Programme (DPAP), Hill Area Development Programme (HADP), Command Area Development Programme (CADP) and Tribal Area Development Programme (TADP). The latest programmes introduced in this sphere are the Integrated Rural Development Programme (IRDP) as well as Regional Development Programme (RDP). However, the third category of programmes included in the Third Plan and subsequent plans were meant for certain special target groups. These programmes included Small and Marginal Farmers and Agricultural Labourers Development Programme, Tribal Sub-Plan, Rural Industries Programme, Rural Artisans Programmes, Crash Scheme for Rural Employment, Pilot Intensive Rural Employment Projects, Employment Guarantee Scheme, Food for Work Programme, Antyodaya Programme, etc.

We shall discuss some of these programmes in the following pages:

Programmes for Increase in Agricultural Production

The programmes which are given for rural development have an objective to remove poverty of the people. The official policy of the government has been as under:

> Rural poverty alleviation has been the primary concern in the economic planning and development process of the country. ... rural development which encompasses the entire gamut of improvement in the overall quality of life in the rural areas can be achieved through eradication of poverty in the rural areas.

(i) Intensive Agricultural Area Programme: Keeping in view the above planning policy in mind, the Intensive Agricultural Area Pro-

gramme (IAAP) was introduced in 1960-61 on the recommendation of the agricultural production team sponsored by the Ford Foundation. It was argued by the committee that there were no reasons in terms of soil and climate for lower yields of the produce. It, therefore, selected one district out of each state on experiment basis for intensive agriculture.

In the year 1964-65, a modified version of IAAP was made. It was implemented in several other parts of the country. The main concern of the programme was growing of special crops. In the beginning, the selection of district was on the basis of assured irrigation facilities, minimum hazards and well-developed rural institutions.

(ii) Intensive Agricultural District Programme: Yet another programme meant for agricultural development was Intensive Agricultural District Programme (IADP). The administrative boundaries of the district had the operation of this programme. The programme could not make any significant achievement. A task force on Integrated Rural Development was constituted by the Planning Commission in October 1971. It submitted its first report on Integrated Agricultural Development Projects in the canal irrigated areas in September 1972. The report highlighted the problems of Command Areas of the River Valley Projects where the realisation of the fullest production potentials could be attempted by mutually reinforcing measures connected with the development of local land and water resources.

The intensive and integrated agricultural development project covered within its operation the following aspects of agriculture:

(i) consolidation of holdings,
(ii) land levelling and land shaping,
(iii) realignment and lining of water courses,
(iv) training and cleaning of *nallahs*,
(v) provision of drainage of ditches,
(vi) provision of supplementary irrigation facilities from ground water resources, wherever necessary, and
(vii) provision of supplies.

(iii) High Yielding Varieties Programme: The High Yielding Varieties Programme (HYVP) has become a popular programme in

agricultural development. It is this programme which has resulted into green revolution. This programme introduced agricultural inputs of high yielding quality in the production. These improved varieties were introduced in chemical manure, seeds, implements and cattle. The improved seeds with the help of agricultural technology and insecticides increased the agricultural growth.

This programme was implemented in 1966. The new strategy for agricultural development was concerned not only with higher yield but also with greater intensity of cropping. The peasants were encouraged to take three crops a year.

Area Development Programmes

Under these three programmes, viz, (i) Drought-Prone Area Programme, (ii) Command Area Development Programme, and (iii) Hill Area Development Programme were started.

(i) *Drought-Prone Area Programme*: The Drought-Prone Area Programme (DPAP) was started in 1973. The objectives of the programme are to (a) minimise the adverse effects of drought on production of crops and livestock and productivity of land, water and human resources through integrated development of the natural resources base of the area by adoption of appropriate technologies; (b) to conserve, develop and harness land, water and other natural resources including rainfall for restoration of ecological balance in the long run; and (c) to improve the economic and social conditions of the resource-poor and disadvantaged sections of society such as landless labourers and women.

The programme is being implemented in 13 states where the conditions of drought are always vulnerable. The effort of the programme is to provide facilities to the peasants who are more than often victimised by drought.

(ii) *Command Area Development Programme*: The second programme within the Area Development Programmes is the Command Area Development Programme (CADP). There has been huge public investment in major and medium irrigation projects. It has been the objective of the government that these irrigation projects are fully utilised by the peasants. This requires that water courses and field channels are properly constructed and planned. If this is not done in a scientific way, there is every possibility of waterlogging, salinity and alkalinity. These are some of the problems which result in the absence of proper shaping of earth and making facilities to avoid waterlogging.

In the beginning (1966-69) eight river projects were taken for area development. Ten more such schemes were taken during the Fourth Plan period. The area increased with the coming Five Year Plans. The implementation of CADP encouraged multicropping and made it possible for the peasants to take as many as four crops a year.

(iii) *Hill Area Development Programme*: The Hill Area Development Programme (HADP) is specifically meant for hill areas. The major thrust of the programme lies in the identification of backward regions in states with sizeable hill areas and formulation of a separate sub-plan for the development of these ares. Pilot projects were taken up under this programme in Himachal Pradesh, Uttar Pradesh and Tamil Nadu. The main strategy of development in these projects was the integrated development of agriculture, animal husbandry, horticulture, land development and soil conservation, minor irrigation and other basic infra-structural facilities on watershed basis.

Programmes for Special Target Groups

It was realised by the Planning Commission that there are some groups in the rural society that have been victims of exploitation since the period of colonial rule. For instance, the small and landless labourers have always suffered at the hands of landlords, *jamindars, jagirdars* and other kinds of intermediaries. Second, there are tribals who have always been dispossessed of their land by non- tribal peasants. Such groups are vulnerable to all kinds of exploitation and bondage. The Planning Commission, therefore, made some development programmes for special target groups. These programmes are discussed below:

(i) *Special Programme for Small Farmers and Agricultural Labourers*: The small farmers, as defined by the government, are those whose holding is less than two hectares. The new agricultural technology increased the number of small farmers. To combat this situation, the All India Rural Credit Review Committee (1969) recommended the establishment of Small Farmers Development Agencies (SFDAs). This agency got recognition by the government.

In order to reduce disparities between big and small farmers certain programmes were taken up during the Fourth Plan period. Two of these programmes were meant for (1) small farmers, and (2) marginal farmers and agricultural labourers. The small farmers were taken to be those who, with the help of irrigation, provision of credit, supplies and marketing and application of modern technology, could be made viable. A limit of one to three hectares of landholding was generally adopted in identifying such farmers. Farmers with holdings below this limit were categorised as marginal farmers. As regards agricultural labourer, this category was defined to cover those rural households which derive more than 50 per cent of their income from agricultural wages. For the sub-marginal cultivators and agricultural labourers two sets of measures were contemplated. The first set of measures was in the sphere of land reforms, and the second aimed at the generation of employment through poultry farming, dairy farming and other supplementary employments.

The agencies-in-charge of these projects are corporate bodies registered under the Societies Registration Act. Each agency had a small membership consisting mainly of the representatives of the institutional agencies and concerned district officers with the Collector or the Deputy Commissioner as the chairman. The agencies were expected to utilise the existing field institutions, i.e., the government development departments, local organisations, particularly those of Panchayati Raj and block development and cooperatives.

Although the special programme was initiated in 1969, it started functioning only in 1971-72. The performance of the programme was reported to be much unsatisfactory. There was improper identification and verification of the variants of farmers. Secondly, the number of agricultural labourers was altogether left out. Thirdly, there were several cases wherein the funds were misutilised. In regard to programmes of subsidiary occupations the beneficiaries were not property selected, and supporting facilities were not provided adequately. As a result of this, instead of generating income, they proved to be a liability for beneficiaries, specially in the case of dairy farming and poultry programmes.

(ii) *Rural Industries Projects and Rural Artisans Programmes*: Rural Industries Project (RIP) was initiated by the Government of India in 1962-63. Its objective was to evolve appropriate methods and techniques for intensive development of village and small-scale industries. The project was started with the objective to provide employment opportunities and generation of income for the rural poor.

The Rural Artisans Programme (RAP) was also a central sponsored programme for upgrading the skills of rural artisans, adoption of new skills through training of artisans and providing tools at subsidised rate at the end of the training period. There was everything good so far as its objectives were concerned. But, due to some difficulties, it was discontinued in the beginning of the Fifth Plan. However, it was revived in 1978. The programme now is in operation.

(iii) *Antyodaya Programme*: *Antyodaya* means the welfare of a person standing at the end of the queue. The programme provides an opportunity to this last man to rise in status. The scheme was introduced during the regime of Janata government in 1978. Under this scheme five poorest families in a village were selected. Each Antyodaya family could be given loan and subsidies not exceeding Rs. 5,000. This money had to be utilised for generation of income.

(iv) *Rural Works Programme*: The objective of this programme is to provide employment to the weaker sections. At a later stage, as an alternative to rural works programme, certain other schemes were taken up in subsequent years to provide employment to the underemployed and unemployed rural people. Some of these schemes are described below:

(a) *Crash Scheme for Rural Employment*: As an alternative to rural works programme some of the states took up crash scheme for rural employment. The scheme had a two-fold purpose: (i) generating employment for 1,000 persons on an average per year in each district, and (ii) production of assets of durable nature in consonance with local development plans.

(b) *Pilot Intensive Rural Employment Scheme*: This was an ad-hoc scheme of crash employment. It was given in the form of employment for time being in the construction of rural roads, sanitary wells, school buildings, primary health centres and other construction works of the village.

(c) *Special Employment Guarantee Scheme*: Special schemes were formulated by some states such as Maharashtra and Gujarat to provide increasing employment avenues in the rural areas. It was also an alternative to the rural works programme. According to it the works proposed to be undertaken under the scheme related to contour-bunding, irrigation, roads and village industry. The Gujarat government's scheme provided for unskilled jobs to the unemployed workers on different projects.

(d) *Food for Work Programme*: It was introduced in 1977 by the Janata government. Its objective was to provide employment to the unemployed/underemployed village workers during the slack season and at the same time to create community assets of lasting value and provide cereals at reasonable price. The wages paid to the workers were in kind, i.e., foodgrains.

(e) *National Rural Employment Programme*: This programme was implemented as a centrally sponsored scheme on a 50:50 sharing basis between the centre and the states. The state government could use some of the procedures adopted in Maharashtra for raising the employment guarantee fund for generating the additional resources needed for implementing such a project. Wages could be paid partly in cash and partly as grain.

(v) *Tribal Development Agencies and Sub-Plan*: This programme is specially meant for the development of tribal areas. The tribal blocks, according to this project, have to work on somewhat different line from the blocks in the ordinary areas. The tribal habitation pattern is scattered and, therefore, the Tribal Sub-Plan area covers a large number of villages within it. In the Tribal Sub-Plan area, the non-tribal population is also existent. However, the tribal population exceeds more than half of the total population of area.

If we review the new programmes of rural development taken up since the Third Five Year Plan we would find that these programmes are either problem-based, area programmes, target group area programmes or development programmes. These programmes stressed on agricultural production, area development and development of special target groups. Some development works had been done by implementation of these programmes.

However, no effort was made to take into consideration all the aspects of village's integrated development. Since the Eighth Plan some programmes have been implemented taking an approach to develop the village on an integrated way. The development scheme, designed on the pattern of integrated village development, is enumerated below.

Integrated Rural Development Programme (IRDP)

IRDP is described officially as a major mechanism for the alleviation of rural poverty. The main objective of IRDP is to raise families of identified target group below poverty line by creation of sustainable opportunities for self-employment in the rural sector. Assistance is given in the form of subsidy by the government and term credit advanced by financial institutions (commercial banks, cooperatives and regional rural banks.) The programme is implemented in all blocks of the country as centrally sponsored scheme funded on 50:50 basis by the centre and the states.

The target group under IRDP consists of small and marginal farmers, agricultural labourers and rural artisans having annual income below Rs. 11,000 defined as poverty line in the Eighth Plan. In order to ensure that benefits under the programme reach the more vulnerable sectors of the society, it is stipulated that at least 50 per cent of assisted families should be from scheduled castes and scheduled tribes with corresponding flow of resources to them. Furthermore, 40 per cent of the coverage should be of women beneficiaries and 3 per cent of handicapped persons.

The programme is implemented through District Rural Development Agencies (DRDAs). The governing body of DRDA includes local MP, MLA, Chairman of Zila Parishad, heads of district development departments, representatives of SCs, STs and women. At the grassroot level, the block staff is responsible for implementation of the programme. The State Level Coordination Committee (SLCC) monitors the programme at state level whereas the Ministry of Rural Areas and Employment is responsible for the release of central share of funds, policy formation, overall guidance, monitoring and evaluation of the programme.

Impact of Development Programmes

Before offering any comments on the impact of development programmes, a few general observations must be made. The programmes are framed and sponsored by the the central government. But there are programmes which are on the 50:50 basis. And, then, there are also programmes which are sponsored and supported by the state governments. The impact of the development programmes has not been uniform all over the country. In some states, a particular programme gets a healthy response while in other states it is a failure. When we evaluate the impact of development programmes, these basic observations should be kept in mind.

Yet another important thing which requires mention is the focus and thrust of programme. All the development programmes beginning from Community Development Project to Integrated Rural Development have stressed on the development of agriculture and irrigation. Second, the programmes have stressed on public health, veterinary and housing. More or less the content of programmes has been the same. What has changed is approach to a particular programme. In the pages that follow we shall discuss some of the impacts of development programmes on the village life. Generally, the impact has to be seen at two levels. If we look at any particular programme we would find that either it falls in the individual beneficiary programme or community beneficiary programme. The provision of infrastructural facilities such as construction of a sanitary well, approach road, school and public health centre falls in the category of community beneficiary programme. On the other hand, subsidy grant, loan for agricultural inputs, grant of a scholarship or hostel facility to a tribal boy come under the individual beneficiary programme. Any evaluation of the impact of development programmes on the village life should take stock of both individual and community beneficiary programmes.

We now categorise and analyse the impact of development programmes on the village life.

High Yielding Varieties and Green Revolution

It was during the Third Plan, to be precise by 1966, that the high yielding varieties (HYVs) were introduced in agriculture. In other words, the agricultural inputs had potentiality to substantial growth and production. It must be admitted that HYVs revolutionised the agricultural production. Hence, it is called green revolution. The impact of green revolution was highly pronounced in the states of Punjab, Haryana, Maharashtra and Gujarat.

The core of green revolution consists in agricultural production and extensive use of technology. It is argued that the green revolution basically encouraged private investment in agriculture. K.M. Raj, the noted economist, very rightly observes:

What the new strategy can be expected to achieve is not so much a sharp acceleration in the overall rates of growth of agricultural output as in giving considerable stimulus to private investment in the bigger sized farms in region which have the necessary climate and soil conditions, as well as source of water supply for adopting the new technology.

The green revolution gave a package programme for agricultural development. The package consisted of all the inputs, such as seeds and fertiliser, for raising production. The programme is also known as new agricultural strategy or policy. It was started with the *kharif* crop of 1966.

The green revolution observed in 1966-67 was studied by both economists and sociologists. The learned journals such as *Economic and Political Weekly* and *Seminar* brought out a series of articles on the impact of green revolution. Some of the impacts are given below:

(1) It is now more than three decades since the green revolution got off the ground. In spite of all the ignominies heaped on it in the initial years by critics of various hues, it has more than amply achieved its primary aim, i.e., a dramatic increase in the production of foodgrains on a scale that would have been unimaginable before the advent of the new technology in agriculture.

(2) Green revolution has also resulted in a large number of by-products. The massive agricultural production has improved transport system, widened educational network and above all introduced rural electricity. All these factors, if combined together, have led the green revolution villages on the road to progress.

(3) The economists argue that one very optimistic outcome of green revolution is that in the long run it would discourage the rural population to migrate to urban areas. The green revolution villages have all the facilities of urban lifestyle. Electricity, tap water, cooking gas, roads and education are the items of infrastructure which give the village people on urban style of life. Non-migration to urban centres would save congestion in the overcrowded urban communities.

(4) Ashok Thapar, on the basis of evidence observed in green revolution villages, concludes:

In short, agricultural prosperity turns villages into expanding markets not just for products of agro-industry but also for a growing range of consumer goods. And herein lies the main hope for preventing the mass migration to urban slums on the part of India's millions of rural artisans who have already been impoverished by the steady, on-going shift in emphasis in farm mechanisation from time-saving to labour-saving devices.[1]

(5) Frankle Francine[2] has different analysis on the impact of green revolution. Admittedly, the green revolution stands for substantial rise in foodgrain production. But, the increase has not improved the quality of life of people. What is worse, the income of the big farmers has increased many times. And, the sharecroppers, marginal farmers and small peasants have registered no growth in their income. In other words, the gap between the big farmers and small farmers has been widened. The 'haves' have got more than the 'have-nots'. The growth in agriculture definitely gives self-sufficiency in foodgrains but it is highly injudicious so far as the social justice is concerned.

(6) When the impact of green revolution is assessed, there is much talk about trickle-down effect. By the early 1960s it was a growing realisation that if the higher segments of rural life develop, its impact would also go to the lower segments. But this, however, did not happen. The growth in economy did not necessarily lead to the improvement in the quality of life of the people, on the other hand it widened the gap between the rich and the poor.

(7) The Economic and Social Survey of Asia and the Pacific (ESCAP)[3] report has examined the impact of green revolution in India's villages. It, in categorical terms, points out that the rural poor have been by-passed in the green revolution. The report observes:

Believing that the benefits of development, as measured by macroeconomic indices, would eventually trickle-down to the masses, propounders of many past rural development policies have given primary attention to the encouragement of capital-intensive, large-scale farming, the results have proved other than expected and the trickle-down theory has been discredited by the fact that its use has served only to widen and reinforce the gap between the rich and the rural poor.

A heap of literature is available to indicate that the HYVs certainly increased agricultural production but the benefits of production remained restricted to the farmers who had large portions of land, assured irrigation facilities, cultivation friendly soil and adequate money to purchase and hire improved technology. The poor peasants, with meagre hand in their possession, could not benefit by the introduction of HYVs. They were obviously deprived of the trickle-down effect.

We would reiterate that we are offering comments on the impact of village development programmes. The first impact that we have mentioned above is only with reference to the programme of HYV which resulted in green revolution. But, the impacts are several and we propose to discuss other impacts of development programmes.

Politicisation of Development Programmes

If crime in this country is politicised, so has village development been politicised. The peasants who have their political orientation to different political parties, particularly the ruling party, have benefited much from the development programmes. There is enough data to demonstrate that a large number of development projects have benefited those who rule over deliberation and involve themselves in decisions, benefit much. The political leaders, Panchayati Raj leaders and members of dominant castes have cornered several of the benefits of development programmes. The poor villagers continue to remain at the lower rung of village hierarchy.

Development Diversity

One of the objectives of rural development programmes was to pull up the backward areas on par with the advanced areas. But, the results that we find do not provide any evidence to support this hypothesis. On the contrary, the backward areas have become further backward and neglected and the advanced areas have gained prosperity.

Increasing Stratification

We have observed it time and again that India's villages had minimum stratification. The inequality was based on religion and tradition. This inequality has got a new edge, it has got new teeth and the position of the village poor has been worsened. The development projects have gone largely in favour of the rich villagers. The newly stratified village society has achieved a new status. There has come caste in class and class in caste. Among the Brahmins there is a class system where the high-class Brahmins do not accept daughters of low-class Brahmins. Such a situation reveals that in India though classes are emerging, the structural aspects of caste continue to remain unchanged.

Urbanisation of Rural Settlement

The infrastructure provided by the development programmes, alongwith individual beneficiary programmes, have given a new direction to rural development. It is a common observation to find that villages are becoming urban communities which we call town community. The census shows that during the last two decades the number of towns all over the country has increased. It is certain that there is a continuous change of rural communities into a town community.

A Grand Failure

The history of development programmes systematically starts from 1952 when the Community Development Projects were launched. Till now tonnes of money have been invested in village development. Scores of schemes have worked for the removal of rural poverty. But, even then, the progress made by the people is in no way demonstrable. It could be guessed that out of the money meant for village development programmes the larger beneficiaries are big farmers, village moneylenders, village officials, development personnel, engineers and political leaders. Much money has been invested, and little has been harvested in terms of the real improvement in the life of the village people.

The best way to conclude this chapter on the benefit of village development programmes, the story of an American anthropologist who wrote on India's development, is given here. The story runs something like this:

> Once there were rains and the rains in currents and sheets. A river was inundated. Close to it a monkey was sitting on a tree. The monkey saw that fish were going up and down the currents of the river. It was really ghastly scene as the monkey saw. His heart melted: "Oh, how the fish are in trouble, immediately I must do something for them." The monkey moved by the piety came down the tree. It took

as many fish as he could under his legs, climbed upon the tree and put these at a safer place in one of the holes of the tree. After putting them he took a sigh of relief and said: "I have done today a good deed of work. A number of lives have been saved."

The lives were not saved and all the fish died. The anthropologist says that the development personnel and the change agents have made the life of the poor villagers compared to the life of fish. If the villagers did not die like fish, surely, their life became miserable. This is one aspect of development life that the anthropologist has painted. The other aspect of 'happy' life can be anybody's guess.

Notes

1. Ashok Thapar, "Prospects for Agriculture", *Seminar*, 365, January, 1990, pp. 49-51.
2. Frankle Francine, *India's Green Revolution: Economic Gains and political Costs,* Princeton University Press, 1971.
3. Economic and Social Survey of Asia and the Pacific (ESCAP), 1975, Economic and Social Commission for Asia and the Pacific, p. 307.

13 Village Cooperatives

Some preliminary observations are necessary to determine the status of cooperatives in rural India. The history of rural society shows it vividly that the peasants always stand in need of some financial assistance or cooperation. The cooperative societies need to be viewed historically. The great malaise of India's villages is the role of intermediaries who are known by different names. They are called *Diku* in Bihar, *Shankar* in Gujarat, and *Bania* in Rajasthan. The peasant in economic paraphrase is a producer. He harvests the crops. In between the peasant and the consumer, there is a trader. This trader is the exploiter. He exploits on the one hand the peasant and on the other the consumer. And, again, in the process of production, some investment of money is inevitable. This money is always required by the peasant. The peasant has to purchase manure, he has to obtain some irrigation facilities, and he must have some money for the purchase of seed. After having made all this investment he would get his crop after a lapse of three to four months. And, there is again a risk, it is possible that the monsoon betrays him and the crop fails. It is also possible that the yields are poor. And, hopefully, it is occasional that the return of crop is quite satisfactory. All these eventualities put the peasant in need of some money. Historically, therefore, the Indian peasant is born in indebtedness, lives in indebtedness and dies in indebtedness. The situation of indebtedness always requires some agency to advance loans. This introduces the role of an intermediary.

The British government and the feudal regime, which was in vogue in princely states, did not do anything to create some institution which could eliminate the intermediary and make provision for the advancement of loan.

The government of independent India took the economic status of the villager into consideration. It was planned to create cooperative societies which could come in help for the peasantry as a whole. A.R.

Desai, while stressing the importance of cooperative societies in independent India, argues for the encouragement of cooperative sector in rural society. He observes:

> The government is attempting to bring about a directed social change based on certain postulates. It has been trying to overcome the debacle of the agrarian social order caused by the British rulers. Alongwith land reforms ... the government has been encouraging co-operation, building up various kinds of village institutions and has been trying to resurrect cottage industries. It is also endeavouring to create a new kind of administrative machinery which can reorganise the rural social system.[1]

The history of cooperative development indicates that the government has made all efforts for the establishment of cooperative societies. It is also a fact that our national leaders, including Gandhiji and Nehruji, made all efforts for the promotion of cooperative societies. However, the present-day working of cooperative societies is quite dismal. Leaving aside the states of Gujarat and Maharashtra, the rest of the country does not have a meaningful cooperative society. The Government of India which claims to be a welfare state should see that how the cooperative societies which were initially established to minimise the role of traders, middlemen and exploiters, have become a party with the exploiters and the big farmers. A.R. Desai has raised certain relevant questions in this regard when he writes:

> Has the "state of independent India" which claims to be a welfare state and which broadcasts that it represents masses, become an active agency undertaking the above mentioned task? Has it been adopting a bold and radical necessary policy which would make a qualitative break in the social set up by smashing the economic, social and political power or the rich? Has it been generating new institutional framework favourable to the poor?[2]

Before we discuss the present status of cooperatives in rural India we must take into account various dimensions of this movement. There are serious criticisms on the functioning of this movement. For instance, B.S. Baviskar argues that power conflict has emerged in the cooperative societies. In other words, there is a special kind of 'cooperative politics' in the major cooperative societies of the country. Daniel Thorner, on the other hand, has come out with the findings based on empirical research that the village cooperatives today are controlled and run by the richer sections and are strengthening those strata.

Yet another observation which needs to be made at the beginning is that like any economic innovation, the creation of cooperatives is largely based on caste. The cooperatives survive and continue to function only on the caste economics which prevails in villages. We may try to make our cooperatives quite secular but caste and religion which are inherent in our villages also turn the cooperatives to fulfil the ritual and religions functions.

We do not want to provide any critique to cooperative movement in India at the stage. We only want to stress that there is a considerable place of the cooperative societies in the development of agriculture, irrigation and above all rural industries. We now discuss some of the vital aspects of cooperative movement in India in a systematic way.

Meaning of Cooperation and Cooperative Societies

The dictionary meaning of cooperation is "to work together". However, the meaning of cooperative societies is quite technical and has the context of village cooperatives in India. In one form or the other some kind of cooperative societies are found all over the world. A few of the meanings of cooperative societies given by the experts are explained as under:

(1) M.T. Herrick[3] is a renowned author on the theme of rural credit. He has extensively examined the situation of credit in rural society. It is in the context of peasantry that he describes the cooperative societies. He writes:

> Cooperation is the act of poor persons voluntarily unite for utilising reciprocally their own forces, resources or both under their mutual management, to their common profit or loss.

Thus, Herrick brings out a few elements which are essential to any cooperative society: (1) it is an organisation of poor, (2) it is voluntary, and (3) it is sharing common resources. The author stresses that the poor peasantry has meagre resources and, therefore, they unite together to pull their resources for common good. The basic idea of cooperative society excludes the role of big peasants. It is supposed to be a union of small and marginal peasants.

(2) The Cooperative Planning Committee, constituted in 1946, has defined the cooperatives in the context of Indian peasantry. It observes:

> Cooperation is a form of organisation in which persons voluntarily associate together on the basis of equality for the promotion of their common interest.

The committee has elaborated further the meaning of cooperatives. It says that the objective of a cooperative society is to promote the economic interests of the common peasants. The association of members is based on equality. The functions of the cooperative society cannot be fulfilled by individuals. The idea is that what individual cannot do because of his limitations can be done by economic enterprise.

(3) P.R. Dubhashi[4] brings out the meaning of cooperative society in an evolutionary way. He says that cooperative societies have undergone a historical change in their structure and meaning. His argument is that we can understand cooperative society not as an institution but as a movement. This movement is not static and is always changing with the changing needs of the peasantry. Dubhashi's definition of cooperative movement runs as below:

> The cooperative movement in the beginning was confined to the credit structure. It was only during the First World War that the cooperative movement was extended to the consumer business. In the case of the scarcity during the war period, the cooperative movement was given the role of making commodities, in short supply, available to the people. The cooperatives were managed essentially by part-time workers. There was an element of social service in the cooperative activities undertaken in the colonial times. This must be considered to be a very precious element in India's cooperative movement in pre-independence phase, despite the rapid development in that period.

The above definition brings out four important objectives of cooperative societies. In the initial stage cooperatives in India as elsewhere in the world were meant only to advance credit to the peasants. Credit was essential owing to several reasons, such as investment in farm production, failure of crop or making provision for irrigation.

Yet another meaning of cooperatives was to serve the consumers in case of a scarcity that could be caused by war, flood, drought, etc. Then, in the 1940s, the idea of social service emerged. It means help given to the peasants. Recently the meaning of cooperatives has undergone a revolutionary change. The cooperatives today are formed for the attainment of development. In other words, cooperatives are constituted to provide loans for agricultural inputs, like purchase of implements, manure, digging of wells, etc.

Basic Characteristics of Cooperatives

As stated above, the scope and meaning of cooperatives has undergone radical change. During the colonial period it was our realisation that peasantry was the most exploited group of people. The industrial policy that the colonial regime had adopted, was fatal for small artisans and workers engaged in cotton industry. Gandhiji realised that if the cultivators were not rescued from the onslaught of industrial development, the village would be ruined. The plough, therefore, has always been the hope and glory of the people. It was emphasised that the cultivators had to be financially assisted to increase there farm product and thus made India self-sufficient.

The salient features of cooperatives which we identify today are the products of the policy adopted by post-independent India. The Rural Credit Survey Committee in 1951 suggested that the cooperatives should provide coverage to the rural poor, who have no chance against the vested interests of the landlord-moneylender-trader class. The committee, therefore, recommended that the state government should participate in the share capital of the cooperatives and also provide managerial support and subsidies.

The committee also recommended that the Reserve Bank of India (RBI) should support the movement by way of reimbursement of loans extended by cooperative societies. The committee suggested a three-tier structure of the large-size credit cooperative societies at the base. The district cooperative banks as central financial agencies, and at the apex cooperative banks at the state level supported by the agriculture division of the Reserve Bank of India.

Thus, on the basis of the above mentioned provisions of cooperative societies we give below a few features of cooperative societies:

(1) *Organisation of the poor*: Theoretically, the cooperative society

has no scope for the membership of the rich. In fact, the major function of a cooperative society is to provide credit facilities to the peasants for productive purposes only. It does not give credit for fulfilling social obligations. *Thus, a cooperative society is an association of the poor peasants for meeting their productive needs.*

(2) *Membership is voluntary*: Membership to a cooperative society is voluntary. A peasant should assess his needs and accordingly take membership to a particular society. For instance, where a person does not have any cattle or sugarcane crop, why should he be member of a dairy or sugarcane growers cooperative society. A cooperative society has definite objectives and those who find possibility of their objectives fulfilled should opt for membership.

(3) *Absence of exploitation:* A cooperative society inherently denies exploitation of its members and consumers. Basically, the society takes care of the mutual economic benefits of its own members. In this way, the cooperative society rejects any exploitation which was the basis of the intermediaries.

(4) *The role of bank*: The cooperative society cannot left to itself. The government being welfare-oriented cannot remain a spectator only. It has to intervene and play its role in providing assistance to the peasants. It is on this theory that the RBI and other nationalised banks provide assistance to the cooperative societies. The RBI, being the apex bank, has made provisions for the working of cooperative banks.

(5) *Subsidies*: There is a always some risk involved in advancing loans. Sometimes it so happens that due to flood and scarcity the peasant is unable to repay the loans. Or it is also possible that the input technology has a price-tag which is beyond the capacity of the peasant to purchase. In such a situation some subsidy has to be given to the peasant. In other words, though the cooperative societies are autonomous, they are also guided and controlled through banks and government cooperative department.

Types of Cooperative Societies

Credit society was the first type of cooperatives. Its objective was to provide credit to the members of the society. Later on, with the increase in the needs of the peasant people, the cooperatives took different forms. If a categorisation of different forms of societies is made today, it would make a long list. However, on the basis of its functioning, the cooperatives may be divided into three types: (1) credit societies, (2) consumers societies, and (3) producers society. These three basic types are further divided into several types. For instance, there is a society of the peasants. This is sub-divided into cotton growers society, sugarcane society, wheat producer society and so on and so forth. In the similar way there are sub-types of consumers cooperatives and producers cooperatives. We shall discuss the three major types of cooperatives below:

(1) *Credit Cooperative Societies*: Credit societies are voluntary and mutual aid associations. The major function of this type of society is to provide credit on personal security or on the basis of nominal security to its members, who are either cultivators, workmen or lower middle class people. They are of two types, viz., of unlimited liability and of liability. The difference between the two is with regard to liability of members, size of shares, territorial scope, division of profits, management, reserve fund, and their business and moral aspect.

(2) *Consumers Societies*: The membership of these societies consists of agricultural workers and the middle class people who organise a consumer store. The members of the society earn their independent living and they are not supposed to depend on the consumer society. The society only helps them in the better utilisation of their income. And, thus lowering their cost of living, correct weighment, quality goods and reasonable prices are the chief aims of consumers society. These societies were originally started in England where the first store of this kind was launched in 1844.

(3) *Producers Societies*: A producers society is organised for the production of goods and services based upon common ownership and management by a group of workers to eliminate the employee-employer relationship.

In our country, the above three types of cooperatives have taken a mixed form. A single society could be a credit, consumer and production society at the same time. Later, we shall have opportunity to discuss this mixed type of cooperative society.

History of Cooperative Movement in India

The experience of British government with India's peasant society on occasions of famine, scarcity gives the idea of providing some financial assistance to the village people. It was also found that Indian peasantry always suffered from lack of funds required for the development of farm produce. The striking factor is that the *jagirdars* and *jamindars* always exploited the peasants when the latter failed to deposit the land tax in time. Even they required money for their subsistence if there was a famine. Realisation of land tax was the first objective of the colonial rule. This prompted the British government to establish credit cooperative societies in the villages. The first Cooperative Credit Societies Act was passed in 1904. To remove the weaknesses of this Act, the new Cooperative Societies Act was passed in 1912. The movement has now made rapid strides. "The government before fostering and supporting it, wanted to be sure if it was developing on right lines. Therefore, it appointed Maclagan Committee in 1914 which suggested certain improvements in its functioning, such as better procedure of audit, emphasis on teachings to members and to have steady progress of the movement. However, in spite of warning given by the committee, the number of societies continued to increase rapidly.

The cooperative movement got a boost during the war period. Various post-war plans were drawn up in the country and they all emphasised the increasing role of cooperative movement. The second report on recommendation and planning issued by the Government of India gave an important place to cooperative movement. As a result, a Cooperative Planning Committee was appointed by the Government of India in 1945.

It was in 1951 that the RBI appointed a committee with the terms of guidance to survey All India Rural Credit Societies. The report of this committee was submitted in 1954. The important suggestions and recommendations given by the committee include the following:

(1) There should be a partnership of the state government in all kinds of societies (such as credit societies) and banks like Central Bank, State Banks, cooperative marketing, storage, warehousing and all other important societies such as dairying, milk supply, transport and industrial societies.
(2) A central committee for cooperative training should be set up.
(3) It would the responsibility of the state government to implement these programmes. Besides, the other two main agencies will be the Ministry of Food and Agriculture of Government of India and the Reserve Bank of India.

(4) The funding for the cooperative societies of all kinds including the cooperative training centre will be from the following sources:
   (i) Reserve Bank of India;
   (ii) National Agricultural Credit (Long Term Operation) Fund;
   (iii) National Agricultural Credit Stabilisation Fund;
   (iv) State Agricultural Credit (Relief and Guarantee) Fund;
   (v) State Cooperative Development Fund;
   (vi) State Cooperative Bank and Central Cooperative Bank.

(5) The credit institutions at the primary, secondary and apex levels need to be reorganised and at least 51 per cent of the shares in apex organisations should be held by state government. These apex organisations will purchase 51 per cent of the shares in central organisations and the central institutions in their turn of primary organisations.

(6) There shall be a Central Land Mortgage Bank in each state and, Primary Land Mortgage Banks at the lower level.

(7) Primary Village Credit Societies should be reorganised as to have a membership of about 500 persons. And, these should be linked up with marketing societies in the marketing centres. Processing function is to be developed substantially and specially for the producing sugar, ginning cotton, crushing oil and baling jute.

Most of the above mentioned recommendations were accepted by the Government of India and put into effect under the Second Five Year Plan.

Some Important Kinds of Societies

While giving the major types of cooperative societies, namely, credit, consumer and producer, there are a large number of big and small cooperative societies working in villages. The implementation of development programmes has added a large number of cooperative societies in the rural areas. For instance, the milk cooperative societies developed in Gujarat have given rise to 'white revolution'. Similarly, the sugarcane cooperative societies in Uttar Pradesh and Maharashtra have brought about massive production. Here, we propose to deal with some of the specific societies which have assumed importance at the national level.

(1) *Agricultural Credit and Multipurpose Societies*

In the beginning, when the cooperative movement was started in 1904, there were only credit societies. During the later years, when there was depression during 1929-30, it was realised that the main weakness of the movement was its absorption in credit activities to the exclusion of others, which went to make up the economic life of the villagers. It was also felt that (i) moneylender could not be dispensed with unless all his functions were taken up, that is, supply credit and marketing; (ii) credit without linking up it with production and marketing offered a dangerous temptation, and (iii) there was paucity of trained personnel to manage various societies in the same village. This idea came to the forefront with the publication of a bulletin by Reserve Bank of India. Since then, it has strongly veered round it, in this country and their formation has also been recommended by various committees including the Cooperative Planning Committee (1946). Since then attempts have been made to organise such societies in various states.

(2) *Farmers' Service Societies*

The National Commission on Agriculture gave the idea of the formation of Farmers' Service Societies in 1970. These societies have been constituted in a few states. The idea ultimately was to convert the service societies into large-sized multipurpose credit societies. The agricultural credit or multi-purpose credit societies supply short and medium credit to members in rural areas. These societies get amount mostly from the Central Cooperative Banks and State Cooperative Banks. The long-term loans are supplied by the State Land Development Banks through the Primary Land Development Banks in the different areas of the states. Recently, the short-term, medium-term and long-term loans are advanced by a single agency only.

(3) *Cooperative Marketing and Processing Societies*

Effort has been made towards the creation of cooperative marketing and processing societies. The marketing societies procure and distribute foodgrains and certain other commodities to be distributed through its branches to the consumers. The processing societies have come out successfully in the field of producing sugar, ginning cotton, crushing oil and baling jute.

(4) *Large Scale Agriculture Multipurpose Societies (LAMPS)*

In the 1970s it was realised that the fruits of economic development were not reaching to the poorer and backward strata of the rural society. The small and marginal farmers who formed the bulk of rural households were not getting their due. The concept of Farmers' Service Society was conceived as a device to provide a say to these people in the management of the credit cooperative societies. We have mentioned about these multipurpose cooperative societies earlier. A form of such society was introduced among the tribals. And, here we discuss the LAMPS working among tribals in Tribal Sub-Plan projects.

It must be stressed that the emergence of LAMPS as a cooperative organisation was specially meant for the tribals. The tribals took to agriculture about 100 years back. They are actually latecomers to agriculture. Earlier to it they lived on forest and forest produce. LAMPS are actually a component of the wider cooperative structure. These are a specific type of cooperatives.

LAMPS are supposed to be an intermediary agency between the tribal cultivator and the tribal consumer. In fact, LAMPS have taken the role of a traditional *sahukar* or moneylender. The moneylender has always been an exploiter of the tribal. Viewed from this perspective the LAMPS are created to remove the moneylender. Following are the main functions of LAMPS:

(1) to provide trade facilities to the people of the tribal area;
(2) to provide loaning facilities to the tribals in order to get them rid of the exploitation by the traders;
(3) to bridge the gap in development between tribals and non-tribal segments and also to eradicate poverty among the tribals;
(4) to help the agriculturists in the procurement and marketing of minor forest produce, agricultural commodities, articles of consumption and to maintain eco-system alongwith the guidance for development; and

(5) to work as an agent of the government or state level cooperative institution and local-self corporation for providing seed, manure, agriculture implements, foodgrains and consumption articles.

Thus, the introduction of LAMPS, therefore, is made with the objective to cope up with the particular economy of the tribals. LAMPS are found in all the states where there is Tribal Sub-Plan area. No specific findings are available, however, on the functioning or the LAMPS. On a general plane it could be said that much of the success of LAMPS rests on the awareness of the members of the LAMPS. As a prerequisite to the success, it must be said that the members must be not only educated but familiar with the ideology of cooperatives. Surely, the development agencies have housed the LAMPS in particular villages but the absence of non-awareness results in the defunct LAMPS. Most of them, all the time, are found locked.

(5) *Milk Supply Societies*

The milk supply societies are also of a specific kind of cooperative societies. There is a network of such societies all over the country. The prime objective of such type of society is to provide good quality milk at reasonable prices to consumers in the urban areas. But, these societies also work for the production of milk in a larger way by the agriculturists. The agriculturists can increase their income by dairy farming. The milk supply societies not only collect the milk available in the villages and supply it to consumers in the town but they also provide agriculturists with funds to purchase more milch animals, feeds to nourish them, and to raise superior cattle. These activities relieve unemployment and underemployment among villagers and convert farming into a paying mixed farming proposition. The number of milk unions and milk supply societies was very small in the beginning. However, there has been tremendous increase in it and the business due to introduction of certain special schemes."

(6) *Sugar Cooperatives*

Sugar cooperatives are essentially processing cooperatives. The sugar cooperatives are formed in the regions where sugarcane is grown in abundance. Generally, the cane growers in a given area, for instance, in a cluster of 100 villages, form a cooperative. The members cultivate cane on their own lands. The sugarcane cooperative society provides a number of services; e.g., it gives crop loans and provides automatic repayment, helps to establish ancillary organisation, such as lift irrigation societies, poultry cooperatives etc., distributes hybrid seeds, chemical fertilisers and research information, provides soil testing services, organises the harvest and transport of cane through contract teams, processes the cane into sugar and markets the sugar and distributes the profits in the form of high cane prices to farmer members.

Politics in Cooperative Societies

There is a network of cooperative societies in all the states of the country. These cooperatives are linked from the grassroot level to the Central Ministry of Cooperation. Besides the government, the cooperatives are also controlled by the Reserve Bank of India and the state apex and cooperative banks. Theoretically, the cooperative movement has nothing to do with politics. Despite this theoretical status of cooperatives there are a few issues which influence the working of the societies. One very common issue with the cooperative societies is the non-payment of loans. When the time for depositing the loan instalment comes, there is always an intervention from the local leaders. Sometimes, when a political party comes to power, it waives the loans taken from the cooperative societies. There are occasions when lakhs of money are waived by the government. And, then, when a cooperative society fails, it is kept continued for political interests. Sometimes, a particular type of cooperative bank is kept functioning in the name of the welfare of the peasants. Rural banks all over the country are running in loss but they are survived because of vested interests of some of the segments of society. There are several issues related to the cooperative movement. However, here we shall refer to one issue only, that is, of politics in cooperative societies.

B.S. Baviskar[5] has explored the role of politics in cooperative societies. He has taken for his study only two societies: (i) the sugar cooperative of Maharashtra, and (ii) the milk cooperative of Gujarat. His study of these two societies very clearly indicates that there is a definite cooperative politics all over the country. His study leads him to make broad generalisations. Before giving details of the sugar and milk cooperatives he makes his statement by saying at ideally there is no place of politics in cooperatives. He then goes on to raise two questions which are relevant in discussing the cooperative politics. He writes:

> In the literature on cooperation there is an idealistic emphasis on keeping cooperatives free from politics. Political neutrality is often considered to be one of the principles of cooperation. *In my view, in real life no cooperative is free from politics* (emphasis ours).

Baviskar has raised two questions in this regard: What is the nature of relationship between cooperatives and politics? What are the implications of politics in cooperatives? Baviskar tries to find answer of these two questions in the field.

Sugar Cooperatives in Maharashtra

The land in Maharashtra is dry and it often witnesses drought. There is failure of rains and the whole region becomes victim of scarcity. It was felt that some irrigation facilities need to be given to the peasants. During 1920s canal irrigation facilities were introduced in Maharashtra. It so happened that despite the availability of canal water facility, the cultivators did not use it. It became a problem with the government. Consequently, the government invited industrialists of Bombay to establish sugar factories in the intensively irrigated areas. By 1930s some farmers were persuaded to take to sugarcane crop. The joint stock company constituted by the industrialists was asked to take the sugarcane for processing sugar. This kind of venture or relationship between the joint stock company and the sugarcane growers did not work well. The growers had so many complaints. They were not paid fully. There was over-weighing and the payments were delayed. Then, by 1946, the cane growers had a meeting at Shrirampur (Ahmadnagar). They took the decision to make a cooperative sugar factory at the *taluka* headquarters. The experiment was successful and at a later stage the government encouraged to launch Shrirampur-type sugar factories in other parts of the state. During 1960s and 1970s a large number of factories came into existence in Maharashtra. According to data available for the year 1994-95 there were 435 sugar factories in the whole of Maharashtra. Of these 244 belonged to the cooperative sector. About three million sugarcane growers were members of the cooperative sugar factories. There are also cooperatives for the marketing of sugar. A large number of members in the sugar cooperative societies are small share-holders.

This is, in short, the organisation and functioning of sugar cooperatives in Maharashtra. The description would allow us to analyse the politics involved in these odd number of sugar cooperatives:

(1) At the level of a single sugar cooperative society there is a struggle to get power. This power to a member enables him to control the cooperative society. Struggle for power acquisition is always in a society, sometimes latent and sometimes manifest.

(2) Each sugar cooperative is related to the local politics beginning from Gram Panchayat to Zila Parishad.

(3) Sugar factories are intimately related to politics at state level. Actually, in the state of Maharashtra, sugarcane growing is an important economic activity. It is the power which a person gets through his membership determines his status in the district or the region. And, if one becomes a member of the Board of Directors of the cooperatives he becomes a leading figure in political circles. Describing the role of politics in sugar cooperatives B.S. Baviskar writes:

> Elections to sugar cooperatives are a major political event in the state. In some ways they create greater excitement than even the general elections, as newspapers have reported over the years. The leaders invest a great deal of money, energy, organisation and other resources to get elected. The interest of the members is equally matched.[6]

Baviskar has demonstrated empirical evidence to lead to the conclusion that the politics in sugar cooperatives is a cut-throat politics. In his yet another statement, he writes:

> The leaders of sugar cooperatives aspire to be—and often succeed in becoming—members of legislatures at the state as well as the central level. Control over the resources of sugar cooperatives enables them not only to get elected to the state assembly and the parliament but also provides their respective parties one of the major avenues of finance and other resources during the general elections so as to enable the party to win as many seats as possible.[7]

Cooperative politics results in several benefits to the members. The influential members of sugar cooperatives get their work done at the district level. If anything else, at least they are not intimidated by the petty officials. Yet another outcome of the cooperative politics is that the Maratha caste has become a dominant caste all over Maharashtra. It is because of the fact that the Maratha caste cane growers are in majority in cooperative societies.

Milk Cooperatives in Gujarat

Baviskar's another case study is that of milk cooperatives of Gujarat. He also finds, though at a different level, the occurrence of politics. The dairy cooperatives first started in western India. He makes special reference of the dairy cooperatives found in the Chorotar track of the Kheda district in central Gujarat. Chorotar is a cultural region largely inhabited by the Patel caste. Patels are known all over the country for their excellent skills in agriculture. They also do dairy farming. The Chorotar region consists of the tehsils of Anand, Patalad, Borsad and Nadiad. During the last century, the Patidars had successfully taken up the cultivation of cash crops such as cotton and tobacco besides the routine crops of *bajra*, rice and wheat. Each Patidar farmer also kept a few buffaloes of the local 'Surati' breed which enabled him to provide milk for domestic consumption and use the surplus for marketing in the form of *ghee*.

In course of time, say by 1929, the yields of milk increased. It was planned to supply the Chorotar milk to Bombay. The government established in 1945 the Bombay Milk Scheme which depended largely on the supply of liquid milk from Kheda district by rail. The milk supply at a later stage was handedover the Polson who was the main supplier. The milk was collected by Polson through his agents in the villages. It was pasteurised at Anand and transported to Bombay. Polson was paid liberally by the Bombay government. But, the former often manipulated measurement of quantity and fat content of milk and delayed payment. They often refused to accept milk during the flush season. To add insult to injury, the government gave monopoly rights to Polson in 1946 to procure milk in Kheda district which deprived the producers of the freedom to sell their milk to anybody else. This created strong discontent among the farmers and local political leaders.

The farmers were much agitated. They stopped supplying milk to Polson and consequently in 1946, the Kheda District Cooperative

Milk Producers' Union was established. In the beginning only two villages were under it. At a later stage Morarji Desai and Sardar Patel gave a lead to the movement. One Tribhuvandas Patel played a significant role at the village level to mobilise the milk producers to take membership.

When the Kheda milk union got its roots, V. Kurien was appointed its manager in 1950. The union and its dairy (Amul) received encouragement and financial aid not only from the state and central Governments but also from international agencies such as UNICEF and OXFAM. They also became objects of praise for their achievements from many quarters.

Lal Bahadur Shastri, the then Prime Minister, once happened to visit Anand in 1964. Being highly influenced by the functioning of Amul Dairy, he suggested to have such a network of milk cooperatives all over the country. This led to the setting up of National Dairy Development Board (NDDB) in 1965. V. Kurien who was the General Manager of Amul for many years was made chairman of the new organisation. It was later in the 1970s and 1980s that Anand pattern cooperatives became very popular in other parts of Gujarat and elsewhere in the country. What we call 'white revolution' in the form of dairy production had its start from the Chorotar experience of Gujarat.

Politics in Milk Cooperatives

The structure of Kheda Cooperative Milk Societies and Amul dairy is such that there is little scope for competition to various bodies. Compared to sugar mill cooperatives there are no privileges even attached to the Board of Directors. This has reduced the competition. As a matter of fact, the Directors are merely rubber stamps. Actually, the Amul Dairy is run by the technocrats. It is they who decide everything. The politicians, in this respect, have very little to say. Denying the importance of politicians in the running of the Amul Dairy Baviskar writes:

> The perishability of milk required the organisation to work efficiently and according to the clock. Only the technocrats, given a free hand, could provide the efficiency. In brief, vis-a-vis the technocrats the politicians were often in a no-win situation.[8]

Actually, the generalisation made by Baviskar is based on the findings of A.H. Somjee.[9] Thus, both Baviskar and Somjee seem to agree with the predominant role of technocrats in the milk cooperative societies. However, Sujata Patel finds another kind of politics in the milk cooperatives. There is political rivalry between the two major caste groups in the district, namely, Patidars and Banias. She argues: "The domination of the technocrats in the Union is a result of a deliberate policy on the part of the *Patidars* to maintain their control over the organisation vis-a-vis their political rivals, the *Banias* ... Amul is very much a creation of the *Patidars*—the dominant, landowning and enterprising caste in the district. Its Chairman and majority of Directors have always been *Patidars.* Most of the new villages were *Bania* dominated. The *Patidars* know that in an open political contest they would no will against the *Banias*, as they have found by experience in the other contest for power including in the State Assembly and *Zila Parishads.* They, therefore, deliberately projected the managers and technocrats as real men of power to make the positions of Chairman and Directors less attractive to *Banias.*"

It appears that the politics in the Kheda milk cooperatives is a two-level. The first level is between the technocrats and the politicians. In this contest, the technocrats seem to be winners. The second level of contest is between the two castes, viz., the *Patidar* and the *Bania.* This contest goes on sometimes latently and sometimes manifestly. But, definitely, there is some kind of politics in the milk cooperatives.

Status of Cooperatives in India

The general impression of the village people at large is that the cooperative movement has largely failed in the country. Despite this common impression it is also agreed by many that in some of the states, namely, Gujarat, Maharashtra and Karnataka, the movement has made a successful story. M.S. Jain and P.C. Trivedi[11] who have made a comparative study of the LAMPS among the two tribal villages of Gujarat and Rajasthan, come with the finding that the LAMPS of Gujarat have succeeded largely whereas, in Rajasthan they have failed terribly. Likewise, Daniel Thorner[12] has made a large-scale comparative study of about 117 cooperatives scattered throughout most of the states of India. Though the field work for the study of these cooperatives was undertaken in 1958-59, some of the general observations made by Thorner are even relevant today. He has also brought out some basic problems with the proper functioning of the cooperatives. We shall, therefore, provide a general critique to the status of cooperatives in the state. Before we do that we must very strongly emphasise that the role of cooperatives as a credit giving institution cannot be challenged in India. The creation of cooperatives, whether consumer, producer or credit, is a result of our long historical experiences.

At the close of this chapter we would enumerate a few of the factors which help us to assess the contemporary status of cooperatives of all kinds in the country.

(1) It is evident that there is some kind of politics in the cooperatives. The politics takes the caste lines or the class lines. And, what is striking is that the cooperative politics is linked with the local state and central level politics. This has been argued and supported by sociologists and particularly B.S. Baviskar, A.H. Somjee, Sujata Patel and Daniel Thorner.

(2) In some cooperatives it is found that most of the power is concentrated in a single family. There are various forms of such power concentration. Thorner refers to such cooperatives. In one cooperative society of joint farms in Gujarat (Vodadara district), he found that the benefits of the members included purchase of school books for their children. This one family show operated on family land. Three brothers of this single family were serving respectively as the Chairman of the Managing Committee, the Managing Director and the Farm Manager. More of the work of the farm appeared to be done by hired labourers than by the members themselves.

Yet another instance of power concentration in a single family given by Thorner is from village Sadoli in Kolhapur district. Seven brothers of a single family wielded the greatest influence in the multipurpose cooperatives of the village. Another example is that of Salem district of Chennai. This society of Salim was the highly celebrated cooperative in the district. In this cooperative one family has dominated a movement for a generation.

(3) There are a few societies which give membership to the moneylenders. The moneylender, on the one hand, sanctions loan to the

members and out of the cooperative realises his dues from the person's sanctioned loan. The very objective of a society is defeated when instead of abolishing the private credit, it encourages the moneylender to become a party in sanctioning the loan.

(4) The cooperative movement is also defeated because in some societies the big farmers also become members. They corner much of the benefits of loans for their own purpose. For instance, if a big farmer takes loan for a tractor or an improved plough, the marginal farmers are definitely deprived of the facility.

(5) Bureaucratic intervention also comes in the way of smooth functioning of the cooperatives. The bureaucrats include the officials of the cooperative department and the cooperative banks. Sometimes illegal money is also transacted under the table. Corruption has occupied a dirty role in the sanctioning of loans. The illiterate farmers are cheated and exploited in the grant of loans and payment of loan money.

(6) Yet another handicap of the cooperatives is the repayment of loans. The peasants even during normal times fail to repay the loans taken by them. This results in the failure of the cooperatives. Much of the loss suffered by the cooperative banks is also due to non-payment of loans.

Daniel Thorner has provided an intelligent prescription for the progress of the cooperatives in India. It must be made very clear that this movement was started to (1) provide easy credit to the poor farmers, in other words, the cooperatives were constituted as a forum of the poor peasants who mutually contribute their share for their development. (2) It was also the objective of cooperatives to eradicate the role of moneylender. In fact, the place of moneylender had to be taken by the cooperative. If the moneylender takes over the cooperative the latter is doomed. (3) When the movement ideally denies any place to politics, the members practising it, should be debarred.

Keeping in view his vast experience of working in various cooperatives, Daniel Thorner very rightly gives his prescription as under:

> Experience in many countries has shown that cooperatives can serve as a means by which peasant cultivators can help each other to improve their position. But the success of rural cooperatives pre-supposes a modicum of social equality, political democracy and

economic viability among the villagers. These pre-conditions have not been present in village India and are still not present today. If the cooperative movement in India is to get anywhere, two things must happen first: (1) the power of the village oligarchs—the leading people, the *Mukhyestaru,* to use the Kannada experience must be curtailed; and (2) the government must become an instrument of the ordinary peoples, and must be considered as such by the ordinary people.

Notes

1. A.R. Desai, *Rural Sociology in India,* op. cit., p. 481
2. Ibid., p. 482.
3. M.T. Herrick, *Rural Credit,* p. 247.
4. P.R. Dubhashi, "Cooperative Movement, Present Status and Further Challenges", *Cooperative Perspective,* July-September, 1991, Vol. 26, No. 2, p. 6.
5. B.S. Baviskar, "Milk and Sugar: A Comparative Analysis of Cooperative Politics," in Volume 4 by A.M. Shah, B.S. Baviskar and E.A. Ramaswamy (eds.), *Social Structure and Change,* Sage Publications, New Delhi, 1997.
6. Ibid., p. 94
7. Ibid., p. 95.
8. Ibid., p. 107.
9. A.H. Somjee, "The Techo-Managerial and Politico-Managerial Classes in a Milk Cooperative in India," *Journal of Asian and African Studies,* Vol. XVII, pp. 122-34.
10. Sujata Patel, "The Anand Pattern: A Socio-Historical Analysis of its Origin and Growth". Paper submitted to IPAD Project at the Institute of Social Studies, The Hague (mimeographed).
11. M.S. Trivedi and P.C. Jain, *LAMPS in Tribal Areas,* Himanshi Publications, Udaipur, 1996.
12. Daniel Thorner, "Context for Cooperatives in Rural India", *The Economic Weekly,* Thirteenth Annual Number, February 1962.

14 Village Environmental Crisis

Forest, Landuse, Water and Fuel

Globalisation is the theme for our contemporary discussion. It is argued that a new kind of cultural entropy-historical process is emerging which is termed as the global cultural melting pot. This global culture ends up in the process of cultural creolisation or rather inaccurately a situation of westernisation. Globalisation, on the one hand, has influenced local culture and on the other hand created awareness for developing a sustainable environment. It is the globalisation which has taken within it an agenda, some of the crises which are today threatening in the world. Among these crises are included decay of environment, ecology and some fatal diseases such as malaria and AIDS.

Environment is a world problem. But the severity of ecology and environment varies from community to community. For instance, the environmental problems of the urban communities relate to inadequate disposal of wastes or overuse of toxic substances. This kind of environmental crisis is very acute in industrial cities. But the other kind of environmental crisis relates to the degradation of the natural resource base. In rural India, the second kind of crisis is quite fatal. It is concerned with the degradation of land, water and forest resources. The village environmental crisis can break the country. On their decay, naturally, there is decay of food, fodder, firewood, fibre and water. The life of the 600 million odd rural people depends on the sustainable development of these natural resources. The environmental degradation of our villages, therefore, occupies an important place in any discussion on rural sociology.

It is indeed a tragedy of fate that the villagers who possess the natural resources and who reside within the natural environment are deprived of the benefits of these resources. Any visit to our villages would show that the school-going children early in the morning leave their house for collecting fuelwood. For them collection of fuelwood is more necessary than to attend to school. One can find women engaged in fetching water from long distances and half of their day thus spent on the management of potable water. The decay of forests has multiplier effect on the village people. They used to earn by the sale of fuelwood collected from their nearby forests; they made some money out of the forest produce. Besides, their implements were also made without any cost from the forest wood. Their houses were also built out of forest wood. The decay of forest, therefore, has multiplied their turmoil.

Environment, Ecology and Development

The term 'environment' has become one of the most overused and obscurantist concepts in today's lexicon of development. Literally, environment means all that which surrounds us. It is an external condition which influences our development and growth. The surroundings not only influence human development but also development of animals, plants—living or working. Environment is a totality which determines the way of the life of the people. In our contemporary situation of world order environment is clubbed with development. There is no discussion about environment without linking it with development. In the Third World countries a debate is cropped up which is hinged on development versus environment. It is argued that development in the end leads to degradation of environment. Or, there cannot be development without exploitation of environment. The debate—environment versus development—has assumed national significance in our country. The environmentalists suggest that all programmes of development should be cancelled as they lead to degradation of environment and ecology. Recently, the environmentalists have become lesser doctrinnaire and have agreed to sustainable development, that is, the development which also maintains the requirement of environment. As, at present, in our country, there appears to be an agreement in the nexus between environment and development that we should make all efforts to attain development to the extent that it does not permit any degradation of environment.

'Ecology' is basically concerned with the relationship between plants and man. As a matter of fact environment is a comprehensive term which relates to man-nature relationship. It relates to plant, wildlife, water, land and man-made things as pollution resulting from industry and other such technological development.

The context of environment, that is, degradation of land, forest and water resources in India's villages occupies a crucial importance. The village people have been living in the villages and they are much closer to natural environment compared to their counterparts in urban communities. A little degradation of environment, natural resource base directly influences the village people. The village life is witnessing a fast transformation. Increasingly Indian villages are becoming towns; towns in their turn are transforming into cities and cities are becoming metropolitans. An appropriate study of village community, therefore, involves an elaborate study of village environment, ecology, land use, water and fuel.

The Policy Framework

During the last three decades environment has quite definitely been put on the world's development agenda. Ever since the Stockholm Conference in 1972 the conscience of the world has been awakened to the limits of growth and the limits of development.[1] The second World Conference on Environment in 1978 established the United Nations Environment Programme (UNEP) with its headquarters in Nairobi. The creation of the Ministry of Forests and Environment, in 1984, is a reflection of India's concern for the degradation of environment. In India, the Centre for Science and Environment's first report on *The State of India's Environment, 1982, The First Citizen's Report*[2] is by far the most wide-ranging document available. The second and third Citizen's Reports (1985 and 1991)[3] are even more comprehensive reviews. Many studies have been made to comprehensively review the state of environmental degradation, both by government and non-government agencies.[4]

The Indian government has linked environment with development. According to official report environment is classified into two broad categories: (1) Environment which has negative effects resulting from the process of development. It argues that our development efforts have led to degradation of environment. (2) Environment that arises from conditions of poverty and underdevelopment. The first category of environment is thus concerned with the impact of efforts to achieve rapid economic growth and development. Poorly planned development projects are usually environmentally destructive. The second category has to do with the impact on the health and integrity of our national resources such as land, soil, water, forests, wildlife, space, etc., as the result of poverty.

Extent of Environmental Degradation

The environmental degradation at the village site has gone to the largest extent. We shall refer to some of the aspects of environmental degradation in the following section:

(1) *Land Degradation*

India's land has an extraordinary capacity to produce, but at the same time nearly one-half to one-third is fast becoming an unproductive desert. The land is becoming unproductive because of several factors. There has been excessive use of chemical manures. The canal water has created waterlogging resulting into saltriness of land. Looking to the man-land ratio one can easily understand that in the context of population explosion land has become scarce. The increasingly becoming scarce land and its unproductive nature resulting from development has given us a deficit farm produce.

The government is conscious about the land being degraded. It has created Landuse Boards which are also engaged in the improvement of the quality of wasteland. But nothing substantial has been done. The National Wastelands Development Board which was launched, resulted into a dead body in no time.

(2) *Water Management*

There has been callous degradation of our water resources. Surendra Lawrence[5] informs that at the level of water management there has been a large scale environmental degradation. On a broader plane the water level has gone very low. The canal water has created waterlogging and salinity. Lawrence describes the degrading status of water as under:

> Equally serious is the downstream effects of the damage done upstream. Indo-Gangetic agriculture, often described as a potential bread basket in the world, is becoming damaged beyond repair as a result of soil degradation. Some areas are facing problems of waterlogging and rising water tables because of poorly planned and

ill-executed irrigation. In other areas, the water table is receding because of overexploitation of ground water. Furthermore, the quality of ground water is being affected due to chemical pollution, and in coastal areas, due to the ingress of sea water.

(3) *Excessive Use of Fertiliser*

In order to get more and more farm produce, there has been excessive use of fertiliser. The use of pesticides and fertiliser imposes threat to human health, to the genetic stocks and reduce the natural soil fertility in the long run. The absence of an integrated land and water use policy for the country is taking a heavy toll on these basic natural assets.

(4) *Degradation of Flora and Fauna*

There is a rich diversity of flora and fauna in our country. These aspects of nature maintain our ecosystem. But the flora and fauna have constantly been indiscriminately exploited. This has affected in the disappearance or scarcity of some of our diverse flora and fauna. The fragile environs of island ecosystems have been subjected to pressures of various forms including migration of people from the mainland.

(5) *Decay of Forests*

Perhaps, the greatest loss to our rural communities has been the decay of forests. Explaining the extent to which there has been degradation to our forest wealth Surendra Lawrence says that our forest wealth has been subjected to overgrazing, overexploitation both for commercial and household needs. There has been encroachment of mining in the forest area. Besides, several developmental activities such as roads, buildings, irrigation and power projects have been based in the forest area. Though the data are not updated, Surendra Lawrence is perfectly right when he observes:

> The recorded forest cover in the country is 75.01 million hectares which works out to 19.5 per cent of the total geographical area against the broad national goal of 33 per cent for the plains area and 66 per cent for hilly regions. Even within this area, only 11 per cent constitute forests with 40 per cent or more of crown cover. According to the state, forest cover in the country, was 64.01 million

hectares during 1985-87 and the annual rate of loss works out to 47,500 hectares. The loss of habitat is leading to the extinction of plant, animal and microbial species. According to the botanical and zoological surveys in India, over 1,500 plant and animal species are in the endangered category.[6]

(6) *Decline in the Domesticated Animals*

Our domesticated animals include a large number of cows, buffaloes, bullocks, sheep and goats. These animals depend for the fodder on the green pasture lands and the forests. Looking to our large size of domesticated animal population we have hardly 3.5 per cent of our geographical area under grassland. For an animal population of about 500 million, the grassland is more than meagre. The degradation of grassland is caused by water and wind erosion, salinity, alkalinity and river action.

(7) *Mines and Minerals*

It must be accepted that our building and ornamental stones, besides the precious metals such as zinc, lead, copper, etc., are a waste material. It means that once they are exploited we cannot exploit them again. They are once and for all. These natural materials after their exhaustion leave the land waste. It cannot be use for cultivation. Nor can it be used for afforestation. Surely, there is economic value of mines and minerals but from the environment point of view it leads to a terrible degradation of our natural resource base.

(8) *Pollution*

As a matter of fact environment is a very wide term which in a loose way includes every conceivable things on earth. But operationally, we could limit it to resources which support, develop or enrich human life. Pollution, viewed from this respect, is also a part of environment. There are various forms of pollution; for instance, water pollution by industrial and domestic wastes, air pollution, that is, smog and soil pollution in the form of excessive erosion. Thus pollution has three major forms: (1) water pollution, (2) air pollution, and (3) soil pollution. As a matter of fact, water, air and land are the basic commodities of life and these are continually getting polluted in the wake of population growth, industrialisation and urbanisation, on account of discharge of sewage, industrial effluent, stack emissions, dust, smoke, solid waste on the one hand and strain on the existing resources on the other.

However, the major problems of pollution are related to urban communities only. The rural community has the least pollution problem. The farmers who have taken to farm technology or the villages which possess small-scale industries, biogas plants, piggeries and poultry farms suffer from soil and air pollution. It could be said that the major sources of pollution in the rural society are as under:

1. The use of fertiliser generally leads to breathing difficulty.
2. The agricultural machinery, particularly threshers, creates problems of pollution. A large number of people suffer from breathing problem and irritation in the throat as result of the use of machines.
3. Burning of by-products also creates pollution in the villages. The villagers burn the by-products of paddy and the left out portion of the wheat crop after the use of combine. The pollution created by the burning of by-products also causes breathing difficulties.
4. Heaps of waste material are found in most of the Indian villages. The waste material of the households and the crops are kept in heaps near the houses. Similarly, dung is also kept in heaps. These practices not only create foul smell but also result in pollution.
5. The disposal of dead bodies of animals also creates pollution in the villages. The *Chamar* generally makes his carcasses out of dead animals close to the village.
6. The *kaccha* lanes of the village create problems of pollution more particularly during the rainy season. The lanes full of mud and water work as breeding places for mosquitoes. Very often it leads to epidemics such as malaria and diseases which are water-borne.

Causes of Environmental Degradation

There has been a definite degradation of rural resource base including landuse, water, fuel and pollution. Compared to the urban life, the losses of rural society are lesser but the degradation in the village community is directly related to their sources of livelihood. The village people traditionally eked out their living from forest wood and minor forest products. With the degradation of forests, the village sources of subsistence, have dried up. Some of the forms of degradation are directly related to the implementation of development programmes. The construction of dams---major or minor---has rendered the cultivable soil as a saline soil. These dams cause multiplier effect on the village life. The big farmers are the gainers of canal water irrigation. Irrigation increases the farm growth and ultimately the village society becomes a class society. The environmental degradation has ruined the village life. Such a deteriorating environmental situation raised some important questions: If the present trend of degradation continues, what is the future of village community? From where will the villagers collect their fuelwood? How the peasants would get their implements repair and how will they be able to build their house? The questions are several, but the basic thing is that those who are guilty of committing the crime of environmental degradation, even if it is the state, who will hang them?

The following section of the chapter would analyse some of the important causes of environmental degradation.

(1) *State Responsibility*

The state in India is a class state. It gives priority to the vested interests of the societal elites, leaders and persons belonging to higher classes. Though the state is armed with legislation to protect the natural environment, at the operational level all legislative measures are thrown asunder. There is a coalition between the forest officials, political leaders and the mafia. The role of state has become suspicious. The state, in its enthusiasm for development, has not considered seriously about the decay of environment. The schemes initiated for the revival of ecosystem have yielded nothing substantial and huge sums of money are wasted.

Anil Agarwal and Sunita Narain have argued that it is very easy for the state to create unproductive employment in the name of enhancing the cause of environment. The authors write:

> The same story goes for afforestation. A British economist once pointed out that it is very easy to create unproductive employment—just dig a hole and fill it back with earth and keep doing that perpetually. The latest name of that game is afforestation. "Dig a hole, put in a sapling, fill it with earth; next year the sapling dies and

> the entire exercise begins again." Between 1980 and 1989 the government claimed to have planted forests over 11.82 million hectares—an area almost equal to Assam and Kerala combined. Can anybody believe such figures? Indian bureaucracy, today, operates such mega-projects with such mega-targets that it does not even care to taste the veracity of its figures. A lot of these hectares have been planted under the very programmes that L.C. Jain was wondering about.[7]

Whether it is the central government or the state government, the development programmes are launched without taking into consideration the interests of the poor who reside in the villages. It is observed that the state is the prime accuse so far as the environmental degradation is concerned.

(2) *Class Interests*

One very serious reason for the degradation of environment is the class interest. The high class people demand much from forest. There are traders who are engaged in the export of the carcasses of wild animals. This affects the population of lions, elephants and other animals. Much furniture is required for decorating the drawing rooms and shopping complexes. Demands from natural resources are so fantastic that it results in the decay of natural environment. It must be observed that it is the class interest which is largely responsible for the loss of environment. Commenting on the responsibility of elites and rich people in the degradation of environment, Madhav Gadgil observes:

> This degradation occurs for two kinds of reasons: first, because we are making increasing demands on the resources of the country; and second, because these demands are being met in a higher undisciplined fashion.[8]

(3) *Inefficient Exploitation of Resources*

Whether the elites, government officials or traders, all exploit the natural resources in a very inefficient way. The forests are axed ruthlessly. The mining is very unscientific. As a matter of fact, the exploitation of natural base is highly characterised by indiscipline and inefficiency. The approach to nature, from all points of view, is wasteful. The tragedy is that both the elites and the masses put the blames on each other for the degradation of environment.

(4) *Fragile Environment*

When there is exploitation of natural resources, whether forest, flora, fauna or water, we must understand that the environment which we find today is of very fragile nature. Pointing to the fragility of environmental resources Anil Agarwal and Sunita Narain comment:

> Environmental resources are extremely fragile. A tree has to be cared for, especially if it is a multipurpose tree which not only provides wood but also fruit or fodder. A pond is also a fragile resource because its catchment must be brought under a good land use system otherwise it will silt up very fast. This care can not be provided by government officials. It can only be provided by the village people themselves.[9]

(5) *The Villagers Themselves*

Last but not the least, the villagers are also responsible partly for the degradation of environment. It is alleged that a part of forest is cut down by the villagers themselves. Either they sell it in the market or use it for their own consumption. They also become a party to the forest contractors and put their axe to the trees quite ruthlessly. It is argued that if the classes are held responsible for the degradation of the forests, the masses of the people are equally responsible. They seldom stand up in the protection of their natural resources. If the class people are hanged for the crime of environmental decay, the masses should also be hanged for the same crime.

(6) *The Iron-Triangle*

If we get a glimpse of our rural India, we would find that there are a few pockets in the country which have witnessed a large quantum of environmental degradation. Among these are included the industrial belt in western Maharashtra, the areas around Coimbatore in Tamilnadu, metropolises like Delhi and Chennai, and tracts of green revolution in Punjab and Haryana. The degradation of environment is traced to some forces. These forces have been explained by what is called as the 'iron-triangle'. This term is used by the Americans. The iron-triangle is explained by the following categories of people who benefit from the exploitation of the resource base:[10]

(1) those who benefit from the subsidies: the industrialists, the urban populations, rich farmers;
(2) those who decide on who is to be subsidised at whose cost: the politicians; and
(3) those who administer the subsidies: the bureaucracy.

Thus, according to the iron-triangle, the benefits of environmental degradation are cornered by the industry, urban populations, rich farmers, politicians and bureaucrats.

Madhav Gadgil argues that the subsidies given to the farmers and people of industry generally go in favour of the rich farmers, contractors and others. This kind of explanation given by the American social scientists describes the situation of America. In our country, agriculture is given top priority because it is concerned with the food production. The farmers are provided subsidies or concessions on the consumption of electricity, diesel and fertilisers including the insecticides. For all these agricultural inputs there are liberal provisions of credit and subsidies. All these benefits are availed of by the big farmers and the absentee landlords. In the context of our country, besides subsidies, there are a large number of other forces also which are responsible for the environmental decay. The iron-triangle thus explains a part of the situation and not the whole.

People's Movement for the Protection of Environment

It is often questioned whether there is an environmental movement in India for the protection of environment. If the question is required to be answered in precise words it could be said that there is no such movement in the country. The fact of the matter is that ours is a vast country which is divided by cultural regions, castes and languages. We very often forget that these ethnic influences also affect environmental politics. Darryl D' Monte has ventured to answer the question whether we have a movement for the protection of environment. He says:

> Paradoxically, there is no movement of the western variety, but there is certainly a coalition made up of scores of small, grassroot organisa-

tions located throughout the length and breadth of the country. Together, these constitute the environmental movement, leading credence to the cliched dogma, 'unity in diversity'. The strange truth is that even if there is no dialogue between different strange there is still the tangled skein which is a distinct entity within the socio-political structure of the nation. This makes the environmental movement in India rather different from that in most other countries of the world."

What D' Monte argues is that we do not have an environment movement in India of the variety of Germany and other countries. On the other hand, what is particular about India is that we have an environment movement at the local level or at the village level characterised by parochial ethnicity. The love for environment, trees and wild animals which the Bishnoi caste of Jodhpur (Rajasthan) has, is absent in other parts of Rajasthan and elsewhere in the country.

One can list some of the prominent movements related to the protection of environment at national level. Undoubtedly, the forest resource is a central issue in Indian context. Prior to the advent of British rule, communities themselves exercised some minimal restrictions on the use of forests. But the collection of what foresters term 'minor forest produce' i.e., twigs, berries, fruit and so on, was not regulated because the forests extended over such a large area that there was no need for control. However, it were the British who introduced the first laws, ostensibly in the public benefit, but with the sole purpose of commercial exploitation of this resource. Possibly, the first environmental movements in India, therefore, were protests against the limited entry into forests, historical records show that these took place in areas as far apart as Garhwal and Chhotanagpur. In the latter case tribals in the forested belt of Bihar launched the Santhal rebellions, the precursor of today's more 'bourgeois' Jharkhand movement.

In contemporary India, the environment movement has taken an entirely different direction. The Chipko organisation which got all the ground in 1973 owes its inspiration to Gandhian passive resistance principles: to prevent contractors from felling trees, women hugged the trunks. From those beginnings—the Chipko movement is probably the best known example of grassroots' protest against environmental destruction in world—it has branched out into a much broader tendency, which looks at the basic causes of resource degradation—poverty and unemployment. This is why it advocates prohibition of liquor as well.

The Chipko movement was led by Sundarlal Bahuguna. The movement caught the imagination of the villagers in other parts of the country. In Karnataka, it is known as 'Appiko'. Here, the people fight against the plantation of eucalyptus. Apart from its adverse ecological repercussions eucalyptus has no social value; it can neither be used as fodder nor as fuelwood since it finds a ready market as pulp for the rayon and paper industries. In Karnataka, there is also another movement waged against Harihar Polyfibres, a Birla company, which has obtained permission to setup a joint venture with state government to plant eucalyptus trees.

Besides forests, there is yet another area where environment movement has taken its roots. It is the mining. The Jharkhand movement of Bihar, which stands for the demand of autonomy, has also a movement against mining. The mining of limestone is opposed by the tribals because it poses a threat to the whole hill region. Women in Garhwal are also concerned about open-caste mining for soap stone and other minerals in a highly sensitive ecosystem.

There has also been protest movements against the construction of big dams. The Tehri Garhwal and Sardar Sarovar dams have continuously been opposed by the environmentalists. It is argued that big dams are against the interests of the protection of environment. Megha Patkar is the leading figure to oppose the construction of big dams.

The Government Initiative

The state is also aware about the protection of environment. As stated earlier, according to official policy environmental problem is classified into two broad categories: (i) those arising as negative effects of the very process of development, and (ii) those arising from conditions of poverty and underdevelopment. The government has made enactments for about 30 areas of environment. Some of the major enactments are given below:

(1) Wild Life (Protection) Act, 1972.

(2) Forest (Conservation) Act, 1980.

(3) Water (Prevention and Control of Pollution) Act, 1974.

(4) Air (Prevention and Control of Pollution) Act, 1981.

(5) Environment (Protection) Act, 1986.

(6) Public Liability Insurance Act, 1991.

(7) The Motor Vehicle Act, 1938 (amended in 1988).

The central and state governments have made many legislations to protect the environment. So far as the government policy is concerned the enactments show the intention of the government. But it is striking to note that there are only a few enactments which concern the protection of rural environment. Water protection is an important area of rural life. But at operational level nothing substantial has been done. In the similar way, the forest and wildlife protection is ensured by legislation. But the corrupt practices of the forest officers and contractors have not prevented the decay of forest. In coalition with the forest bureaucracy there is shooting and poaching of forest game. The hides of precious wild animals get a clandestine foreign market. What is required is an institutional involvement of the village people in the protection of environment. The environment movement should be organised at the grassroot level. It should then further be vertically linked with the central level movement. Only such a movement can protect the environment at the village level.

Notes

1. Barbara Ward, *Only One Earth*, Harmandsworth, Penguin, 1972.
2. Centre for Science and Environment, The State of India's Environment-I, 1982, The First Citizen's Report, New Delhi.
3. The State of India's Environment-II, 1985 and III, 1991.
4. Madhu Mishra, *Selected Bibliography on Environmental Studies*, Indian Institute of Management, Calcutta, 1991. Also see *The Hindu's Annual Survey of the Environment*, 1990.
5. Surendra Lawrence, "Environmental Implications", *Seminar*, 395, July, 1992.
6. Ibid., p. 45.

7. Anil Agarwal and Sunita Narain, "The Village Republic", *Seminar* 377, January 1991, p. 76.
8. Madhav Gadgil, "Population, Resources and Environment", *Seminar*, 365, January, 1990, p. 53.
9. Anil Agarwal and Sunita Narain, op. cit., p. 78.
10. Madhav Gadgil, op. cit., p. 53.
11. Darryl D'Monte, 'Green' at the Grassroots, *Seminar*, 355, March 1989, p. 16.

15 Panchayati Raj

An Era of Empowerment

Panchayati Raj means democratic decentralisation. It falls within the great tradition of our country. We often talk about *Panch Parmeshwar.* It means that the god speaks through the *Panch. Panch Parmeshwar* can never be prejudicial to anybody. It is how we understand about the Gram Panchayats. Our tradition of Gram Panchayat is elaborately manifested in our languages. Besides, we also have tradition of Caste Panchayat. The Caste Panchayat looked after the problems at local level. Sometimes, it also functioned as inter-village *panchayat*. Among tribals, even today, the role of traditional *panchayat* is so much important that the member of the tribe makes his first approach to it. If he is dissatisfied at this level, then he goes to the court of law. In some villages, the Caste Panchayat is also important. A large number of decisions pertaining to social and marital conflicts and disputes are solved by the Caste Panchayat.

The role of Panchayati Raj has to be analysed with reference to this great Indian tradition. Gandhiji had a conviction that Gram Panchayat should be made all-powerful so that it could take all decisions pertaining to its administration and development. Gandhiji often talked about and actually stood for *Gram Swaraj.* Literally, it means autonomy of village. The village as a collectivity should rule over itself. The theory of *Gram Swaraj* as given by Gandhiji runs as below:

> My idea of village *swaraj* is that it is a complete republic, independent of its neighbours for its own vital wants and yet interdependent for many others in which dependence is a necessity. Thus every village's first concern will be to grow its own food crops and cotton for its cloth. It should have a reserve for its cattle, recreation and playground for adults and children... The government of the village will be conducted by a panchayat of five persons annually elected by the adult villagers, male and female, possessing minimum prescribed

> qualification. These will have all the authority and jurisdiction required. Since there will be no system of punishment in the accepted sense, this panchayat will be the legislature, judiciary and executive combined to operate for its year of office... here there is perfect democracy based upon individual freedom. The individual is the architect of his own government. The law of non-violence rules him and his government. He and his village are able to defy the might of a world. For the law, governing every villager, is that he will suffer death in the defence of his and his village's honour.[1]

Why Study Panchayati Raj?

In social science paraphrase Panchayati Raj is an area of study taken up by political science. When the political scientists look at Panchayati Raj, obviously their perspective is power-sharing and administration. They study the offices of *Pramukh*, *Pradhan*, *Panch* and other officials as well as non-officials. Thus, in the social science, the study of Panchayati Raj comes within the framework of political science. Then, why does rural sociology and for that matter sociology study Panchayati Raj? The basic question is: What is perspective of sociology in studying the Panchayati Raj? The question is right. Sociology has a focus on the structure of society and its various groups such as caste, class, religious organisations, polity and economy. When a rural sociologist studies Panchayati Raj he is not interested in the administration of this organisation. Nor is he interested in the ways the people are ruled or administered. His focus is the group structure of the village, the people who are involved in decision making, and the groups that have a share in the power invested in Panchayati Raj. To be short, when a sociologist studies Panchayati Raj, actually he makes inquiries in the decentralisation of power. In the present chapter, we shall inquire about the status of different groups, particularly women, scheduled castes, scheduled tribes and varying power groups including the subalterns. This perspective would guide our analysis here.

A.R. Desai has yet another point for the study of Panchayati Raj in sociological perspective. He says that India is engaged in the task of nation-building. The country cannot progress in an integrated way unless we take into consideration the village land problems, cooperatives, Panchayati Raj and village development. Desai's observation runs as below:

> Land reforms, cooperatives, Panchayati Raj and community development movements are supposed to be the four solid pillars on which a prosperous, dynamic and genuinely democratic rural social system is attempted to be built by the government of independent India.
>
> Panchayati Raj is also claimed as a real democratic political apparatus which would bring the masses into active political control from below, from the vast majority of the weaker, poorer sections of rural India. According to some it will 'decentralise' democracy.[2]

The study of Panchayati Raj, according to sociological perspective, thus, is the study of (1) the decentralisation of democratic power; and (2) the study of groups which wield power and an enquiry into the impact of development projects on the subaltern people of the village. In short, Panchayati Raj is studied in terms of the structure of rural society and its transformation.

Historical Backdrop

The concept of Panchayati Raj is relatively a new. Earlier, it was termed as Village Panchayat or District Board. It was used for rural self-government. Actually, the Village Panchayats were meant for rural administration and particularly administration in the fields of social service and rural reconstruction. The Village Panchayat is a link between the people and the bureaucracy at the state level.

In our country, the system of Village Panchayats is very old, though its structure varied from time to time. There were Village Panchayats in ancient and medieval periods. During the last phase of medieval India the Gram Panchayats became oblivious or ineffective. During the British Raj an effort was made to revive the Panchayati Raj. When popular ministries were formed under the Government India Act, 1919, various provinces passed the Village Panchayat Acts in 1919.

The Gram Panchayats which worked during the British period largely consisted of the higher castes of the village. The poor and the lower castes had no representation in these bodies. The powers which were given to the Gram Panchayats were very few. Their main concern, however, remained limited to social reform and administration of welfare measures. The Gram Panchayats during the British period could not make any success. Actually, the area under the Gram

Panchayat was very large. And, what is worse, the funds given to them were not sufficient. These Gram Panchayats could not be effectively linked to the District Boards. And, this resulted in the failure of the Gram Panchayats.

A Constitutional Obligation

The constitution of Panchayati Raj is not the sweet will of the state government. It is the result of the provisions made in Indian Constitution. The Directive Principles of State Policy lays down that the state shall take steps to organise village panchayats ...to enable them to function as units of self-government.

The objective of the constitution of Panchayati Raj was mainly two-fold: (i) decentralisation of power, and (ii) development of villages. Yet another reason for the creation of Panchayati Raj was to seek the cooperation and participation of masses of people in the national reconstruction and development. Initially, in 1952, the Panchayati Raj bodies were entrusted with the implementation of Community Development Projects (CDPs). The institution of *shramdan*, voluntary labour, was created to involve the people in the development of their own village. The Panchayati Raj, however, did not make any headway in the development of village. The CDPs were considered as projects of development from the above, that is, the government. It was essential for development that the initiative should have come from the below, the masses of people and in fact, from the grassroots. To overcome this difficulty a committee headed by Balwant Rai Mehta was constituted. This committee made initial experiment in Andhra Pradesh and Rajasthan. The Mehta Committee was the watershed in the development of Panchayati Raj.

Balwant Rai Mehta Committee

The Balwant Rai Mehta Committee found that the CDPs when came at the Gram Panchayat level were considered as programmes of the government and not programmes of the village people. The village self-sufficiency could not be attained without the active partnership of the village people. The Mehta Committee, therefore, suggested that the villagers should be given power to decide about their own felt needs and implement the programmes accordingly. Bidyut Mohanty, while explaining the recommendations of the Mehta Committee, observes:

> In 1959, the Balwant Rai Mehta Committee suggested that an agency should be set up at the village level which would not only represent the interests of the village community but also take up the development programmes of the government at its level. The Gram Panchayat which was to constitute this agency was, therefore, perceived as an implementing agency of the government in a specific, namely, developmental sphere.[3]

The Panchayati Raj, which came into existence following the recommendations of Mehta Committee, had the following major objectives:

(1) to represent the felt needs of the village community;
(2) to give power to the non-officials for the development of village communities; and
(3) to give power of implementation or execution of programmes to the people.

Thus, the Balwant Rai Mehta Committee legislatively made the villagers active partners in the task of village development. The responsibility of the execution of development programmes was left to the elected members of the Panchayati Raj.

The Panchayati Raj, as suggested by Mehta Committee was first implemented in the state of Rajasthan. It was an irony of fate that the state of Rajasthan which experienced feudal rule throughout the medieval period was first to implement the Panchayati Raj. The experiment was further taken over by Andhra Pradesh and other states. The Mehta Committee suggested a three-tier structure for Panchayati Raj. These tiers could be altered vis-a-vis the needs of the state. The bottom tier consisted of *Gram Sabha* which was constituted on the basis of population size. Sometimes it included a big village but generally two or three villages on the strength of their population size constituted a *Gram Sabha.* This was the lowest rung of Panchayati Raj. The second tier was coterminous with the *tehsil* or *taluka.* And, at the apex level was the district. The three-tier structure thus consisted of the elected non-officials who implemented the programmes of development on the technical and bureaucratic guidance of the officials.

The pattern of Panchayati Raj was thus developed on the coordination between the officials and the non-officials.

The Panchayati Raj could not come out as a successful story. Though, theoretically, the decisions had to be taken by the non-officials at all the three tiers of Panchayati Raj, the officials become the major decision makers. The non-officials being illiterate and uneducated could not wield their power. And, what is worse the Panchayat Samiti which implemented the development programmes at the tehsil level, cornered most of the benefits for the high castes and big peasants. The poor segments of society remained neglected as before. The apex tier at the district level did not have any power of implementation. It also failed to bring coordination among the three tiers. The three-tier pattern of Panchayati Raj as recommended began to crumble down, and a new pattern was evolved on the basis of the recommendations made by the Ashok Mehta Committee.

Ashok Mehta Committee

Ashok Mehta, an economist, headed over a committee to suggest changes in the pattern of Panchayati Raj recommended by Balwant Rai Mehta Committee. In 1977, the Ashok Mehta Committee recommended a fundamental change in the Panchayati Raj system. It asked for transformation of the panchayat from an implementing agency to a political institution.[4] In order to implement this recommendation the need for constitutional amendment was felt. It, however, took more than a decade for the first steps in this direction to be taken in the form of the 64th Constitution Amendment Bill which was defeated in Rajya Sabha. In 1992, another legislation, the 73rd Amendment Bill was introduced in parliament which adopted it in the same year.

73rd Constitution Amendment Act

The present Panchayati Raj differs from the Balwant Rai pattern in two respects. First, the earlier Panchayati Raj was not a political institution but only an implementing body. In this pattern there was no role of political parties. Elections to panchayat bodies were held on individual basis. The candidates contesting for elections were not nominated by the political parties. The 73rd Constitution Amendment Act allows political parties to enter into election fray. In other words, elections to Panchayati Raj today are contested on party basis.

Second, the present Panchayati Raj is not an implementing body to the development programmes. It is a decision making body and rules over the governance of the village. One very conspicuous aspect of the present Panchayati Raj is that it empowers the women and weaker sections of village in the wielding of power. The members of weaker sections including women are given representation by a fixed quota fixed by the constitution. In other words, membership to Panchayati Raj Institution (PRI) is reserved vis-a-vis the members of the weaker sections. The Panchayati Raj thus has empowered the women, scheduled castes and scheduled tribes.

The present Panchayati Raj is constituted as an amendment to the Constitution of India. It is, therefore, the central Act which is adopted by all the states of the union. Some important features of the Act are given below:

(1) Panchayats will be considered political institutions in a truly decentralised structure.

(2) The *Gram Sabha* shall be recognised as the life-line of the Panchayati Raj. The voters of the village of clusters of villages will constitute its membership.

(3) There will be direct elections in all the three tiers of governance: (i) Gram Panchayat at the village level, (ii) Panchayat Samiti at the intermediate level; and (iii) Zila Parishad at the district level.

(4) So far as the empowerment of women is concerned, the Act has provided that at least one-third of the total seats at all levels shall be reserved for women of whom one-third shall be from the scheduled castes and scheduled tribes. In this context it is important to note that at least one-third of the total posts of the office bearers at all levels will also be reserved for the women.

(5) Each PRI will have a tenure of five years and in case it is dissolved by the state government fresh election will be held within a period of six months.

(6) The election to local bodies has to be conducted regularly.

(7) There will be a separate Election Commission and also a Finance Commission for PRIs in every state.

(8) It is obligatory on the part of centre as well as the state to provide adequate funds for the PRIs to enable them to function properly.

In addition, the PRIs will have their own fund raising capacity on the basis of the local resources.

(9) Some states like Rajasthan, Haryana and Orissa have debarred the candidates, having more than two children, from contesting in the election with a view to controlling population growth, given the low average age of marriage of girls (19), they would have crossed the two children norm by the time they contest for elections. Hence, it will be difficult for the states to get suitable women candidates for the Panchayati Raj elections.

(10) Some states like Bihar, Himachal Pradesh, Uttar Pradesh, Haryana and Karnataka have provision of *Nyaya Panchayat* to settle the disputes at all the three levels.

However, the 73rd Amendment Act does not make it obligatory for states to provide for *Nyaya Panchayats* to solve local disputes. Secondly, although the objective of the Act is to build the Panchayati Raj as an effective decentralised political institution at the grassroot level, the division of functions in its XI Schedule makes it in reality, essentially an implementing agency for developmental activities.

Functions of Panchayati Raj

The structure of Panchayati Raj is designed in such a way that the 73rd Constitution Amendment Act gives certain powers and functions to the three-tier structure of the Panchayati Raj. The idea is to decentralise the power of rural administration to the elected representatives. The Act enables the elected representatives to take their own decisions within the framework of Act. Some of the important functions of the Panchayati Raj are enumerated below:

1. Agricultural development and irrigation facilities;
2. Land reforms;
3. Eradication of poverty;
4. Dairy farming, poultry, piggery and fish rearing;
5. Rural housing;
6. Safe drinking water;
7. Social forestry, fodder and fuel;
8. Primary education, adult education and informal training;

9. Roads and buildings;
10. Markets and fairs;
11. Child and women development;
12. Welfare of weaker sections, scheduled castes and scheduled tribes.

Some Special Provisions:

1. Enforcement of prohibition;
2. Protection of land;
3. Minor forest produce;
4. Water resources;
5. Village markets;
6. Development.

If we analyse the functions of Panchayati Raj, it is found that the Act is highly elaborate. The functions of Panchayati Raj in terms of Gram Sabha, Panchayat Samiti, and Zila Parishad are spelt out separately. Quite like functions the administrative powers are also ascribed to each tier. On the whole, the Panchayati Raj system empowers the total functioning of the village system. It stresses on the limited autonomy of the village but also encourages it for interdependence with other clusters of villages.

Empowerment of Women

All over the world and particularly in south and east Asia the gender problem has loomed large during the current years. The gender issue has become a crucial point of argument. The United Nations, in its various declarations, have made it clear that women now cannot be asked to wait for any more time. Their sufferings are historical. Thus, the gender problem, in the context of new forces of development, assumes vital importance. Underline the problem of the empowerment of women is the plea for shared responsibility between the male and female. The simplest way to distinguish between sex and gender is to define sex as biological and, therefore, given and gender as socially and culturally constructed and, therefore, variable over space and time. Whereas multiple sexual encounters for men are seen as the sign of their virility, menstruation for women is seen as polluting in many cultures. Actually gender is constructed in part through the organisation of our culturally experienced bodies.

The gender disabilities are, therefore, not uniform all over the country. There are regional variations in the power status of the women. For instance, in north India, there is much discrimination against women. There is a limited public space for them. Young girls are not allowed to move freely. However, such a hard discrimination is relatively lesser in the southern states. In Kerala, because of the high rate of literacy, there is least discrimination against the women. However, in Tamilnadu, there are instances of female infanticide. On a broader plane it could be said that all over India and generally in south-east Asia there is much discrimination against the women. They are considered to be a weaker section of society. Such a state of socio-economic affairs warrants for a plan to give special political status to the women.

The 73rd Constitution Amendment Act has made an effort to give some special powers to women in all the three tiers of Panchayati Raj. It is argued that women have acquired some improvement in their social and economic life. There was a time in the earlier part of 1930s when Bombay University did not allow a woman to take courses in graduation. The candidate was informed that the university rules did not permit women to take admission in graduate courses. The framers of 73rd Constitution Amendment Act had the argument that social and economic status of women could not be improved much without political power. The females in the village need to be given some political power. They should have their share in the decisions made about the development of their village. The new Panchayati Raj is a part of the effort to empower the women at least at the village level.

The reservation of one-third seats for women alongwith the scheduled castes and the scheduled tribes, is, therefore, a bold step towards the empowerment of women. It is quite interesting that the women who have been working as farm labourer, cleaning the utensils and fetching the water, are legally permitted to share the jajam with the males of the village in matters of decision making. The provisions of Act for the women are in no way less than a revolution.

But the question remains to be answered: Why do the women require empowerment?

Efforts to empower women are not statutory only. Women are

empowered through women emancipation movement, education, communication, media, political parties and general awakening. The Panchayati Raj effort of empowerment is one of the several efforts made simultaneously in the society. And, above all, the empowerment action, whether to women or poor and weaker sections of society, has a multiplying effect. For instance, when a woman in the village gets a berth in the Panchayat Samiti, she becomes automatically powerful in the family, kin and village. She is listened to by the people, for she is a decision maker; she can do and undo certain things in the village. She can get her school raised to higher standard, she can get a water pump installed at a particular place in a village and so on and so forth. Surely, she is not everything by becoming member of the *samiti* but definitely she can influence the decisions of the samiti.

We give below some of the reasons which explain the need for the empowerment of women:

1. *Health*

One of the reasons for empowerment is health. It is found that women suffer from poor health condition. There is a general practice in India that the women first serve food to the male members of the family, then comes the turn of children and finally they take food whether it is adequate or not. They have to bear children and they do not get the required calories which are desirable for pregnant women. Thus, the women suffer in the matter of health because of the surrounding cultural and social set-up.

In the matter of medical treatment also the women are sufferers. We have enough research evidence which shows that both women and children are discriminated against medical treatment. Bidyut Mohanty, for instance, referring to the neglect of women and children health, observes:

> With regard to health care, discrimination against females is also reflected in the type and relative frequency in utilising the same. The data show males receive better medical treatment than females in all age groups but this is more prominent in case of children.[5]

Mohanty further providing evidence to his generalisation says that even in Punjab the second girl child is often neglected in terms of medicare. He argues that "this kind of discrimination against women cuts across castes and classes. Even though there are monetary transactions among the low caste women which are kept hidden from the male family members, these do not go very far in enhancing their social power. Though they are slightly better placed in this respect than the lower middle class women.

However, women in Kerala are better off compared to their counterparts in other states of the country. Such a state of Kerala women is explained by the fact that in this state the rate of women literacy is very high.

2. *Literacy*

The need for empowerment is also for the poor state of illiteracy among women. In absence of literacy and education the women have to suffer a lot. They work in the fields, but the fields legally do not belong to them; they live in and work for the upkeep of a house which does not belong to them. It is a real tragedy. In 50 per cent of the states the sex ratio is below the national average. With regard to women literacy rate, only 39 per cent of the total female population above seven years of age is literate. In some of the northern states female literacy rate is much below the national average. For example, the female literacy rate in rural Rajasthan is only 12 (Census of India, 1991). Besides, so far as the school enrolment is concerned, there is a huge gap between boys and girls. Of course, recently, the life expectancy at birth of females has exceeded marginally to that of males. This can be explained in terms of more females in the age group of 60 and above compared to males. However, in the younger age groups, the female mortality rate has been higher than that of males leading thereby to a missing 100 million women in successive censuses.

3. *Economic*

Economically too, women all over the country are weak. They are dependent on males, the latter being their bread-earner. Only a small proportion of women is gainfully employed. They are also culturally so much dominated by the males that they cannot take any decision against the wishes of the males. A females is boss in the office but she is subordinate mistress while in the house.

4. *UN Declaration and Women's World Congress*

Empowerment of women is not only a regional matter. The UN declaration of 1975 compelled the national government to shift its emphasis on women's programmes from welfare to development. Earlier to this declaration the national governments including our own floated a large number of welfare programmes for the women. But these programmes do not provide any long-term solution to the problems of women. And, therefore, the declaration prescribed for the development of women.

Yet another effort made towards empowerment of women is the document released in 1985 after the Women's World Congress at Nairobi. Following this conference a national document was prepared laying down forward-looking strategies for women's development. In this document, the question of women political participation was highlighted and it was recommended that 35 per cent of the total seats should be reserved for women. It was also recommended that some posts should be reserved for women at the block and village level bureaucracy. On the economic front, a number of income-generating schemes were introduced for women. In addition provisions were also made to keep certain proportion of women as beneficiaries in all the developmental schemes like Integrated Rural Development Programme (IRDP), Jawahar Rozgar Yojana (JRY), and Training of Rural Youth and Self-Employment (TRYSEM). Thus, we find a host of national and international events, coupled with the complex social and economic factors influencing the decisions as regards the status of women, culminating in the reservation of 33.3 per cent of the total seats for them at the panchayat level.

5. *Atrocities*

Much injustice is done to women all over the country. There is female infanticide observed in different parts of the country. The motivation to get a son is so strong that girl children before they are even born are killed in the womb. Such a practice is found even in metropolitan cities like Delhi and Mumbai. There is a striking evidence from Bihar where midwives are hired for killing female babies on payment of only Rs. 60 and a *saree* only. There are cases of rape, dowry, deaths and incest sex relations. Women in all walks of their life are discriminated against men. They are victims of atrocities.

As observed earlier, the need for female empowerment was never so urgent as it is today. The 73rd Constitution Amendment Act is just only one step towards the development of women.

Empowerment of Weaker Sections

Empowerment of weaker sections goes back to the constitutional provisions which provide for developmental and protective safeguards for scheduled castes, scheduled tribes and other backward classes. These groups have been given protective safeguards through legislation and reservation of seats in Vidhan Sabhas and Lok Sabha. They are also given protection through the provision of reservation in services, professional institutions, schools and colleges. The Prevention of Atrocities on Scheduled Castes and Scheduled Tribes Act is a major mechanism to protect the weaker sections.

The developmental safeguards include Tribal Sub-Plan area for implementing area development in tribal majority parts. The development programmes implemented in these areas provide for individual beneficiary schemes and Community Development Programmes. The objective of these programmes is to improve the lifestyle of the weaker sections of society. The end result of these programmes is to empower the weaker sections of the society. These weaker sections, it must be mentioned, are largely concentrated in India's villages.

A Critique of 73rd Constitution Amendment Act

It was in April 1993 that the 73rd Constitution Amendment Act came into force and following it, the different states amended their laws accordingly. Since then, hardly five years have passed. During this period not much empirical research has dwelt on the evaluation of the programme. However, some analysis has been made. Some of the drawbacks of the Act have been pointed out by the critiques which we propose to discuss below:

(1) *Bias towards elites and middle class*: Though the Act has a focus on women and weaker sections of society, it is guessed that the creamy-layer of these disadvantaged groups would corner most of the benefits. It has been the experience in our country that though the development schemes are oriented to weaker sections, the beneficiaries

have always been the higher echelons among the weaker sections. The speciality of the new Panchayati Raj is that it gives reservation to women also. But the question is: What class of women would take benefit of this reservation? Surely, the better off women of the scheduled castes, scheduled tribes and general sections of people would get their place in the Panchayati Raj. The weakest of the weak, the poorest of the poor would continue to suffer in the new pattern of Panchayati Raj also.

(2) *Illiteracy*: The kind of Panchayati Raj which we have floated presupposes some level of education among the village women. As we find today, the female literacy rate is very poor in our villages. In such a situation what would happen to the female members at different tiers of Panchayati Raj. It is believed that as members of PRIs they will work according to wills and wishes of the male members.

(3) *Non-availability of Women*: Looking to the socio-economic status of women in rural India, it is difficult for us to find out adequate number of females to work as members of the Panchayati Raj committees. Either we would have inadequate number of women or less qualified women to work as members in various committees. Such a poor situation does not assure us for healthy working of the Panchayati Raj.

(4) *Corrupt leadership and bureaucracy*: India's bureaucracy is notorious. It never works without greesing its palm. It is our experience that an overwhelming part of our development money goes to the purse of bureaucrats. The same applies to our leadership also. The rural leadership is more than shrewd. It knows the art of grabbing money. In such a situation, what will be the fate of development in village India is anybody's guess.

Notes

1. Raghavan Iyer (ed.), *The Essential Writings of Mahatma Gandhi*, Oxford University Press, Delhi, 1996, pp. 358-359.
2. A.R. Desai, *Rural Sociology in India*, Popular Prakashan, Bombay, 197, p. 534.

3. Bidyut Mohanty, "Panchayati Raj, 73rd Constitutional Amendment and Women", *Economic and Political Weekly*, December, 30, 1995, p. 3346.
4. George Mathew, *Status of Panchayati Raj in India*, Concept, New Delhi, 1955.
5. Bidyut Mohanty, op. cit., p. 3347.
6. Jocelin Kynch and A.K. Sen, "Indian Women: Well Being and Survival," *Cambridge Journal of Economics*, Vol. VII, Nos. 3 and 4, 1983; and Monica Das Gupta, "Selective Discrimination Against Female Children", *Population and Development Review*, Vol. XIII, 1, 1987.

16 Changing Rural Society

Rural society is not static. It has been changing fast. The changes have been more rapid during the last four decades. It is quite interesting to mention that not only in India but in almost all the Third World countries, much amount has been spent on rural development. It has been stressed by economists and sociologists that key to our development lies with the development of rural people. International agencies have provided focus on the economic development of the rural society. Various aspects of rural life, namely, education, industry, cooperatives and entrepreneurship are stressed by national government. It should also be mentioned that sociologists have made intensive studies on the rural life, particularly during 1950s and 1960s. Rural social formations such as caste, class and family have received a popular attention of sociologists. It would not be wrong to say that about half of our sociological literature in India belongs to the study of rural society. The economists who concentrate on macro studies have also come down to district level studies.

There is a logic to study the village society. Our country has spent crores of rupees in the development of villages. Village economy and its diversified dimensions have been studied by sociologists. It is agreed that the targeted goals of village development have not been achieved, but the fact remains that much awakening has come among the village people. Perhaps, the objective development of village people is debatable, but subjective development has definitely come to the people. Much of the rural development may not be through the directed planned change but the village people and surely the elites and the middle classes have been marching well on the road to development. Stressing the need for studying the village society with a social-historical bias, Chitra, Shivkumar and S.S. Shivkumar rightly observe:

> Rural social change has been among the most important subjects of study in the Third World countries since 1950, partly because major national efforts in these countries have been directed towards economic development and partly because such efforts have been located in, predominantly, agrarian social settings. The entire future of development efforts rests on what happens in rural areas. While this is well known, the fact that all changes, including rural changes, are historical process, is ignored. We say 'ignored' because the research efforts of various statistical and planning organisations in many countries (including the Planning Commission in India) are characterised by an absence of historical perspective. All share a historicity in their efforts.[1]

The authors plead for the application of historical method in the study of rural development. They have been critical about the statistical and econometric approach to rural study. The authors may be contested for pleading the monolith method of historicity, but the fact remains that all-out efforts should be made to study the development of village communities. One could differ on the suitability of a particular approach—functions, conflict and ethno-methodology. The reality is that we should make a fair and bold assessment about the outcome of development efforts. The basic question is: What is the direction of social change in rural society? A.R. Desai has tried to identify some of the trends of rural transformation resulting from development programmes. He identifies four major trends of rural social change:[2]

(1) rapid transformation of agrarian society from subsistence economy to market economy;
(2) rapid transformation followed by the introduction of modern technology;
(3) abolition of intermediaries such as jamindar and biswedar; and
(4) emergence of various associations and institutions having linkages with urban and national organisations.

Notwithstanding the criticism of the development attained by rural society, it must be admitted that there has been a definite change in rural society. There are some higher strata in the society which have benefited the most out of the development investment. This benefit has deprived the poorer sections of rural society. Surely, on the basis of social justice, this kind of one-sided development cannot be in the interest of the formation of a democratic society. But the fact remains that the villages as a whole have developed. It is also interesting to know that a new class society has emerged in rural India. This class society consists of big farmers, elites of weaker sections and political leaders. In fact, the rural society has swung in favour of the well-to-do classes of rural people. There has also emerged a new kind of leadership which is characterised by an ideology very much influenced by the superiority of higher caste culture. The basic institutions of the village life have undergone tremendous changes.

In the remaining part of this chapter we would discuss the institutional and organisational changes which have come in the Indian rural society.

Subsistence to Market Economy

Throughout the periods of history the village economy has been a subsistence economy. It is because of this that we characterise the rural society as an agrarian society. Opposite to it is the industrial and urban society. As a result of the development programmes and the consequent emergence of infrastructures of technology, education, transport, media, the village economy has moved towards diversified economy. In this economy market has assumed an important space. It will, therefore, be interesting here to mention something about the role of market in the village economy.

Even when the villages survived under subsistence economy, there was some role of market. Despite the villages being self-sufficient in the fulfilment of their needs the village people depended on weekly or occasional markets. These markets gave interrelationship between the clusters of villages. The weekly markets provided place for limited exchange of goods and services. Though the production in the field was meant for the consumption of family only, a part of produce was brought to the weekly markets. People living in hills and forests, specially the tribal people, climbed down to plains in the weekly markets to exchange their goods. This kind of market was quite rudimentary and primary in its functions.

With the coming of modernisation in India, say from the British rule, there came a new kind of capitalistic economy in agriculture. Land became a property. Commercial crops gave rise to market economy. It means that the villagers now produce not only for their own consumption but a part of it for market too. This was initial stage for the development of market. Recently, the market has become an important mechanism for linking the village to the capitalist mainstream of the country. There has been a systematic expansion of market. It has now reached to the doorstep of the village. The tooth-pastes and for the matter the beverages of all kinds have made their entry in the village life. The eggs and milk of a simple remote village have reached the metropolitan market. This is by no means an ordinary change. The expansion of market has various explanations. In the similar way there is also a hierarchy of markets. All markets are not uniform. There are markets for the class, there are also markets for the disadvantaged people. In whatever way we may explain the expansion and hierarchy of market, the fact remains that the market has played a key role in the expansion of rural society.

(1) *Market: A Theoretical Thrust*

In the Third World countries, today, the market has occupied an important concept of analysis. In western social science, the present era is said to be the era of post-modernity. Though there is debate on the definition of post-modernity, by and large it is accepted that hyper differentiation, that is, stratification, commodification of all the things, including fine art and aesthetics and rationality are the basic traits of post-modernity. The post-modernity discusses elaborately the concept of market. Jean Baudrillard, who is considered to be not only a postmodernist but is also understood to have influenced the present generation of post-modern sociologists, argues that market is the crucial variable in the development of hyper capitalism.

During 1960s and 1970s Baudrillard analysed the contemporary European society which he labels as a consumer society. Though, in his earlier life, Baudrillard was a follower of Marx, in his later life he broke away with Marx and Marxism. He says that in the consumer society market is the pre-dominant determinant of the ways people consume things. He argues:

> When we consume objects we are consuming signs and in the process are defining ourselves.[3]

Baudrillard says that people can be identified with the things that they consume. If the people consume high cost articles, they are bracketed into a status society. He says that "people are what they consume and are differentiated from other types of people on the basis of consumed objects. To the lay person, the word of consumption seems, on the surface, to be quite free. After all, if we have the money, we seem to be free to buy whatever we want. But, in fact, we are free to consume only marginally different objects and signs, further in consumption, we all feel quite unique, but in fact we closely resemble everyone else in our group, members of that group consume much the same thing. Thus, it is clear that we are not as free as we think we are."

The post-modern society has attained hyper capitalism, hyper rationality and hyper technological development. India does not have such a situation. We have yet to move forward in the direction of post-modernity. But the advanced countries such as that of Europe and US consider Asia to be a 'giant' for the expansion of their market. With the one set of globalisation and liberalisation, India has become a potential market in Asia. Multinationals are pushing their commodities for sale in this new market.

The Indian industrial market, in its turn, is also expanding its horizons. In this expansion network, the rural society has also been caught. The remote corners of our villages, even in high lands and forests, have received the new commodities of various brands. Thus, the local rural market is fast becoming a consumer market. The development of consumer market is through mass media and technology. The advertisements through print and electronic media are approaching the local rural market. One can easily get products of national standard companies even in the villages. The network of new market has also provided opportunities to the rural market to send their raw material to towns, cities and metropolises. Milk, tomatoes and raw fruits produced in the villageside move towards the city and town side. The *Krishi Upaj Mandis*, that is, agricultural produce markets, have emerged close to the clusters of villages. The villages are linked with the approach road and thus the new infrastructure has brought the villages close to the regional, state and national markets.

(2) *Hither Levels of Consumption*

The new market system has created and strengthened the rural class system. In the villages, a new class of big traders, big peasants and petty officials, along with the elites and political workers, has emerged. This class being influenced by media has begun to consume objects of new culture. They demonstrate a style of life which differentiates them from the other rural groups and brings them closer to the urban consumer society. Market in this way provides a nexus with the regional and national markets.

(3) *Development of Market: Credit Facilities*

The development of market has also provided a large number of facilities. It has created shopping malls or centres. It has also created credit cards. In these markets which are also making their entry in the rural areas, all objects, services, bodies, sex, culture and knowledge are considered to be items of exchange. Portraying the image of this new market George Ritzer observes:

> Consumer society is a place where everything is for sale. Not only are all commodities, but all signs are commodities. Given the latter all 'objects, services, bodies, sex, culture, knowledge' are produced and exchanged.[4]

The image of the developing market though is far away from India, the fact remains that in the contemporary world society market as a place of exchange has assumed greater importance. If, in the initial periods of the development of capitalism, production forces and production relations were stressed, in the present era means of consumption are emphasised by social scientists. The Marxian stress on production relations has been replaced by consumerism. And, this new wave is steadily but surely moving towards rural society.

In any analysis of rural social change, the role of market in the context of consumerism requires to be analysed in all details.

Rural Society and Technology

The Indian agrarian society for longer periods of history cultivated its fields in a primordial way. It carried out its agricultural operations through indigenous breed of bullocks, plough and leveler. Such a method of cultivation, coupled with organic fertiliser, did not give any surplus to be taken to the market. Such a state of agriculture got a revolution by technological innovations. These innovations on the one hand saved much of manual labour and on the other increased the productivity. Technology, thus, has proved to be a multiplier. Some of the major impacts of technology are given below:

(1) *Improved Implements*

Since the introduction of Community Development Projects in 1952, the development programmes introduced new technologically inputs in the villages with the objective of giving self-sufficiency to the peasants. Improved variety of plough, cattle, alongwith an appropriate technology, have been introduced to the peasants. The tractor, lorry, thresher and a large number of techniques have been given to the village people. There are some parts of our country such as Punjab, Maharashtra and Gujarat where the use of bullocks has become oblivious. Bullock-cart has also become outdated. All this clearly shows the role played by new technology.

(2) *New Agricultural Inputs*

The Five Year Plans throughout their history of implementation have given many new agricultural inputs. The electric or diesel oil-run water pumps have revolutionised the old pattern of irrigation. The construction of dams—major and minor—has also added great facilities of irrigation. The chemical manure and insecticides have added much to the farm produce. Much of our food deficiency has been covered by the agricultural growth. The green revolution is the result of this new input.

(3) *Improved Cattle*

India despite its being an agrarian society suffered from scarcity of milk. But the supply of improved cattle has revolutionised the dairy produce. India is now at the stage of white revolution. The production of milk has given rise to a large number of by-products which have assumed importance of export.

Abolition of Intermediaries

The system of intermediaries in the forms of *jamindars* and *jagirdars* which was abolished by the middle of 1950s in parts of India where there was feudal rule, a structural change has been observed. The breakdown of the feudal order brought a large number of changes in rural society. K.L. Sharma, in his study of rural Rajasthan where there was feudalism, brings out two major changes in the rural society: proletarianisation and bourgeoisiefication.[5] By the process of proletarianisa- tion, the *jagirdar* and his kin people took to cultivation and menial work as a result of the withdrawal of power. Actually, the abolition of *jagirdari* system obliged the landlords and their tenants to take to the status of a proletariat. Thus, in different states of India, such as Rajasthan, Punjab, Gujarat and Karnataka where there were princely states, there came a structural change in rural society.

Quite close to the process of proletarianisation, a similar process of bourgeoisiefication also took place in villages of princely states. The big landlords took to different sources of earning a living. Most of them had enough money in their possession owing to the benefits given to them by way of compensation. This money was invested by them in big business such as hotel, transport and trade. The resultant of the abolition of *jagirdari* system thus was seen in the social formation of elites and rich classes.

K.L. Sharma has analysed the impact of abolition on rural society as under:

> Thus, the abolition of the *jagirdari* system affected not only the landowners and the tenants, but a whole lot of rural people. This has provided a ground for the emergence of a new social formation. It is not that the entire change has emanated from the initial land reforms alone. Several other subsequent factors have equally been responsible for social transformation including education, migration, adult franchise and electoral politics, electrification and rural development programmes.[6]

Emergence of Various Associations and Institutions

The emergence of new associations and institutions in the rural society also marks a watershed in the process of transformation from pre-independence to post-independence, the later characterised by planned development. Among the institutions are caste and class which assumed new definitions and formations in rural society. We shall discuss some of the major changes which are observed in caste and class.

(1) *Caste*

Sociology has enough research material which indicates changes that have come in rural caste system. We shall restrain ourselves only to changes which are observed in rural caste system. Some of the changes are as below:

(i) It is observed that caste barriers to economic mobility have slowly given way to secular occupations. The village traditional occupations, such as that of oil pressures (*Teli*), weavers (*Julaha*), have now observed mobility. All kinds of occupations have been taken over by the village people notwithstanding their caste and religion. The occupational changes, therefore, have a revolutionary content.

(ii) There has been a clear-cut drift of rural population towards cities and towns. People are migrating to cities because of several reasons. Burden on land has increased. People have got some education which can provide them new employment opportunities in cities and towns. And, then, there is a fascination to live in a city for the rural people. Urban life also makes available facilities of different kinds such as health and education.

(iii) Though caste has taken new functions in rural society, it continues to remain a mark of identity among the village people.

(iv) Surely, the caste as a system is weakening in rural life; it has assumed new political dimensions. Actually, from several considerations because of the caste system, rural stratification is closed rather than open. There has been some correspondence between caste and landholding. For instance, the Rajputs and the Jats possess larger portions of land compared to intermediate and lower castes.

(v) One very structural change which has come in the rural society is the empowerment of the women and formation of Panchayati Raj. Panchayati Raj is an effort to develop the village through the decisions made by the people themselves. There is a decentralisation of power in the formation of Panchayati Raj. This formation has substantially weakened the traditional caste associations. Though the caste associations have taken over matters related to marriage, succession and family matters, the ultimate authority to be approached is the court of law.

(2) *Class*

Sociologists are recently talking about caste-class nexus. The argument that the caste is changing into class, is a misconception. Caste and class are not dichotomies. There is a nexus between the two. The caste is both a cultural structure and an economic organisation also. In rural society, both these variations of caste and class are observable.

One very significant feature of class formation in the rural society is the emergence of new classes. The planned development has given green revolution and white revolution. These two revolutions have resulted in class polarisation in rural society. As a result of planned development and reservation of seats for scheduled castes and scheduled tribes, a new class from these sections has emerged. Now, there are classes in scheduled castes and scheduled tribes. These classes are integrated into the classes belonging to higher castes and thus the whole rural society is polarised into two categories of classes: (1) classes emerging out of the higher castes who have benefited from rural development programmes, and (2) classes belonging to weaker sections who have cornered a larger portion of the benefits from the programmes of rural development.

(3) *Associations and Organisations*

The rural primordial associations and institutions have now given way to new associations and institutions such as cooperatives, educational societies, religious organisations and political parties. Besides, a new crop of non-governmental organisations (NGOs) has also spread its network in the rural society. There are also peasant organisations of various ideological orientations. Though these peasant organisations claim to be non-political they have some implicit alliance with some political party. These organisations advocate programmes of rural social change.

Contemporary Rural Cultural Changes

People of India (POI), a giant effort made by the Anthropological Survey of India, identifies 91 cultural regions within India.[7] The project informs that each state has plural cultural regions. At the regional level, there is regional self-consciousness or identity of castes, tribes and minorities or other regional groups. This kind of regional or village self-consciousness is increasing but happily this regional consciousness also results in the growth of a holistic consciousness. As a result of the two kinds of cultural consciousness, the village society has assumed a particular cultural identity. On the plane of cultural changes some of the characteristics of the emerging rural society are given below:

(1) It must be admitted that across the nation, the lifestyle and leisure time activities of the people have changed. It includes modes of consumption, style of dress, uses of synthetic material or artifacts, modes of transport and the weakening of the traditional interdictions about the consumption of meat, poultry etc. The consumption of fruits, vegetables and milk products now has a much wider base. The green revolution that took place in the 1970s is now supplemented by a white revolution.

(2) Yogendra Singh argues that in the contemporary social change that India witnesses, there is profound significance of culture. He argues that the higher consumption level which is being attained by the rural people, indicates that despite being quite traditional, the rural society has taken to new cultural ways of life. He writes:

> The past orientalist pronouncement, that Indian culture being other worldly and fractured by segmentary divisions into caste, tribe, etc., would not only help or rather hinder the growth of a modern economy and democratic polity, has been proved erroneous. Castes, tribes, family institutions and religions as illustrated by sociological studies, have richly contributed to the growth in agricultural and industrial entrepreneurship, and modern systems of profession, education, technology and science.[8]

Rural India which was described by the British anthropologists as a republic—isolated from the mainline civilisation, now ceases to be republic. It is, on the one hand, an autonomy having its own production system and a kind of identity but on the other hand it is dependent on other villages, the region and the country as a whole. The villages are fast changing. It would be erroneous to think that the road to change is only economic growth. Villages have changed in all walks of life. The long history of village development shows that our people are quite resilient. They have observed their traditions but at the same time have changed. What is important about village society is that it has also brought about cultural changes within its web. The best way to understand rural India is to identify its economic, social and historical linkages with the regional and national trends of economic, social and cultural changes. The changes thus are both structural and cultural.

Notes

1. Chitra Shivkumar and S.S. Shivkumar, "Rural Change, Social History and Participant Observation", in Shah, A.M., Bhaviskar, B.S. Ramaswamy, E.A.(eds.), *Social Structure and Change*, Vol. IV, Sage Publications, New Delhi, 1997, pp. 115-5.
2. A.R. Desai, op. cit., p. 389.
3. Quoted by George Ritzer in his, *Post Modern Social Theory*, The Mcgraw-Hill Companies, Inc., New York, 1997, p. 81.
4. George Ritzer, op. cit., p. 84.
5. K.L. Sharma, , op.cit., p. 255.
6. Ibid., p. 256.
7. S.K. Singh, *People of India: An Introduction*, Anthropological Survey of India, Calcutta, 1992.
8. Yogendra Singh, *The Significance of Culture in the Understanding of Social Change in Contemporary India*, Presidential Address, XXI All India Sociological Conference, December, 19-21, 1991, New Delhi.

Index

aesthetics
meaning of, 214-215
Agarwal, Anil and Sunita Narain, 321
agrarian unrest, 229
in India, 229-230
agrarian population
categories of, 131-132
agrarian social structure, 115-119
in India, 114-123
— history of, 119-122
— study of, 114-115
agrarianism, 115
agricultural classes
classification of, 175
Akha Teej, 199
Alvi, Hamza, 230, 253
anthropology
characteristics of, 29
outline of, 27-29
area development programmes, 281-282
art forms
types of, 215
Ashok Mehta Committee, 334
Atal, Yogesh, 60, 61

Baden-Powell, B.H., 55
Bahuguna, Sundarlal, 326
Bailey, F.G., 52, 64
Balwant Raj Mehta Committee, 333-334
Bardoli *satyagraha*
of 1928, 240-245
— causes of, 241-242
— course of events leading to, 242-245
Baudrilland, 348
Baviskar, B.S., 294, 305, 309
Bealtie, John, 25
Berger, Peter, 37
Bertrand, Alvin, 98, 105, 108
Beteille, Andre, 48, 65, 77, 114, 116, 118, 132, 134, 136, 151, 165, 166, 169
Bhai-Bhatijavad, 192
Bharucha, Rustam, 213
Bhave, Vinoba, 17, 139
Boas, Frnz, 26
bonded labour, 152
Bose, P.K., 154
Bourdieu, Pierre, 21, 22, 37, 39, 191
Brahminisation, 82
Breman, Jan, 131, 132, 151, 164, 171, 226, 241
bride price, 199
Briffault, R., 189

British Raj, 15, 32, 56, 57, 59, 90, 120, 125
  development efforts made during
  — by government, 267-269
  — by voluntary organisations, 269-272
  emergence of tenants during, 128-129
Brown, A.R., 189

caste
  and economic life, 158
  and joint family, 159
  in rural India, 154-155, 353
  in rural society
  — specificities of, 155-159
  new horizons of, 166
caste associations, 156-157
caste-class nexus, 175-176, 354
Chandra, Bipan, 223, 243
Chanparan peasant struggle
  in Bihar (1917-18), 234-238
  — course of events leading to, 236-237
  — causes of, 235
  — outcomes of, 237-238
child marriage, 199
Chipko movement, 326
Chitambar, I.B., 33
Choudhary, Sukhbir, 239
Classes
  in India, 153, 354
  — types of, 153
Community Development
  Project (1972), 274-278, 332
  critique of, 227-228
  salient features of, 276-277
Community Development
  Programmes, 32
Comte, Auguste, 20
Concurrent List of the, 137
  Directive Principles of State Policy in the, 15
  Panchayati Raj in, 79, 223
Constitution of India, 11, 32, 41, 335
Cooley, C.H., 188
cooperation
  meaning of, 295-296
cooperative movement, 296
  in India
  — history of, 299-301
cooperative society(ies)
  elements of, 295
  politics in, 305-306
  types of, 298-299, 301-305
cooperatives
  characteristics of, 297-298
  in India
  — objectives of, 312
  — status of, 310-313
cult war, 211

D'Monte, Darryl, 324
Damle, Y.B., 89
Davis, Kingsley, 21
de-sanskritisation, 162
Deb, P.C., 34
Democratic decentralisation, 330
Derrida, Jacques, 23
Desai, A.R., 30, 31, 33, 34, 65, 125, 128, 131, 158, 159, 183, 184, 185, 187, 203, 204, 205, 207, 214, 219, 229, 293-294, 330, 346

Desai, I.P., 12, 164, 184
Desai, Mahadev, 241
development
  programmes/schemes
  in India, 279, 341
  — for special target groups, 282-285
  — impact of, 287-292
  — politicisation of, 290
Dhanagare, D.N., 230, 241, 245, 246, 251, 254, 255
dominant caste
  characteristics of, 73-76
  concept of, 63, 72-79, 157-158, 173
  — criticism of the, 76-79
Dube, S.C., 18,59, 63, 157, 181
Dubhashi, P.R., 296
Dumount, Louis, 31, 60, 210
Durkheim, Emile, 20, 201, 202
Dutt, Ramesh Chandra, 237
Dutta, R.C., 121

East Indian Company, 32, 54
ecology, 182-183, 315-316
Elwin, Verrier, 111
endogamy, 197-198
environmental legislations
  in India, 326-327
environment, 315
  classification of, 316
  problem of, 314, 326
environmental protection
  people's movement for, 324-325
  — in India, 326-327
environmental degradation
  aspects of, 317-320
  causes of, 320-324
Epsteen, T.S. 45
Evans-Pritchard, 48, 49
Eriksen, T.H., 27, 28, 46, 49, 206
exogamy, 197

family, 183-184
Fernandes, Walter, 144, 146
Fitcher, J.H., 179
Folk instruments, 218
Frankel, Francine, 174, 289
Frazer, 201
Freud, Sigmund, 26

Gadgil, Madhav, 322, 324
Gadulia Lohar, 184
Gandhi, Mahatma, 11, 17, 54, 68, 122, 223, 235, 239, 265
Geertz, Clifford, 27, 202
Ghurye, G.S., 25, 64
globalisation, 314
Gough, Kathleen, 229, 259
Gould, Harold, 86
Gram Swaraj
  Gandhian concept of, 17, 329
Gramdan movement, 139
green revolution, 225, 288
Grores, E.R., 195
Gupt, Maithilisharan, 11

Haddon Alfred, 49
Hali system, 242, 245
Haque, T., 139
Hasan, Zoya, 174
Herodotos, 25
Herrick, M.T., 295
Hind Swaraj
  theory of, 223
Hindu Marriage
  objectives of, 195
Hinduism, 83, 84

horticulture, 182
Horton, P.B., 179
humanitarianism, 91

ICSSR, 32, 37
ideal folk society
  concept of, 60
India
  rural population of, 12
Indian National Congress, 56, 236
Indian National Movement, 57
Indian agriculture
  aspects of, 224-225
Indian social structure, 94
Ingold, Tim, 24
institution, 179
Integrated Rural Development Programme (IRDP), 286
Intermediaries
  abolition of, 140-142, 351-352
  iron-triangle, 323

jagirdari system, 141-142
  in Rajasthan, 142
Jain, M.S. and P.C., Trivedi, 310
jajmani system, 67, 156
jamindari system, 128, 131, 141
Jenkins, Richard, 46
joint family
  characteristics of, 185
Joshi, P.C., 115, 119, 120, 122, 139
Joshi, Sharad, 260

Kalbelia, 184
Kalekar, 58
Kamat, A.R., 167
Kant, Immanuel, 25
Kapadia, K.M., 180, 185, 188
Karve, Irawati, 182, 184, 191
Kheda peasant struggle
  of 1918, 238-240
  — achievements of, 239
  — causes of, 238
Kinship, 188-191
  and marriage, 192
Kolenda, Pauline, 170
Kuriem, V., 309

Lal, Morley Mohan, 144
LAMPS, 303- 304
  functions, 303-304
land ceiling, 142-143
  exceptions in, 144
  limits of, 143
landlord-tenant relationship, 133, 135
  in India, 134-135
  — caste context in, 135
  — types of, 134
landlordism, 125
land problem
  in India
  — Gandhi's approach to, 122-123
Land reforms
  in India, 137-148
  — access to, 139-140
  — approaches to, 139
  — attributes of, 140-145
  — failure of, 145-148
  — objectives of, 138
land tenure system, 126
land, 125
  as private property, 145
  forms of, 125
Lawrence, Surendra, 317, 318
Laxmi Narayan, H. and S.A. Tyagi, 130

Leach, Edmund, 28
Learner, Daniel, 92
Levi-Strauss, Claude, 27
little community
  concept of, 64
little and great traditions,
  concepts of, 93-96
little republics, 150
Lynch, Owen M., 88

MacIver, R.M. and C.H. Page, 110
Mackenzie, Holt, 55
Madan, T.N., 191
mahalwari system, 140-141
Maine, Henry S., 31, 40, 150
Majumdar, D.N., 18, 64, 77, 78, 181, 195
Malinowski, Bronislaw, 26, 49, 190, 196
Mandelsohn, Oliver, and Marika Vicziany, 118
Manor, James, 174
market economy
  subsistence to, 347-350
marriage
  forms of, 195-196
  — monogamy, 196
  — polyandry, 195
  — polygyny, 196
  institution of, 193-195
  rules of, 196-198
marriage by exchange, 199
Marriott, McKim, 18, 63, 93, 210
Marx, Karl, 20, 56, 201
matriarchal family, 185
Mauss, Marcel, 26
Mayer, A.C., 180, 192
Merton, Robert K., 20
Metcalfe, Charles, 32, 55, 68
milk cooperatives, 304
  in Gujarat, 308-309
  — politics in, 309-310
Min, Herry, 26
Mohanty, Bidyut, 332-333, 339
modernisation, 92, 161
monogamy, 196
Moplah rebellion
  in Malabar (1921), 249
  — causes of, 247
  — course of events leading to, 247-249
Morgan, Lewis Henry, 26
Mukheryei, Rama Krishna, 32, 54, 55, 57, 59, 62, 153, 154
Myrdal, Gunnar, 120, 137

Naipaul, V.S. 163, 164
Namboodripad, E.M.S., 237
Narain, Iqbal and P.C. Mathur, 174
Naxalbari peasant struggle, 255-259
  causes of, 257-258
  course of events leading to, 258-259
Nehru, Jawaharlal, 226
Nehru, S.S, 159
NGOs
  in British Raj
  — development efforts made by, 269-272
Nikah, 196
Nyaya Panchayats, 336

Panch Parmeshwar, 79, 329
'Panchayati Raj', 11, 79, 329
  in India
  — emergence of, 278

— historical backdrop of, 331-336
— objectives of constitution of, 332, 333
reasons for study of, 330-331
Parochialisation
concept of, 63, 96
Parvathamma, 85
Passons, Talcott, 20
Patel, S.J., 57
'atel, Sujata, 310
atnaik, Utsa, 228
triarchal family, 185
sant movements
post-independent India,
-261
Naxalbari peasant struggle,
5-259
angana peasant struggle
7-51), 249-255
dependent India,
satyagraha (1928), 240-245
— Champaran movement in Bihar (1917-18), 234-238
— Kheda peasant struggle (1918), 238-240
— Moplah rebellion in Malabar (1921), 246-249
— peasant revolt in Punjab (1930), 233-234
— Santhal insurrection (1855-56), 231-233
peasant proprietors
types of, 131
peasant revolt
in Punjab (1930), 233-234
— causes of, 234
— outcomes of, 234
peasant, 226-227
categories of, 227
peasantry
erroneous assumptions about, 225-226
in India
— categories of, 227-229
— importance of, 223-225
Permanent Land Settlement of 1793, 127, 128, 231
Pocock, David and Louis Dumont, 12
pollution
forms of, 319
sources of, 320
polyandry, 195
polygyny, 196, 199
poverty removal programmes, 14
Prabhu, P.N., 195
Prasad, Rajendra, 236
Prem Chand, 11, 183
PRIs
functions of, 336-337
proletarianism, 163

Raj, K.M., 287
Ranade, M.G., 120-121
Ranga, N.G., 229
Redfield, Robert, 60
religion, 201-203
Ritzer, Geoge, 350
Rivers, 191
Royal Commission on Agriculture, 32, 119, 268-269
Rudra, 228
rural
what is it ?, 99-101

rural India
caste in, 154-155
cultural change in, 95
rural aesthetics, 213
characteristics of, 216-22
rural caste stratification
changes influencing the, 159-168
— de-sanskritisation, 162
— modernisation and sanskritisation, 161-162
— proletarianism, 163
SCs/STs/OBCs in changing, 166-168
rural class system
changing patterns of, 168-175
rural community, 99-100
rural development, 265-266
in India
— after independence, 272-286
— before independence, 266-272
rural family
in India
— characteristics of, 184-188
rural life
sociology of, 98-113
rural people, 101
rural religion, 205
characteristics of, 205-208
rural social formations
determinants of, 101-113
— cultural environment, 110-113
— geographic environment, 103-107
— social environment, 107-110
rural social institutions, 181-182
types of, 181-211
— family, 183-188
— kinship, 188-193
— marriage, 193-201
— religion, 201-211
rural social stratification, 153-159
rural society
and technology, 350-351
art in
— status of, 215-222
changes in
— trends of, 346
cultural changes in, 354-356
kinship in
— importance of, 191-193
marriage in
— specific aspects of, 198-201
religion in
— significance of, 203-205
Rural sociology, 98
characteristics of, 35-36
emergence of, 29-30
methods of study of, 43-50, 136
nature of, 37-40
newly acquired significance of
— in contemporary India, 12-19
— reasons for, 13-19
origin and development of, 30-35
— in India, 31-35
— in the US, 30-31
studies in, 54-61
— by administrators, 55-56
— by economists, 56-59
— by sociologists/anthropologists, 59-61
subject matter of, 40-43
tools of, 50-52
ryotwari system, 131, 140

Saith, A. and A. Tankha, 228
sanskritisation, 161
  characteristics of, 82-84
  concept of, 81-89
  — criticism of, 84
Santhal insurrection
  of 1855-56, 231-233
  — causes of, 231-232
Saxena, N.C., 147
Seligman, Charles, 49
73rd Constitution Amendment
  Act, 334-336
  critique of, 342-343
  empowerment of women in,
  338
  features of, 335-336
Shah, Ghanshyam, 167, 174
Shah, S.M., 159
Sharma, K.L., 85, 86, 117, 130,
  141, 151, 154, 160, 161, 162,
  163, 164, 167, 172, 173, 229, 352
shifting cultivation, 184
Shivkumar, Chitra and S.S.
  Shivkumar, 345
Singer, Milton, 83, 93, 95
Singh, Yogendra, 40, 43, 66, 67,
  68, 74, 86, 87, 89, 93, 94, 96,
  155, 167, 175
Slater, Gilbert, 32, 56
social anthropology
  meaning of, 24-26
social stratification
  approaches to, 151-152
  forms of, 152-153
  — caste, 152
  — class, 153
  — estate, 152-153
  — slavery, 152
  meaning of, 150-151
sociology
  meaning of, 19-24
Somjee, A.H., 310
Sorokin, P.A. and C.G.
  Zimmerman, 217, 219
Spencer, 201
Srinivas, M.N., 18, 41, 44, 45, 46,
  63, 72, 73, 74, 75, 80, 81, 82, 89,
  91, 157, 161, 162, 172, 180, 181
Strabo, 25
Stuart, Chapin F., 34
sugar cooperatives, 304-305
  in Maharashtra, 306-307
Sundarayya, P., 255
swadeshi
  movement of, 225
swaraj, 122

Tagore, Rabindra Nath, 11
Telangana peasant struggle
  of 1947-51, 249-255
  — causes of, 250-252
  — course of events leading to,
  252-254
  — outcomes of, 254-255
tenancy
  and agricultural backwardness,
  135-137
  aspects of, 134
  in India
  — systems of, 140
  — variations in, 129-133
tenancy systems
  in British India, 140-142
  — types of, 140
Tenant (s), 128
  emergence of, 128-129
Tendulkar, D.G., 235
Thapar, Ashok, 288

Thorner, Daniel, 135, 227, 294, 310, 312
tribals
classification of, 184
twice-born, 89
Tylor, 201, 202

United Nations Environment Programme (UNEP), 316
Universalisation
concept of, 63, 96

varna system, 82
varnas, 82
village community
social framework of, 180-181
village cooperatives, 293
village studies, 61-62
issues included in, 62-68
village unity
characteristics of, 80-81
concept of, 79-81
village(s), 100
in India, 100-101

Washbrook. D.A., 174
Weber, Max, 20, 201, 208
Weiner, Myron, 18
Westermark, Edward, 49, 194, 197
westernisation
and modernisation, 92-93
characteristics of, 91-93
concept of, 89-93
— origin of the, 90-91
white revolution, 301, 309
women empowerment, 337
reasons for need of, 339-342
through Panchayati Raj, 338-339
Wright Mills, C., 40

Zimmerman, C.G., 33

Admittedly, the village [illegible] the law courts.

(c) [illegible]

In [illegible]

[illegible]

(d) [illegible] standards

[illegible]